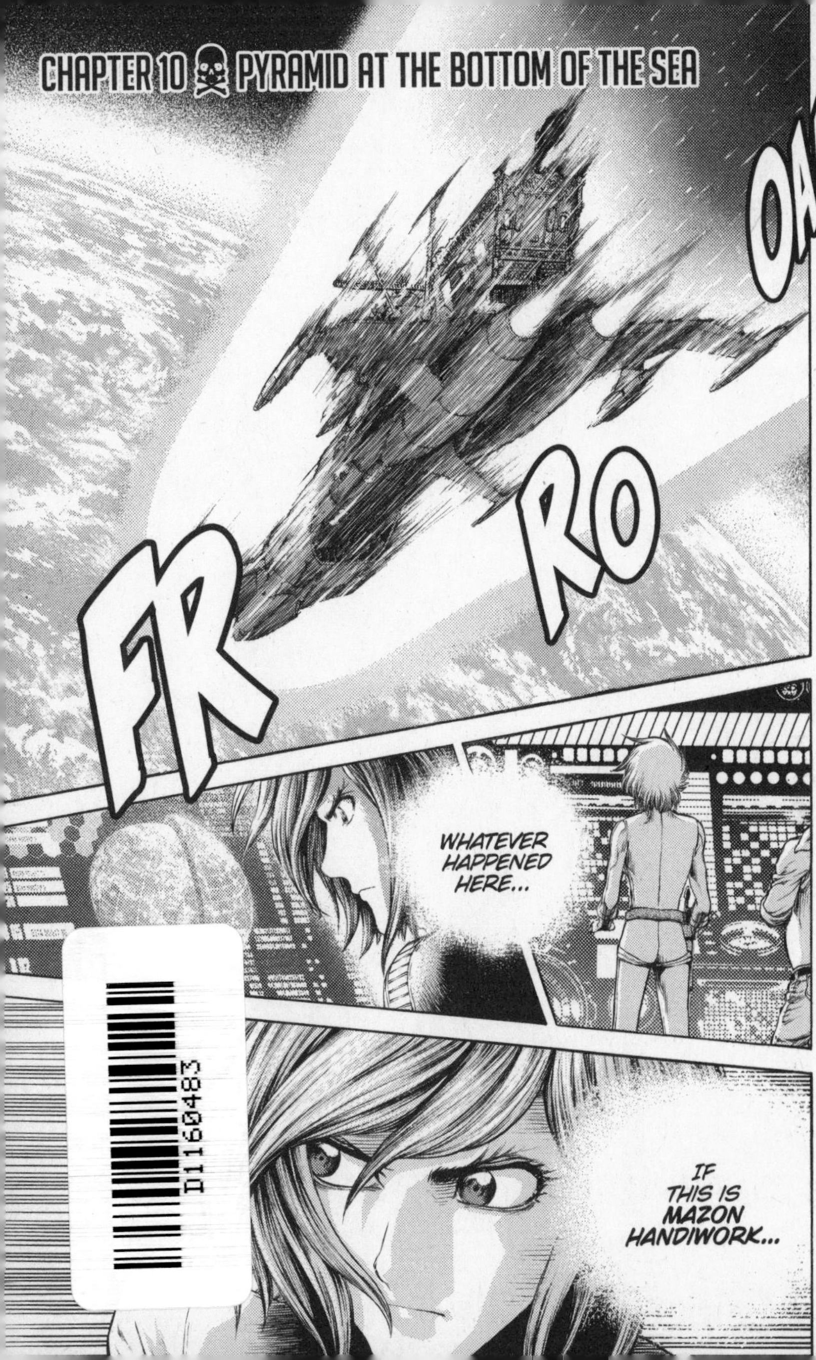
CHAPTER 10 PYRAMID AT THE BOTTOM OF THE SEA
FR
RO
OAAR
WHATEVER HAPPENED HERE...
IF THIS IS MAZON HANDIWORK...

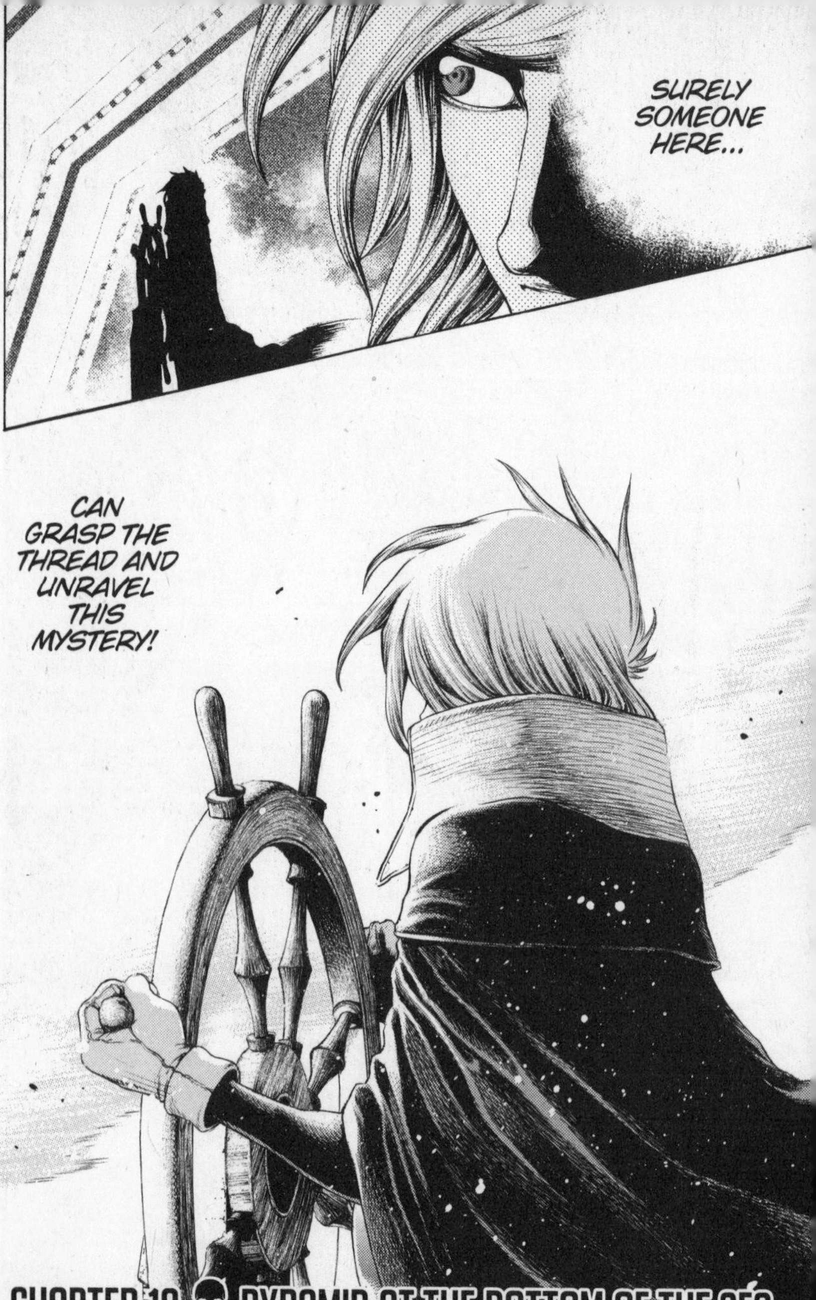
SURELY SOMEONE HERE...
CAN GRASP THE THREAD AND UNRAVEL THIS MYSTERY!

CHAPTER 10 PYRAMID AT THE BOTTOM OF THE SEA

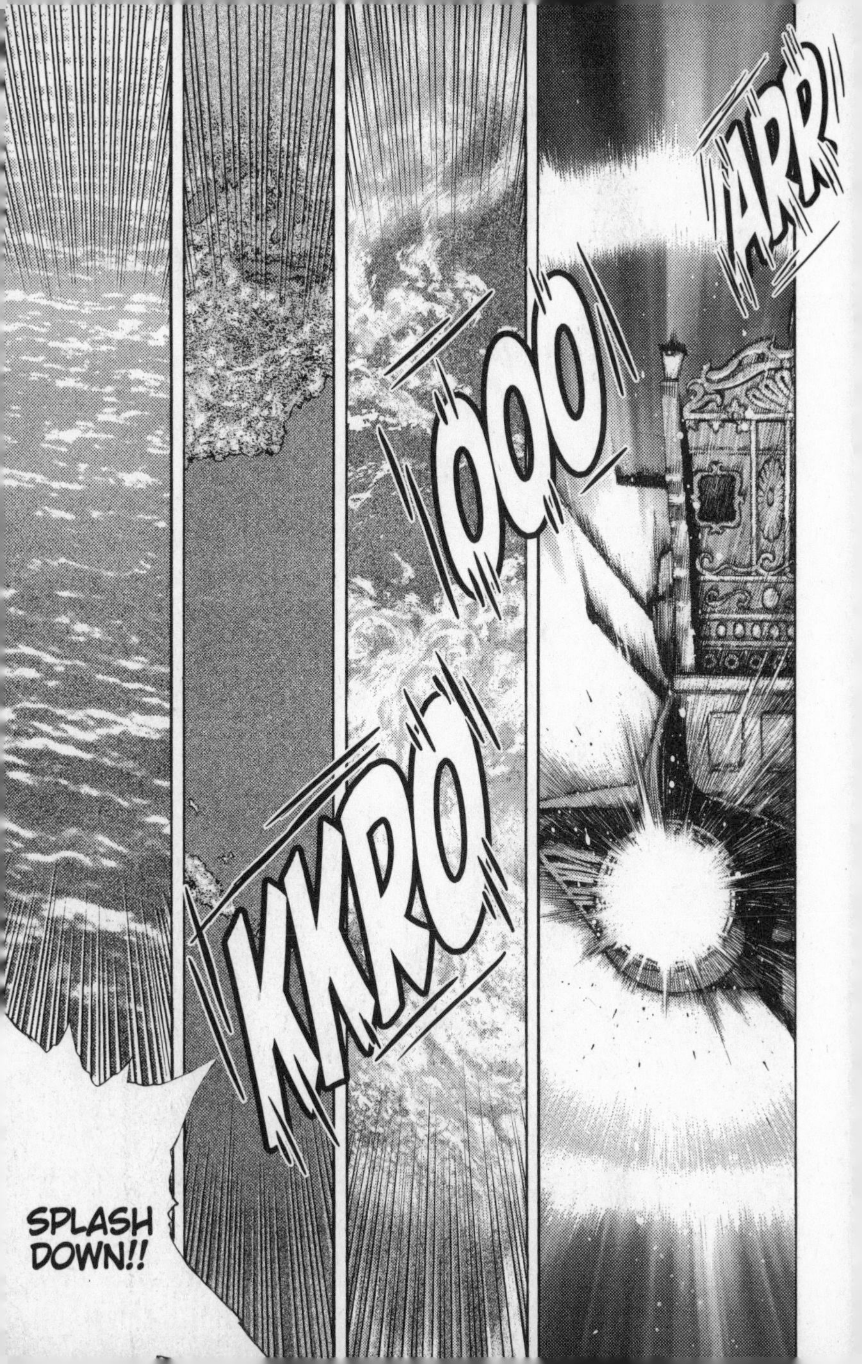
KKRO
OOO
ARR
SPLASH DOWN!!

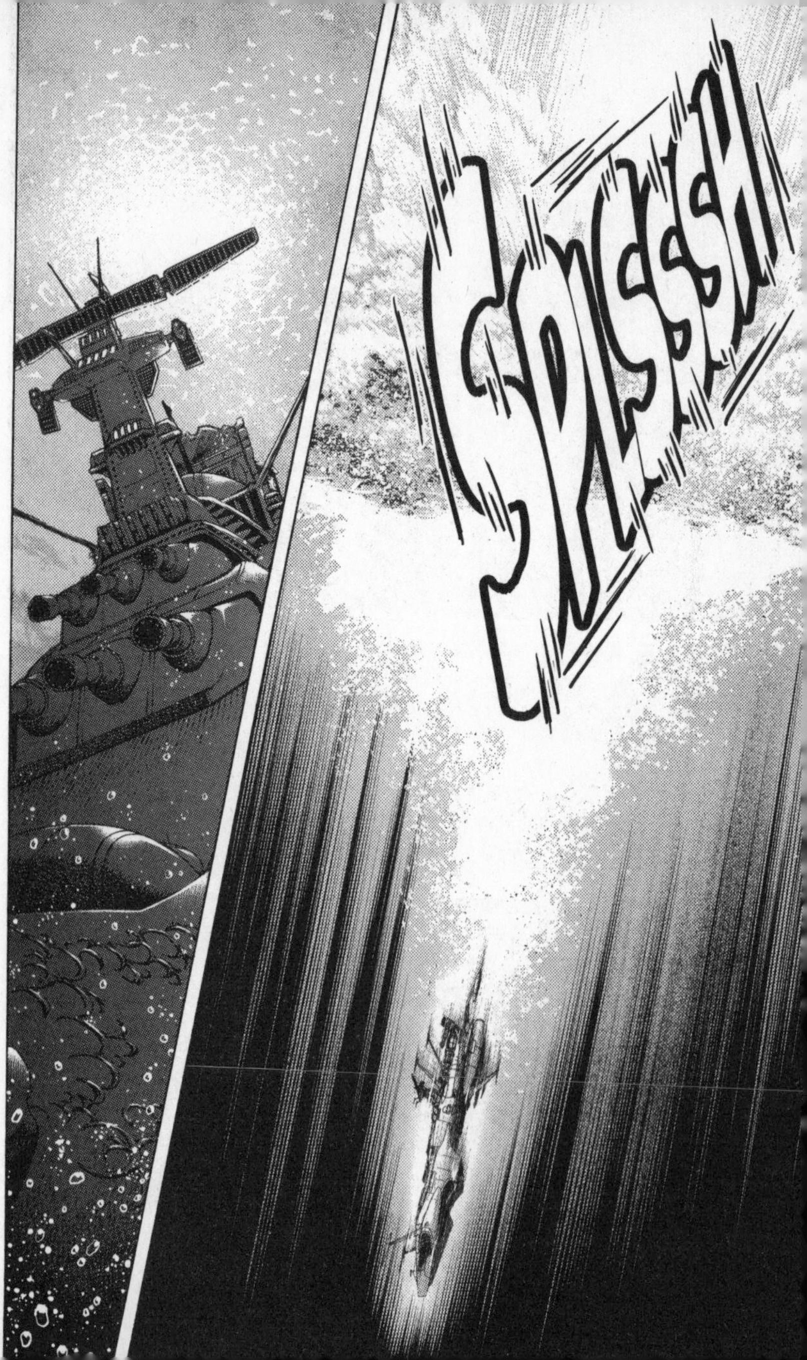
SPLASSSH!

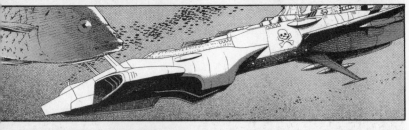

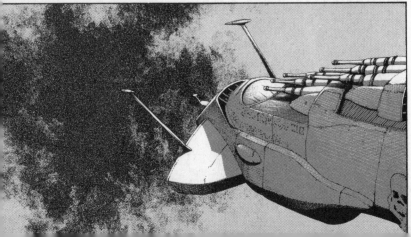

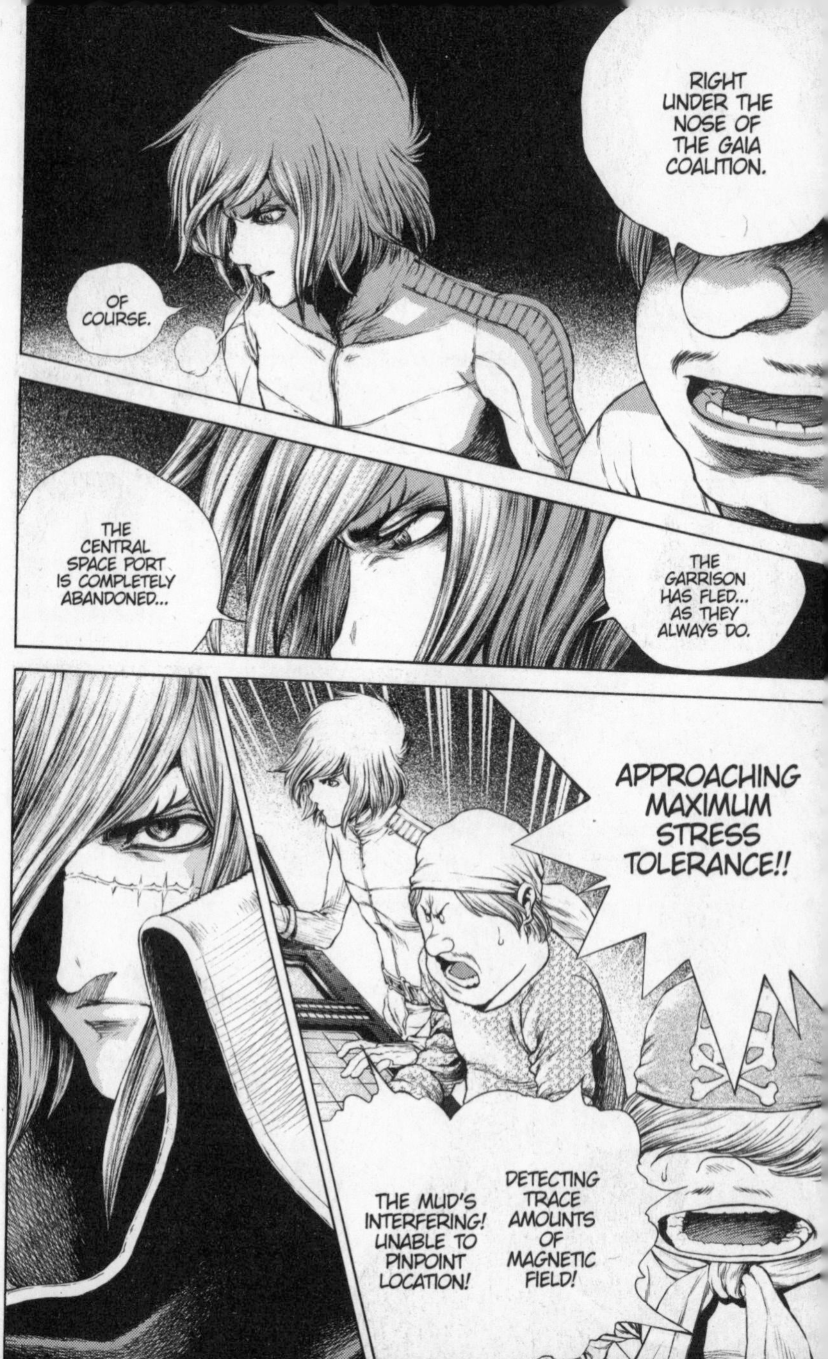
RIGHT UNDER THE NOSE OF THE GAIA COALITION.
OF COURSE.
THE GARRISON HAS FLED... AS THEY ALWAYS DO.
THE CENTRAL SPACE PORT IS COMPLETELY ABANDONED...
APPROACHING MAXIMUM STRESS TOLERANCE!!
DETECTING TRACE AMOUNTS OF MAGNETIC FIELD!
THE MUD'S INTERFERING! UNABLE TO PINPOINT LOCATION!

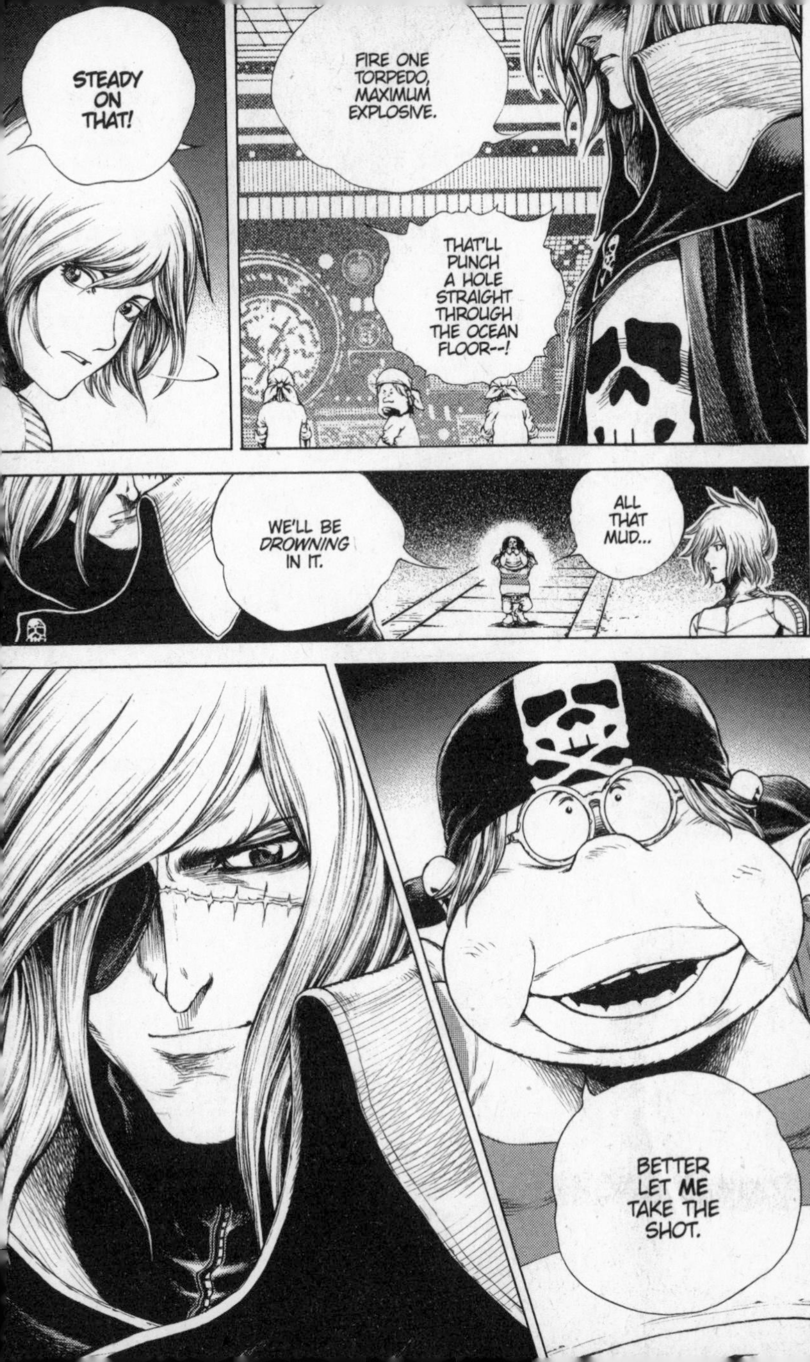
FIRE ONE TORPEDO, MAXIMUM EXPLOSIVE.
THAT'LL PUNCH A HOLE STRAIGHT THROUGH THE OCEAN FLOOR--!
STEADY ON THAT!
ALL THAT MUD...
WE'LL BE *DROWNING* IN IT.
BETTER LET ME TAKE THE SHOT.

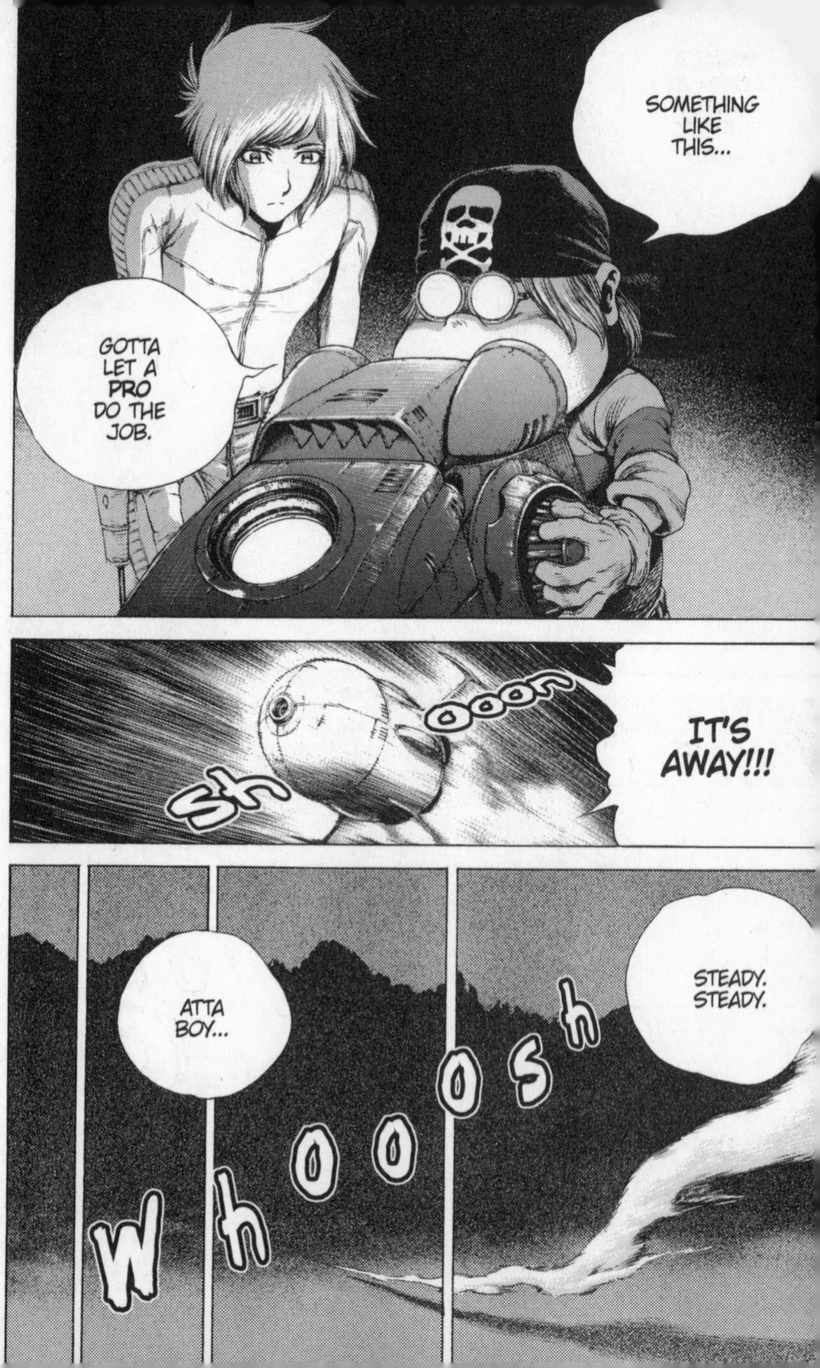
SOMETHING LIKE THIS...
GOTTA LET A PRO DO THE JOB.
IT'S AWAY!!!
Shoooon
STEADY. STEADY.
ATTA BOY...
Whooosh

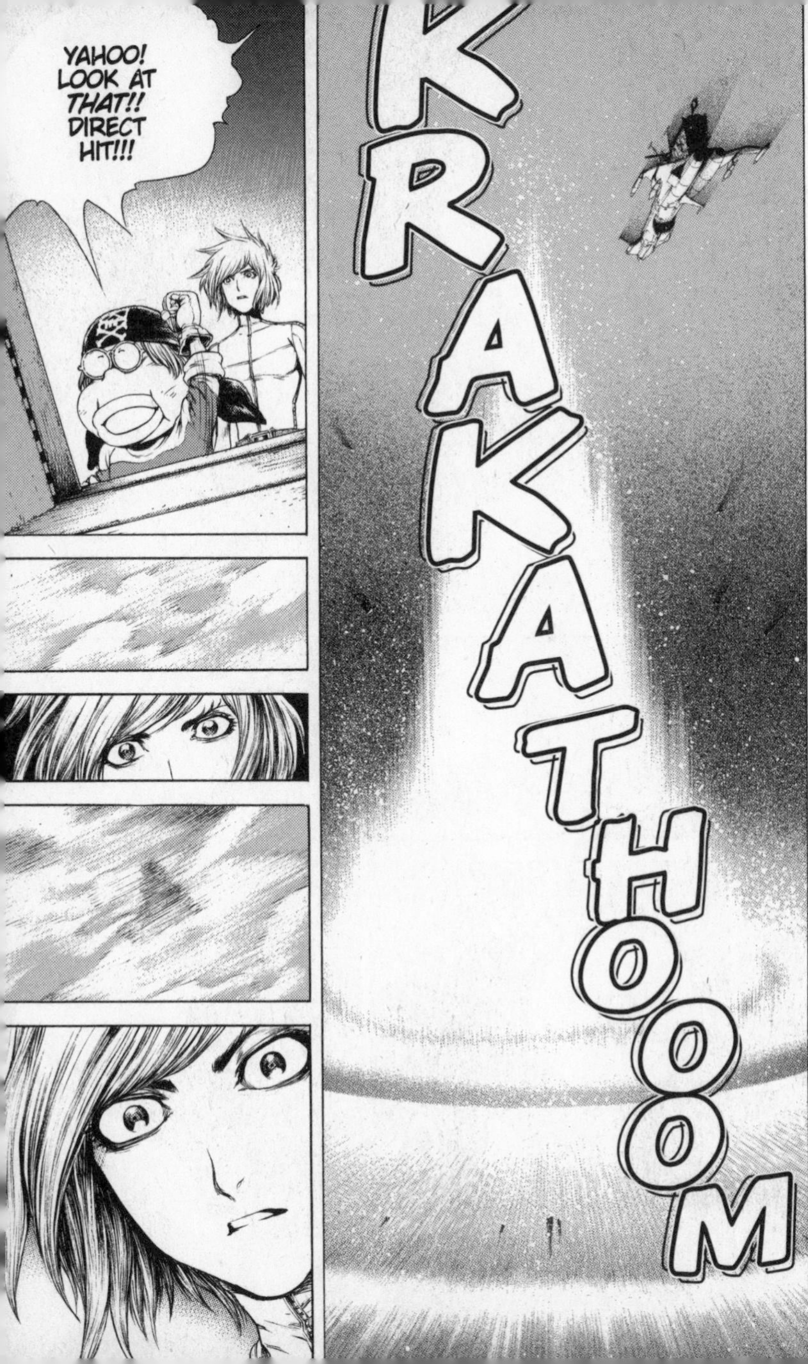
KRAKAKATHOOOOM
YAHOO! LOOK AT *THAT!!* DIRECT HIT!!!

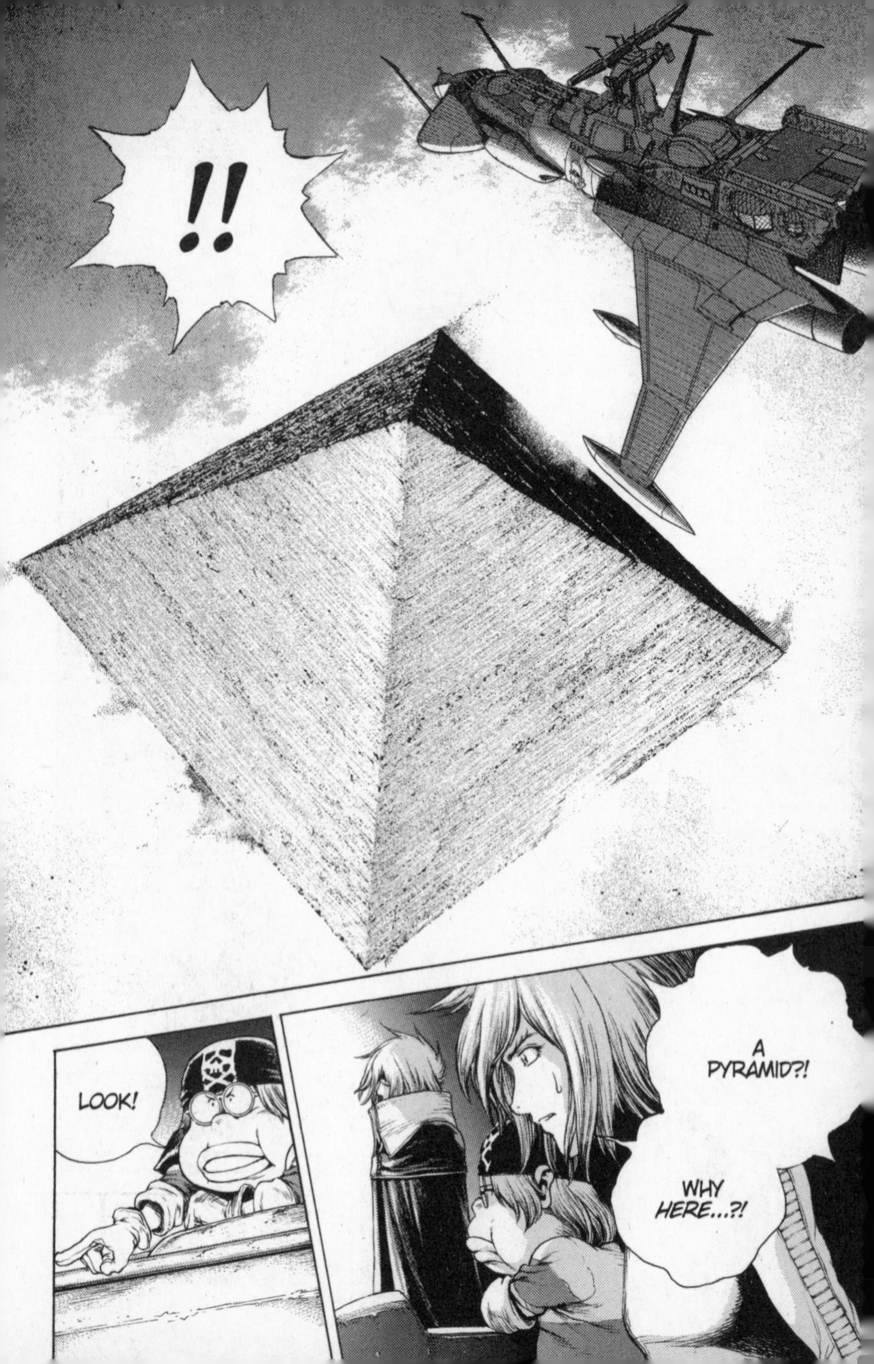
!!
A PYRAMID?!
WHY HERE...?!
LOOK!

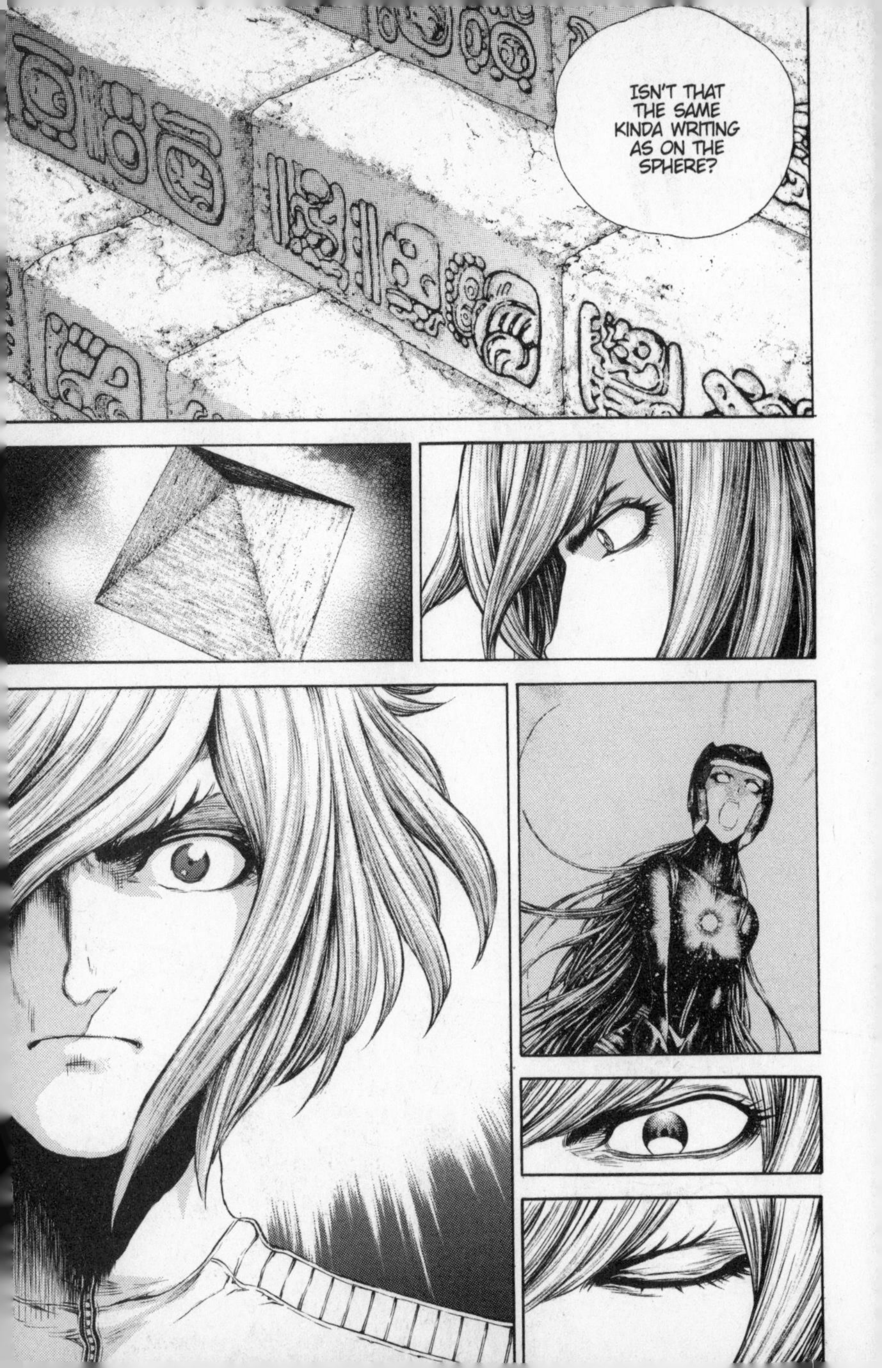
ISN'T THAT THE SAME KINDA WRITING AS ON THE SPHERE?

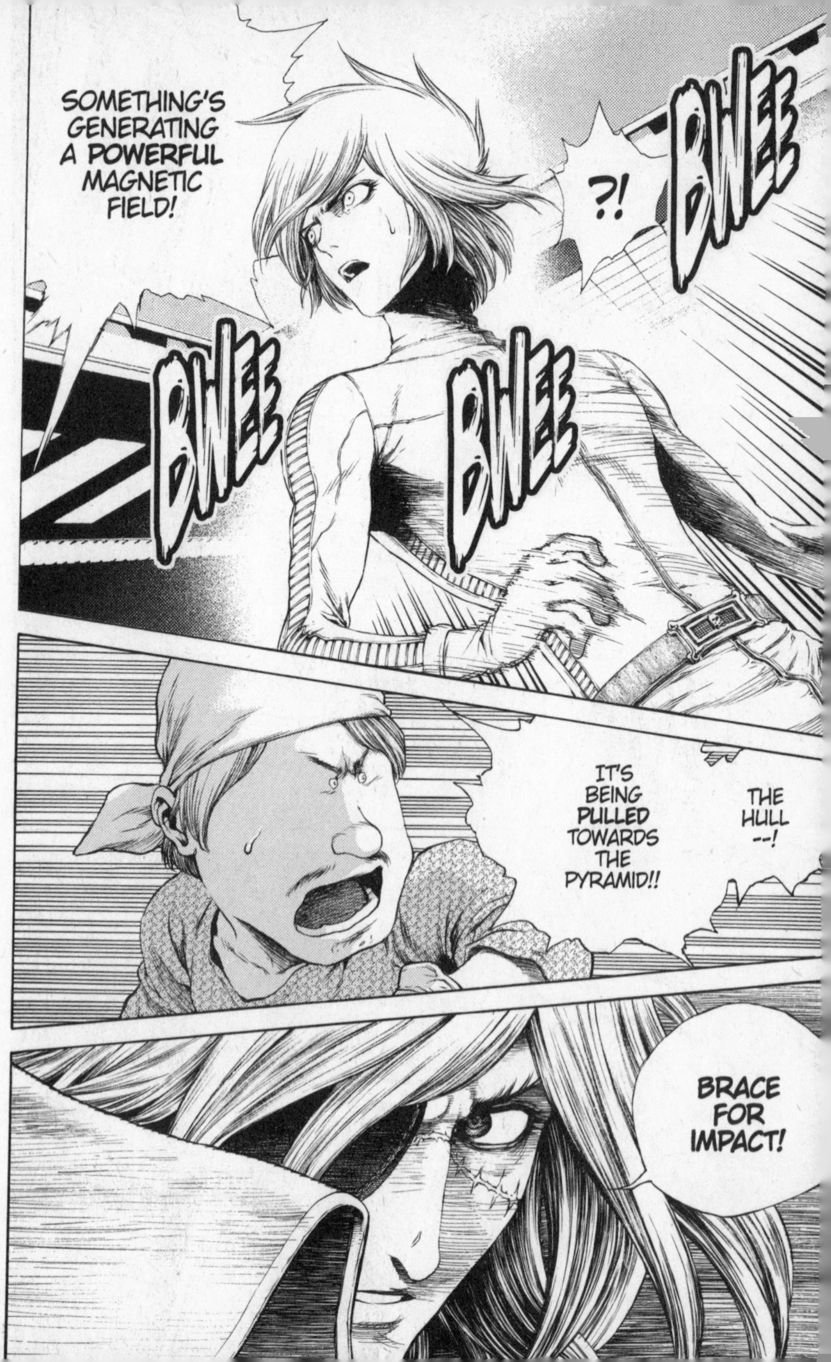
BWEE
?!
SOMETHING'S GENERATING A POWERFUL MAGNETIC FIELD!
BWEE
BWEE
THE HULL --!
IT'S BEING PULLED TOWARDS THE PYRAMID!!
BRACE FOR IMPACT!

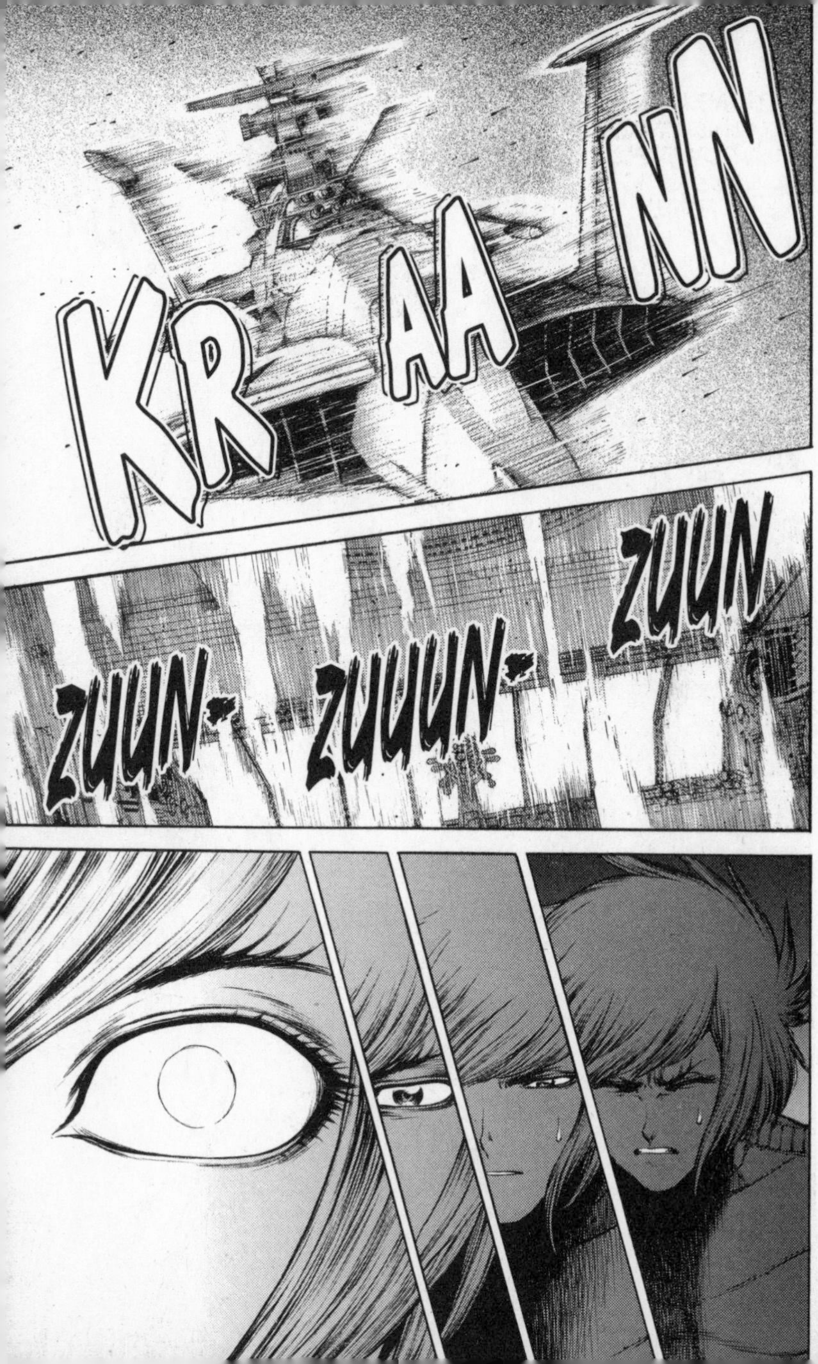
KRAANN
ZUUN
ZUUUN-
ZUUN-

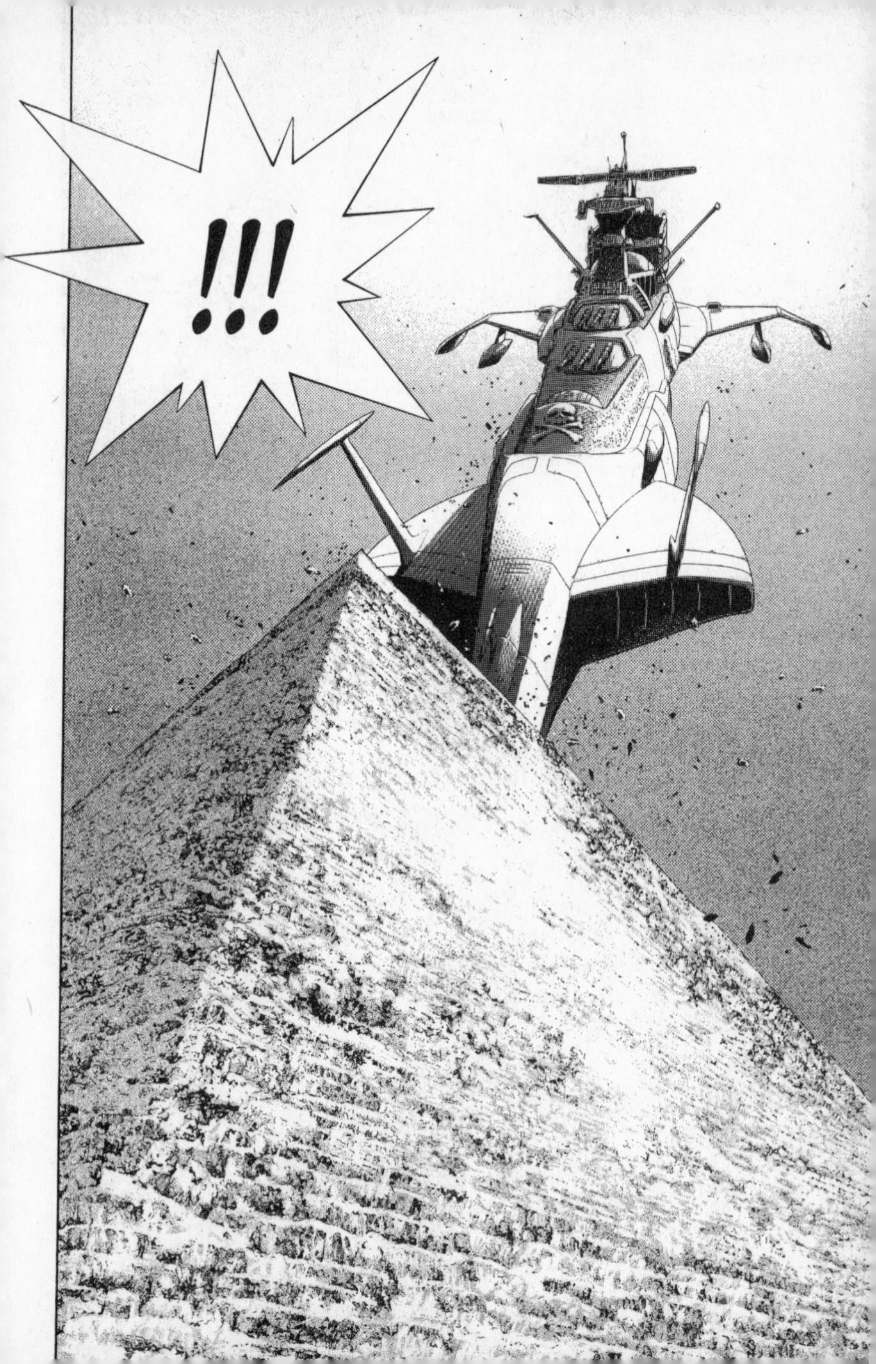
!!!

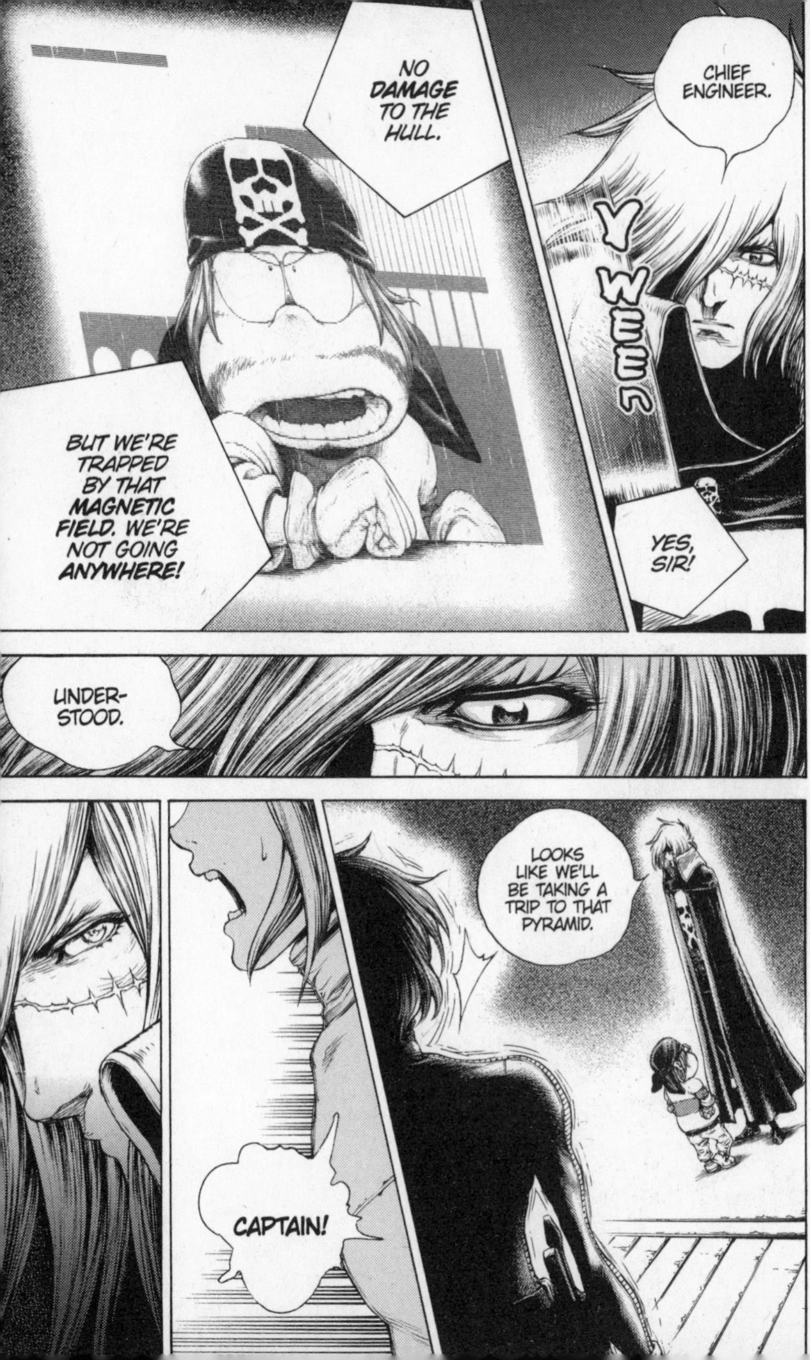
CHIEF ENGINEER.
YWEE
YES, SIR!
NO DAMAGE TO THE HULL.
BUT WE'RE TRAPPED BY THAT MAGNETIC FIELD. WE'RE NOT GOING ANYWHERE!
UNDER-STOOD.
LOOKS LIKE WE'LL BE TAKING A TRIP TO THAT PYRAMID.
CAPTAIN!

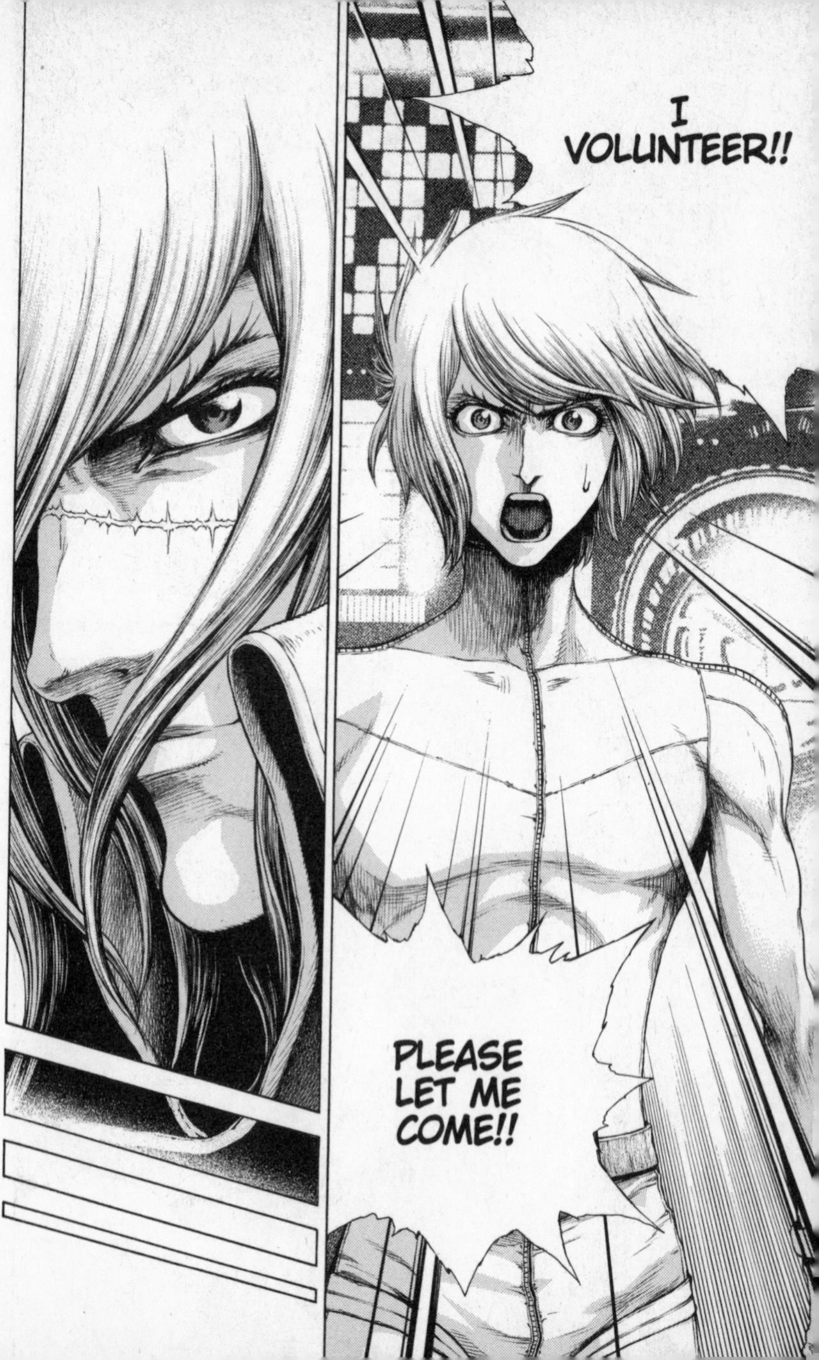
I VOLUNTEER!!
PLEASE LET ME COME!!

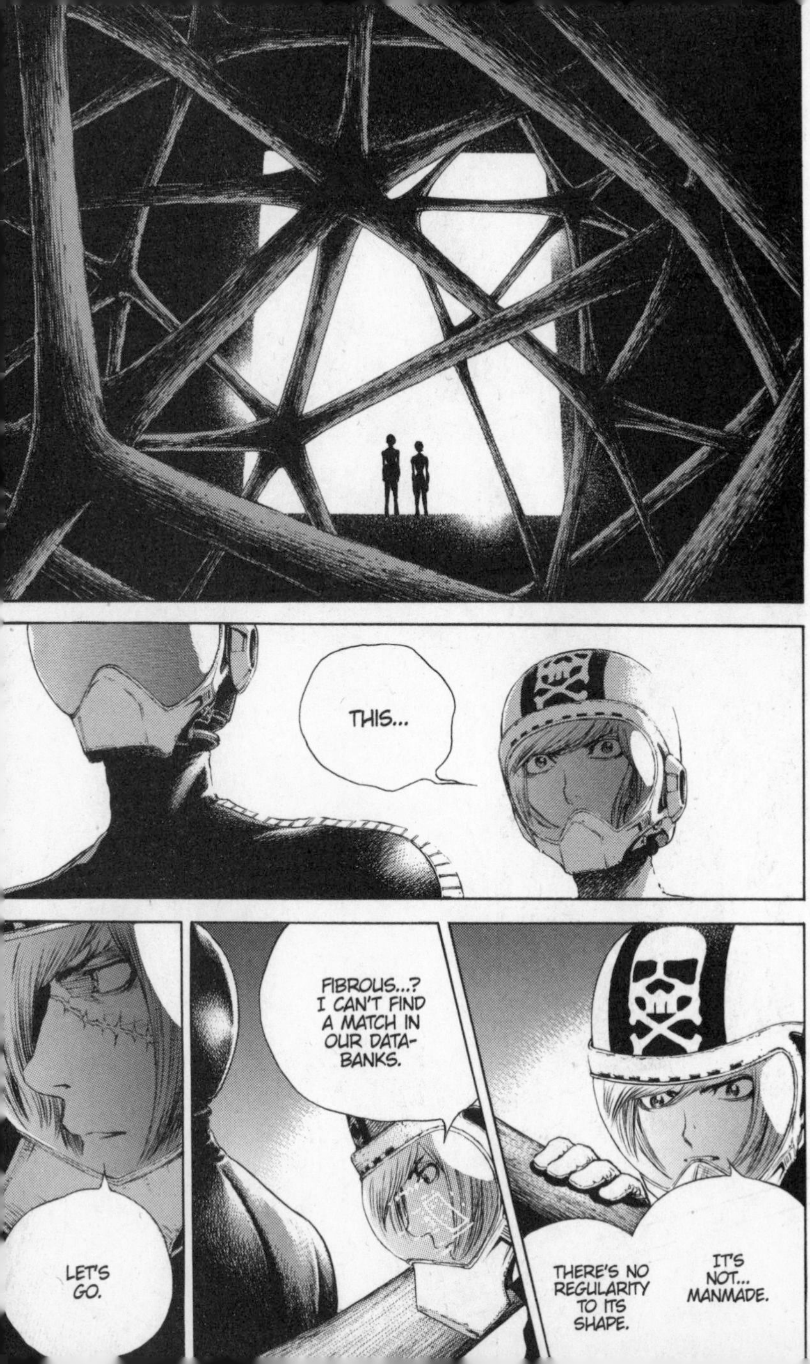
THIS...
IT'S NOT... MANMADE.
THERE'S NO REGULARITY TO ITS SHAPE.
FIBROUS...? I CAN'T FIND A MATCH IN OUR DATA-BANKS.
LET'S GO.

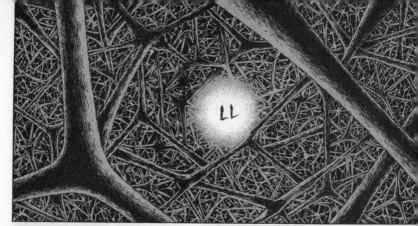

THE CARBON DATING MUST BE WRONG.

JUST HOW LONG AGO WAS THIS PLACE BUILT?

!!

ZUMM

ZUMM

ZUMM

ZUMM

ZUMM

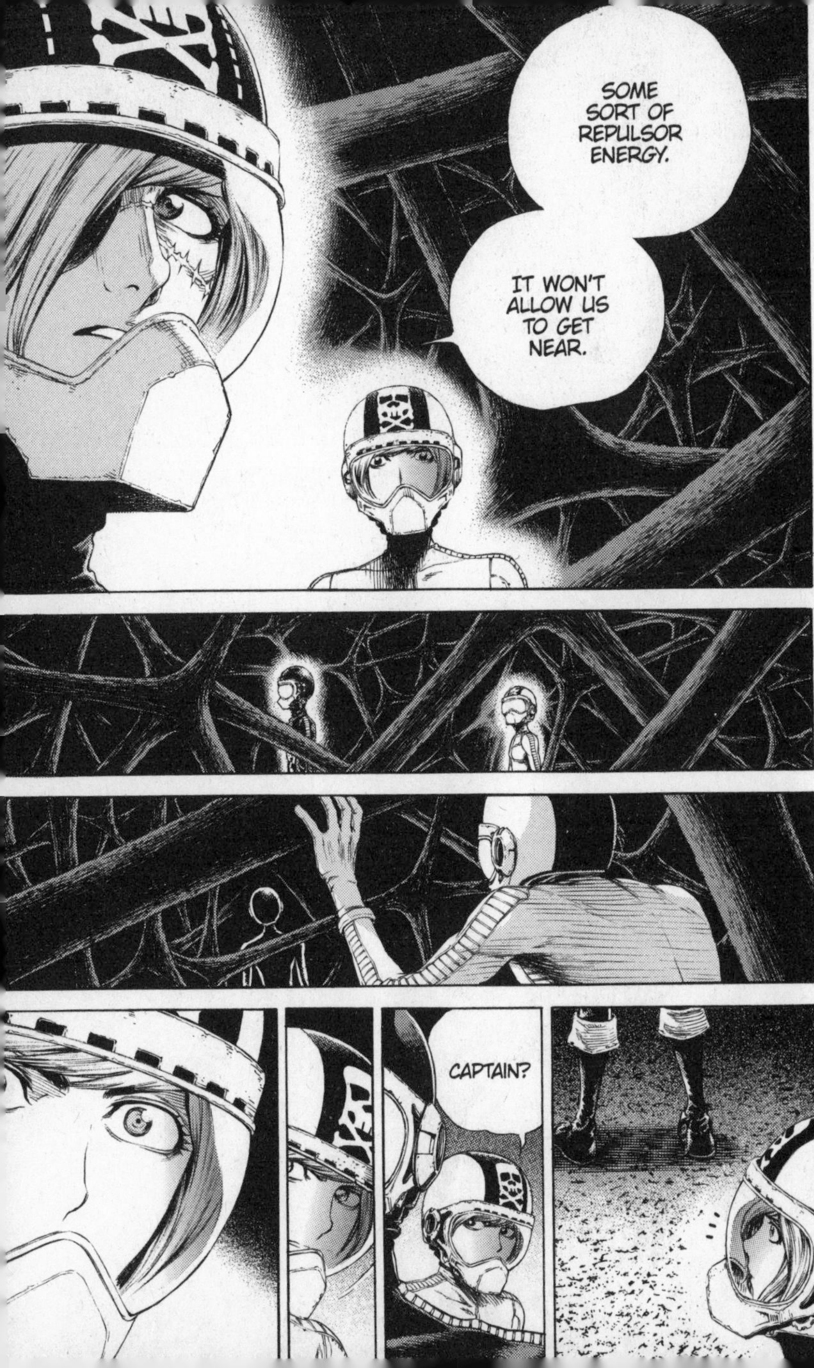
SOME SORT OF REPULSOR ENERGY.
IT WON'T ALLOW US TO GET NEAR.
CAPTAIN?
...

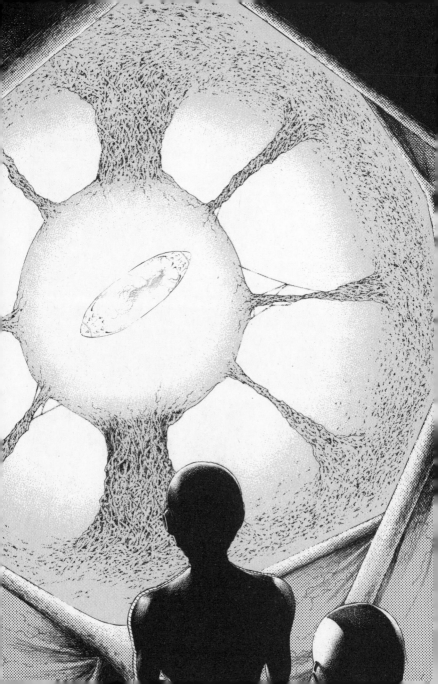

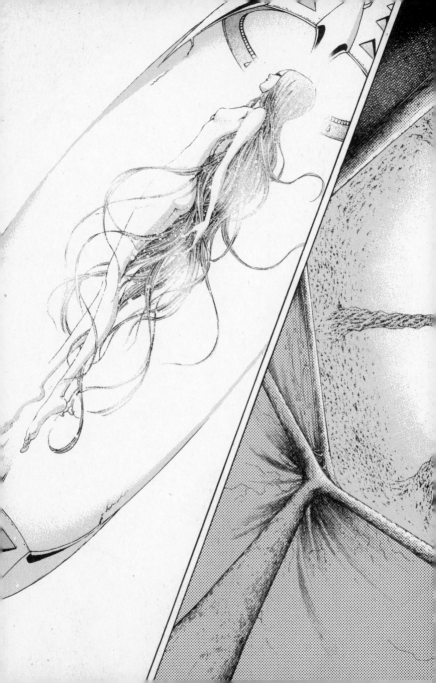

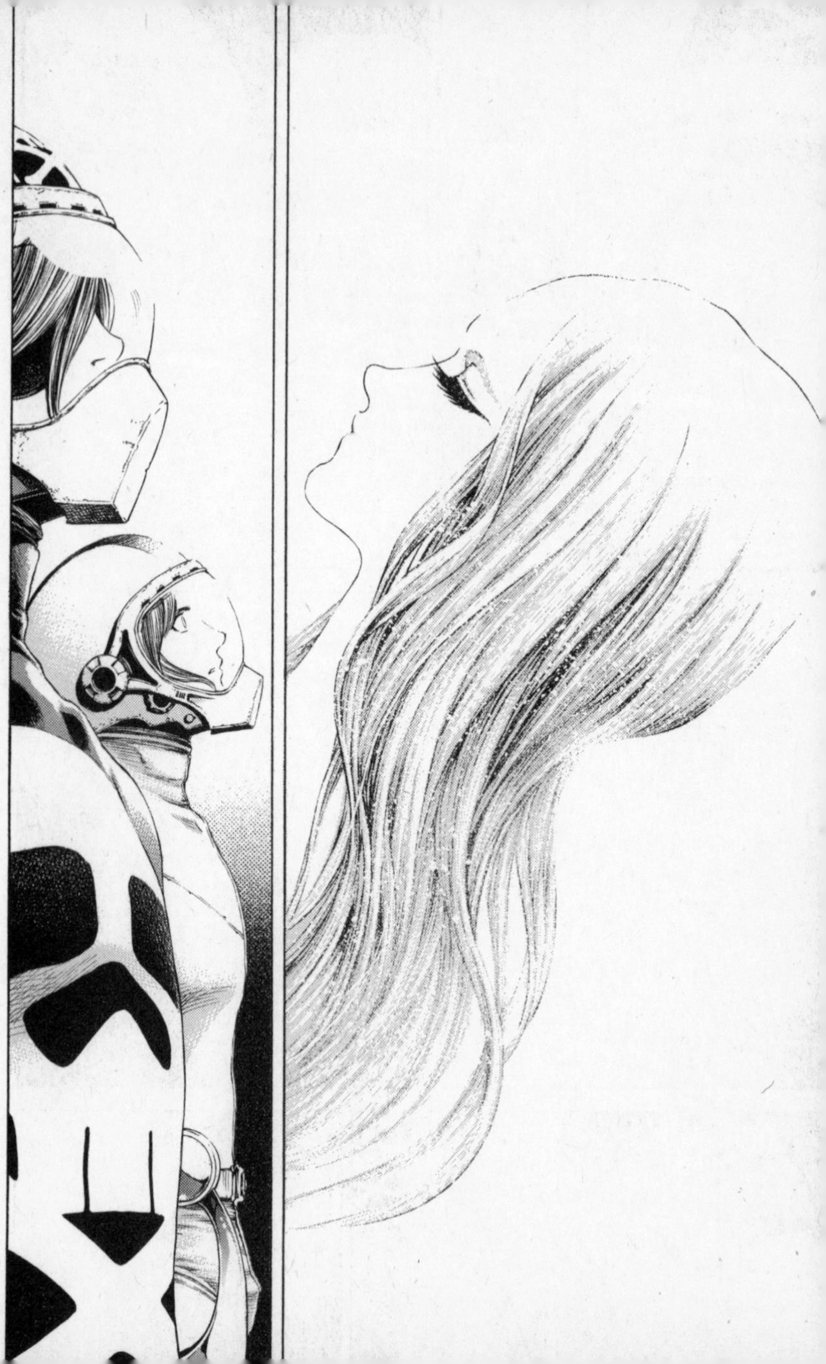

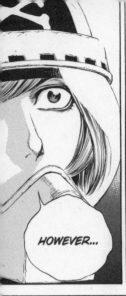

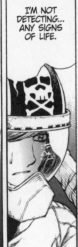

SLEEPING BEAUTY? IN THE PYRAMID AT THE BOTTOM OF THE SEA?
NO...A COFFIN.
I'M NOT DETECTING... ANY SIGNS OF LIFE.
HOWEVER...
THIS IS A MAZON.
DID YOU IMAGINE THEY WOULD BE SO BEAUTIFUL?
IF... IF WE TAKE HER BACK. STUDY HER...
TADASHI.

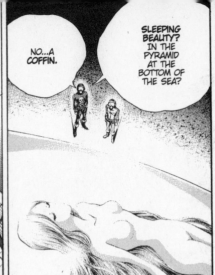

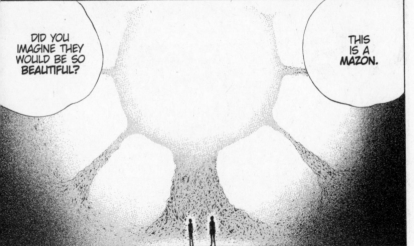

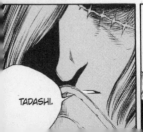

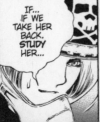

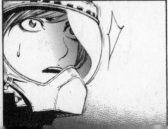

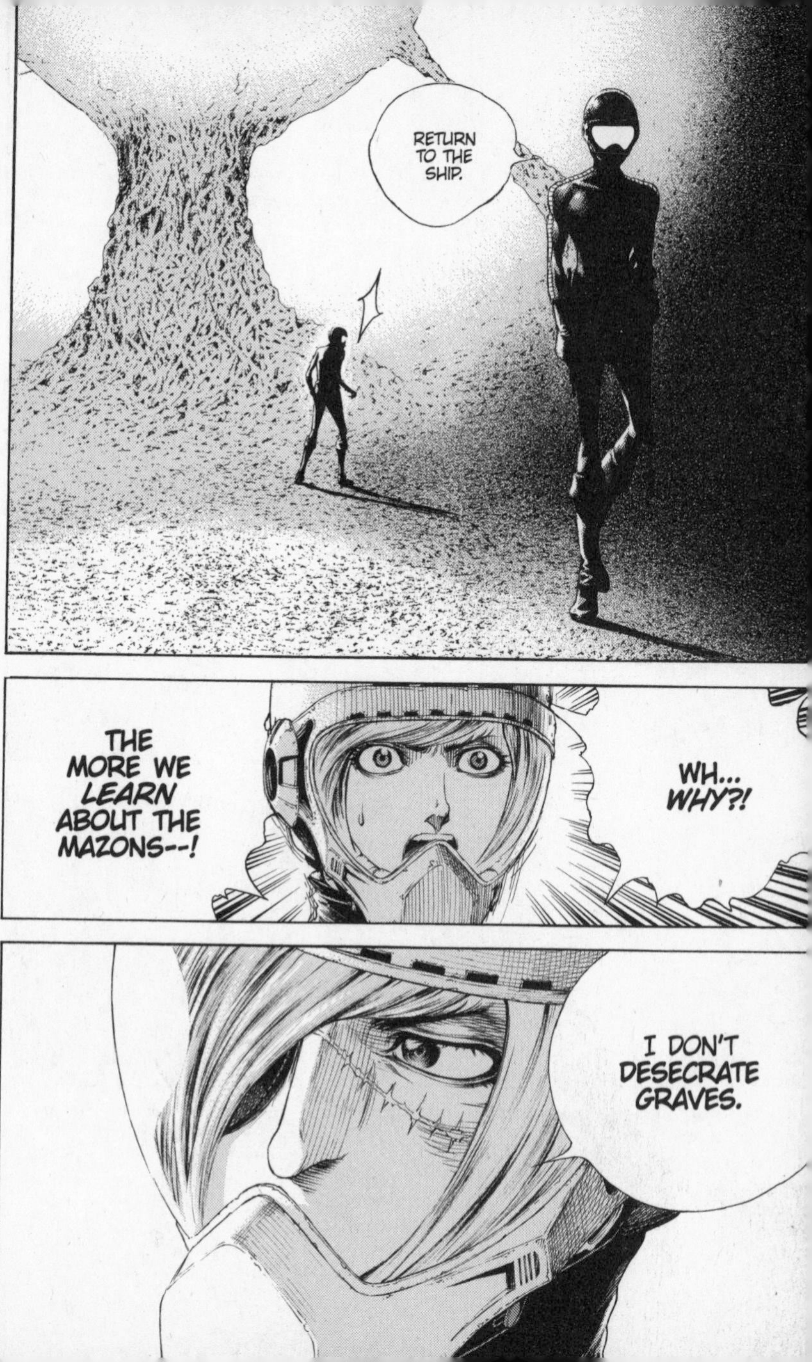
RETURN TO THE SHIP.
WH... WHY?!
THE MORE WE LEARN ABOUT THE MAZONS--!
I DON'T DESECRATE GRAVES.

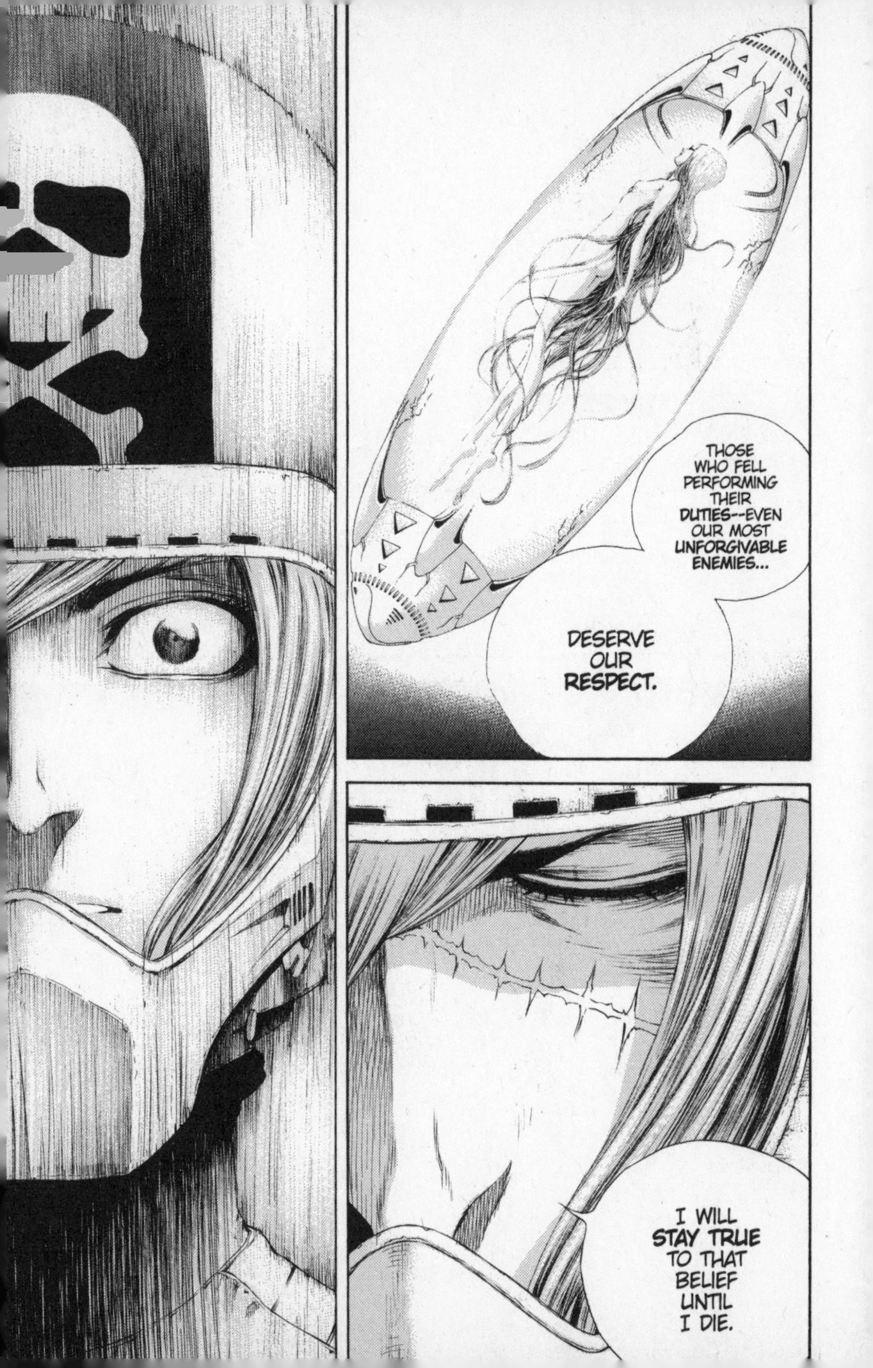
THOSE WHO FELL PERFORMING THEIR DUTIES--EVEN OUR MOST UNFORGIVABLE ENEMIES...
DESERVE OUR RESPECT.
I WILL STAY TRUE TO THAT BELIEF UNTIL I DIE.

THIS WOMAN DIED IN A FOREIGN LAND, PERFORMING HER MISSION. SHE WILL SLEEP HERE FOREVER.

IS THAT NOT A WORTHY EXISTENCE?

MY SELFISH-NESS...

I APOLOGIZE...

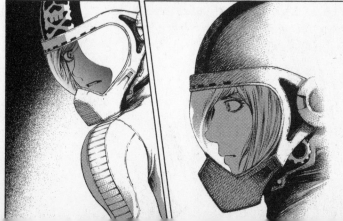

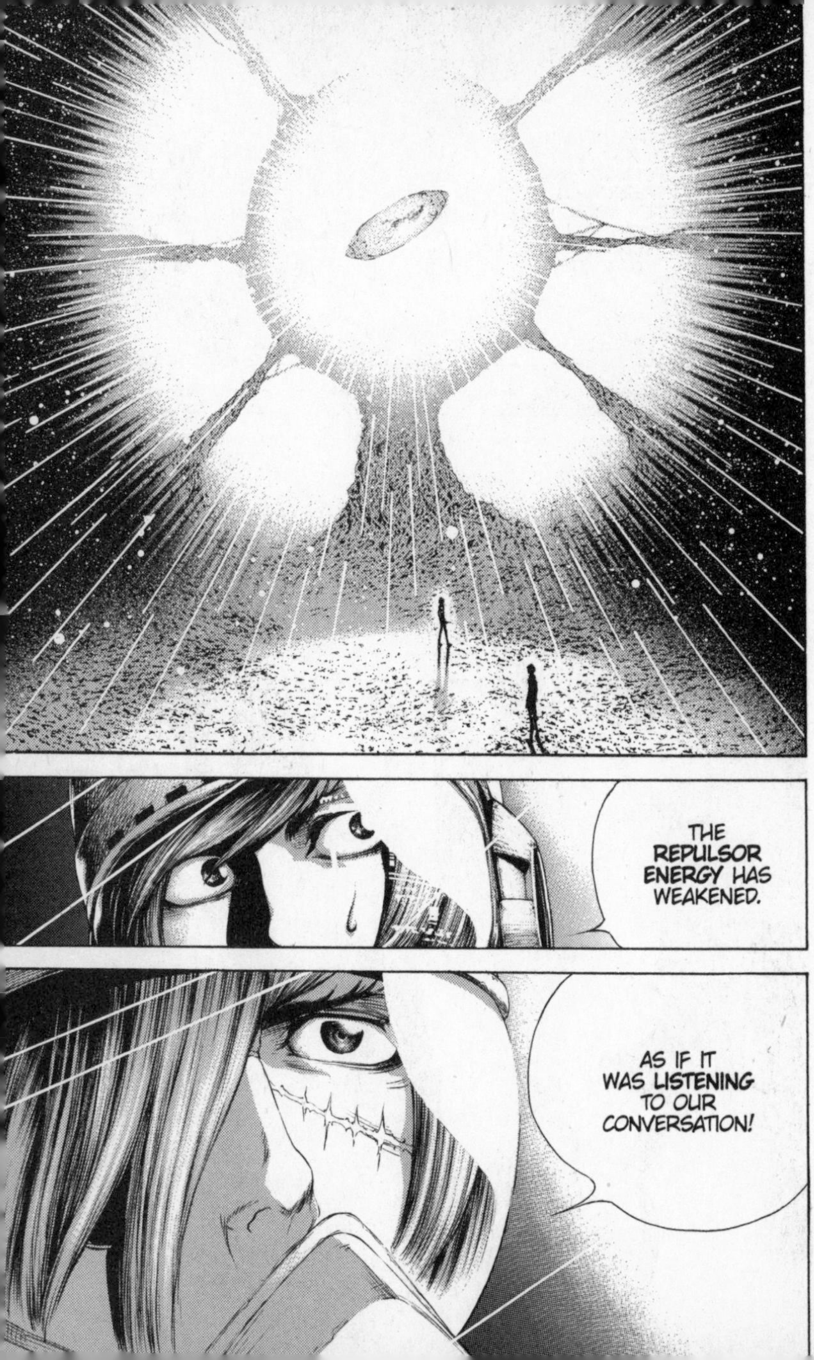
THE REPULSOR ENERGY HAS WEAKENED.
AS IF IT WAS LISTENING TO OUR CONVERSATION!

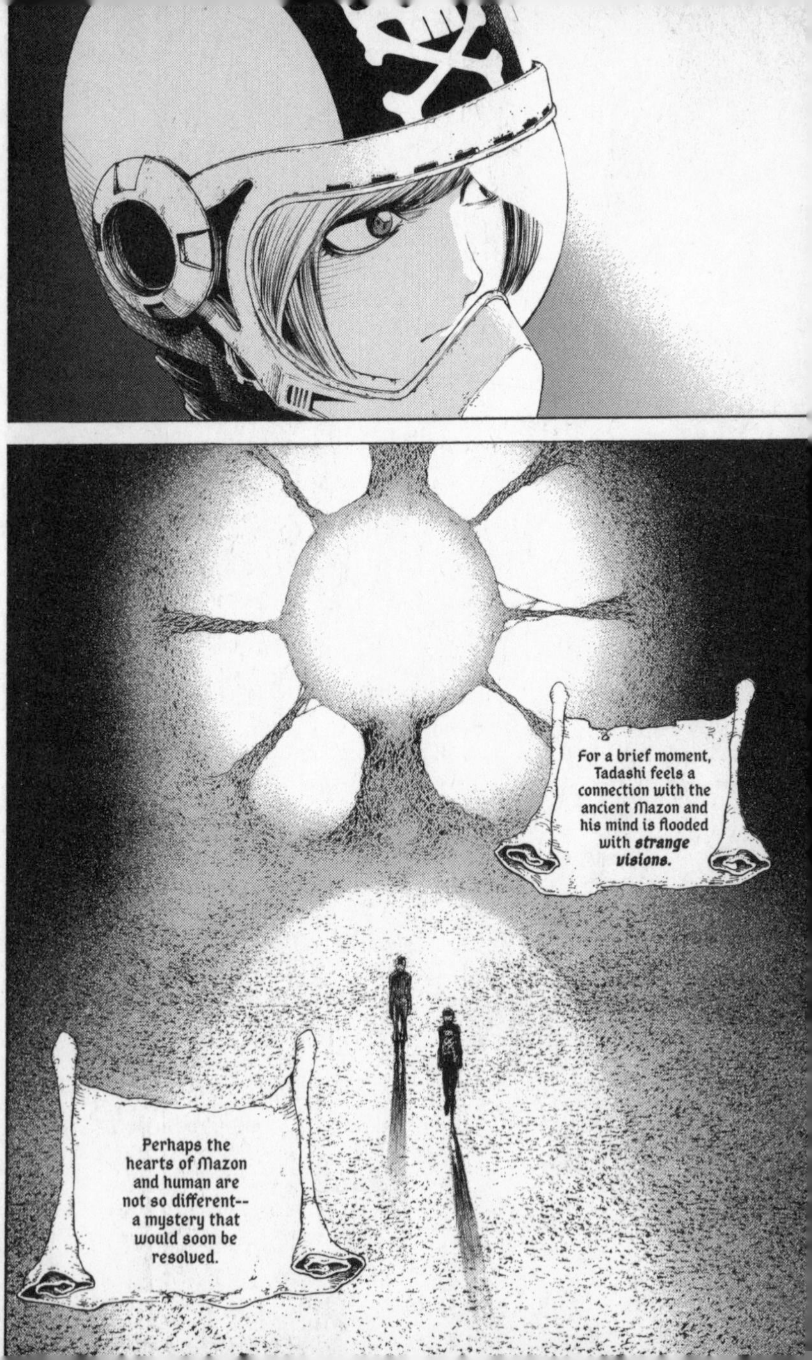
For a brief moment, Tadashi feels a connection with the ancient Mazon and his mind is flooded with ***strange visions.***
Perhaps the hearts of Mazon and human are not so different--a mystery that would soon be resolved.

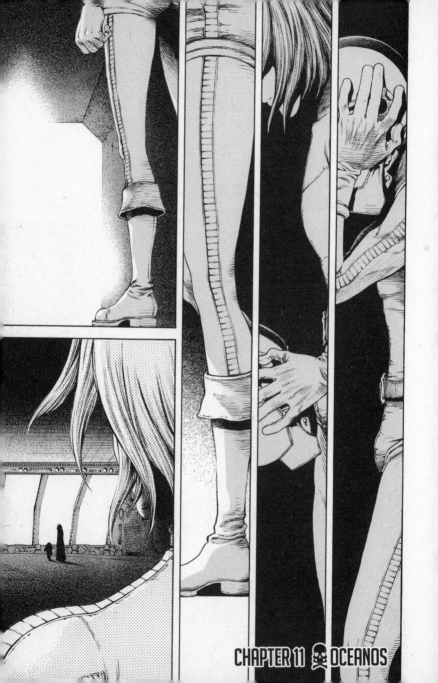

CHAPTER 11 OCEANOS

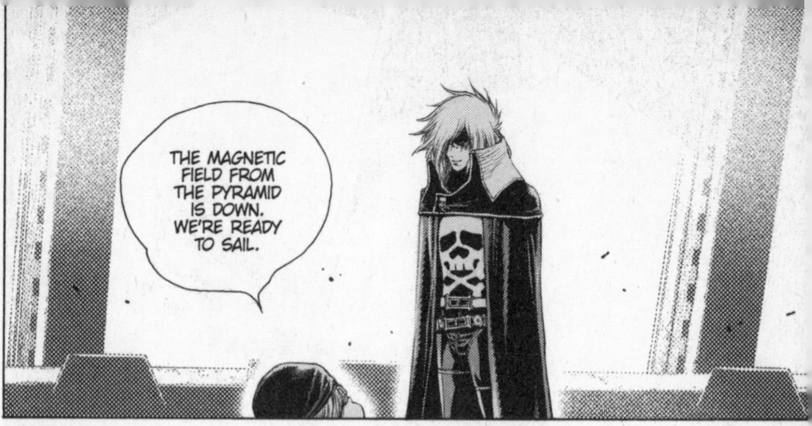
THE MAGNETIC FIELD FROM THE PYRAMID IS DOWN. WE'RE READY TO SAIL.

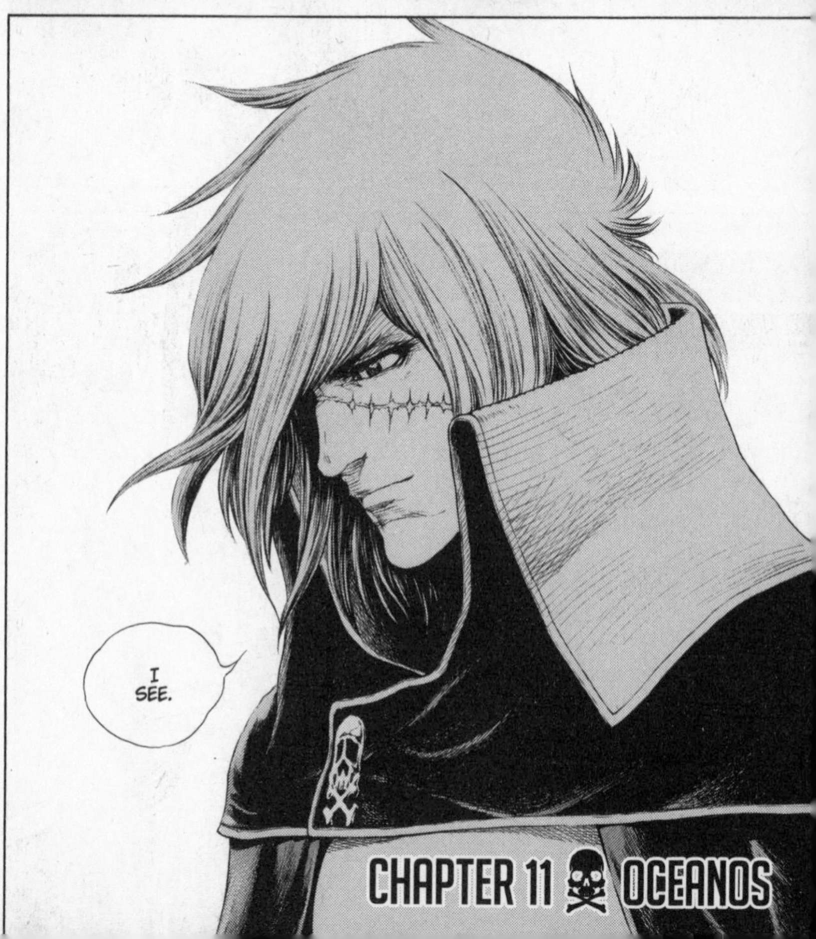
I SEE.

CHAPTER 11 OCEANOS

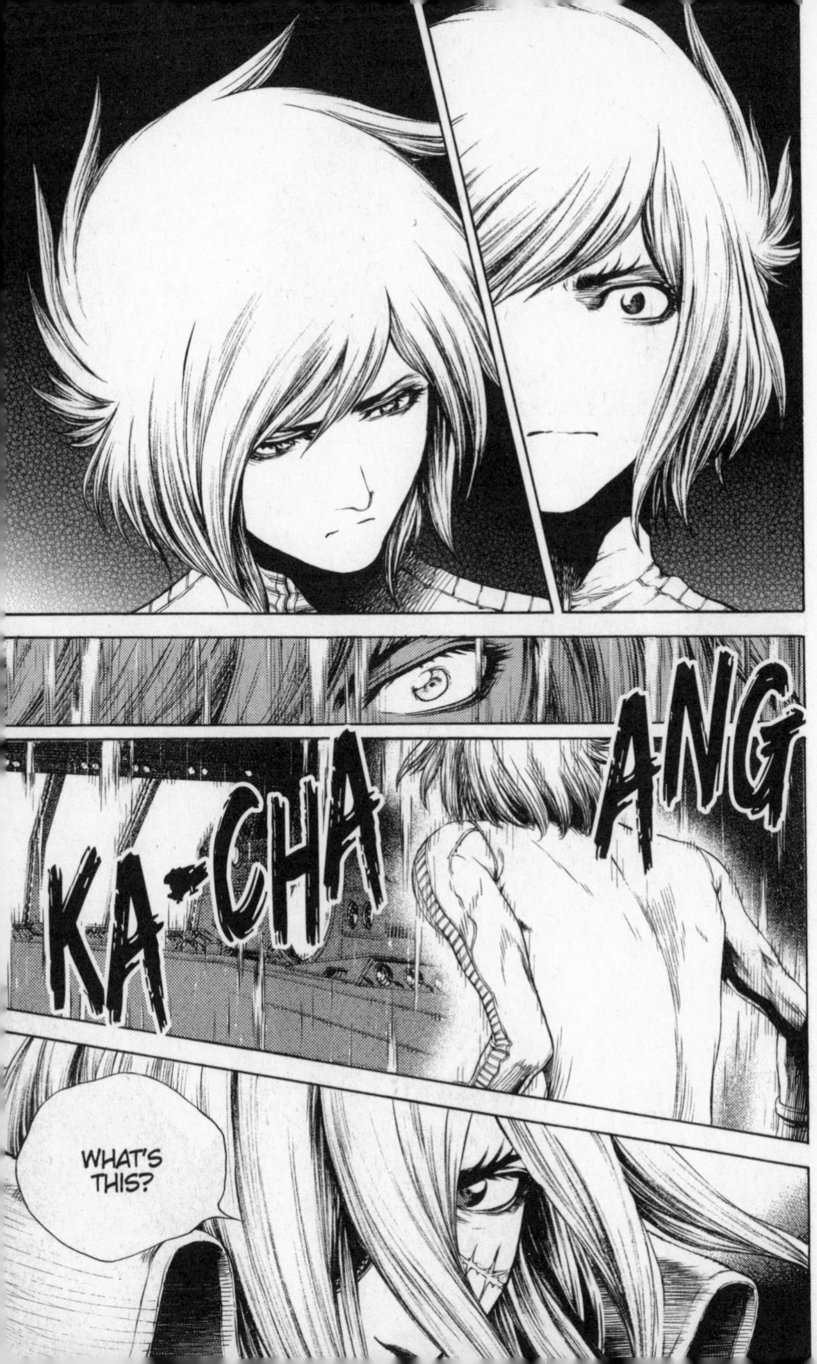
KA-CHA ANG
WHAT'S THIS?

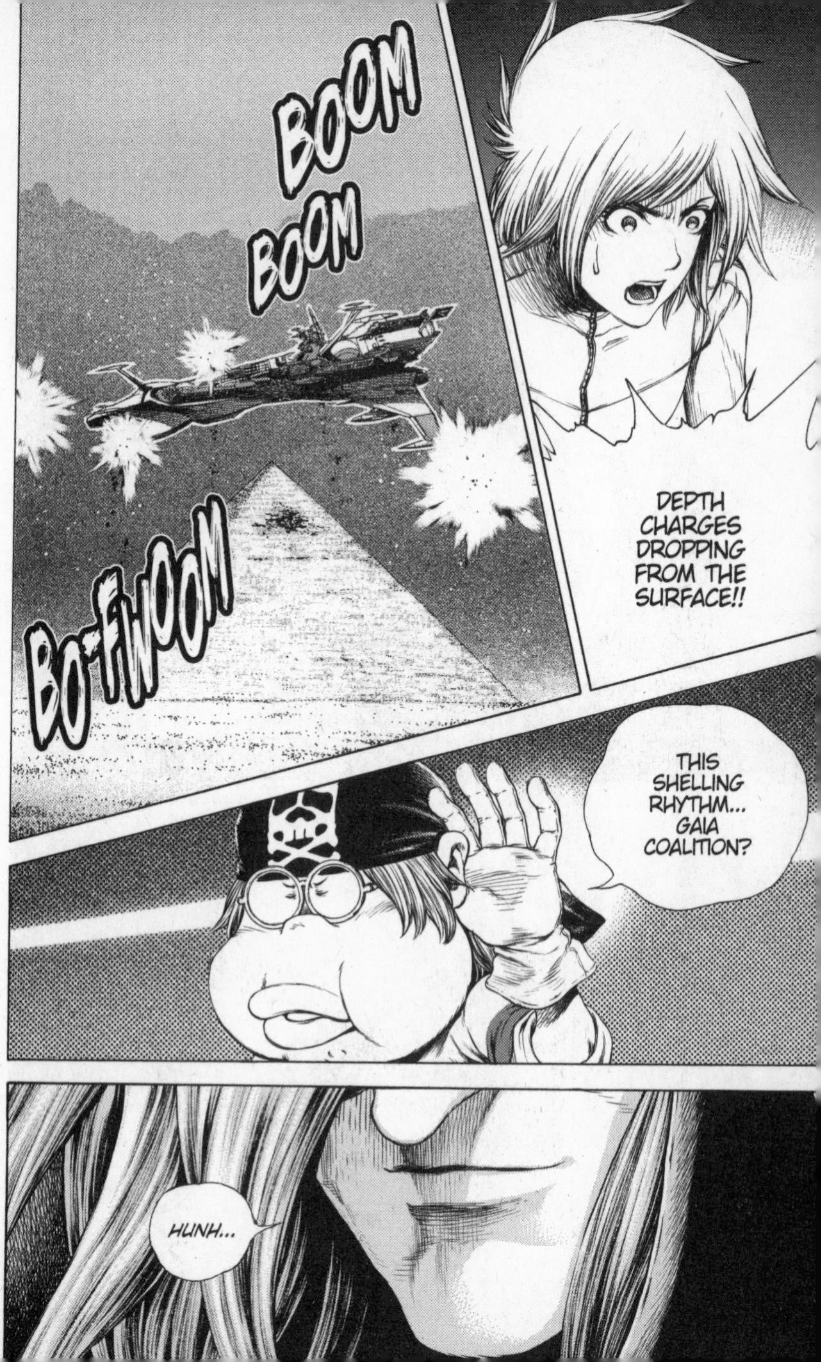
DEPTH CHARGES DROPPING FROM THE SURFACE!!
BOOM BOOM
BO-FWOOM
THIS SHELLING RHYTHM... GAIA COALITION?
HUNH...

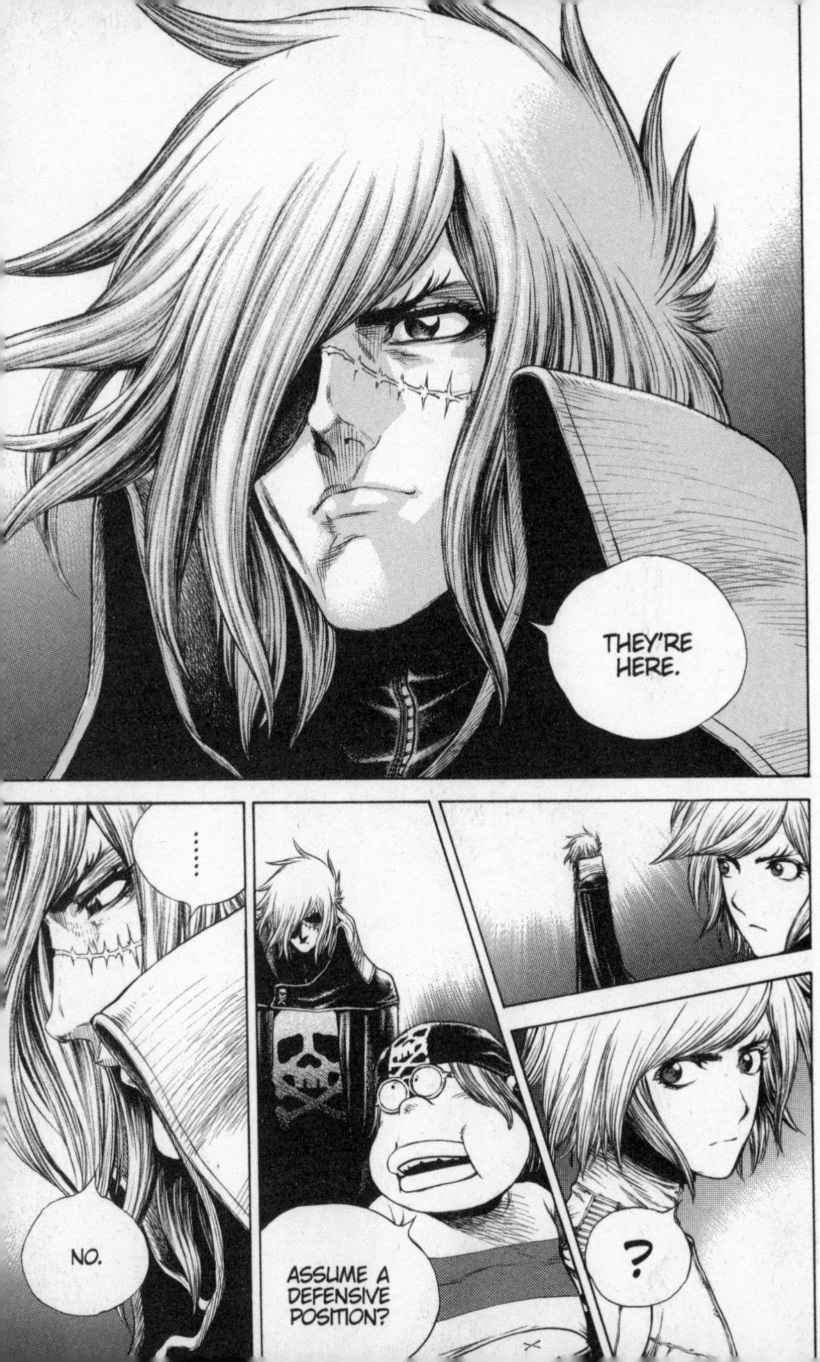
THEY'RE HERE.
?
ASSUME A DEFENSIVE POSITION?
......
NO.

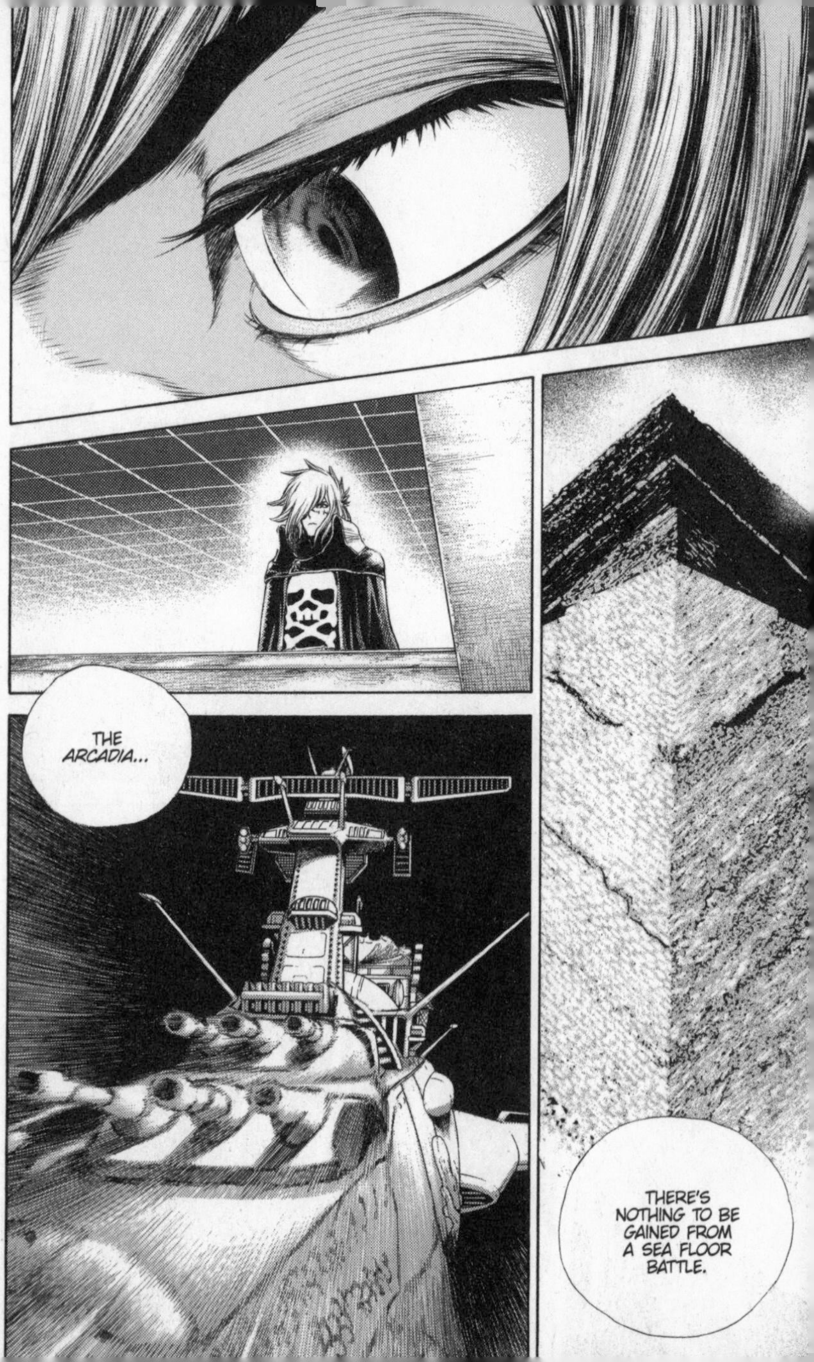
THERE'S NOTHING TO BE GAINED FROM A SEA FLOOR BATTLE.
THE ARCADIA...

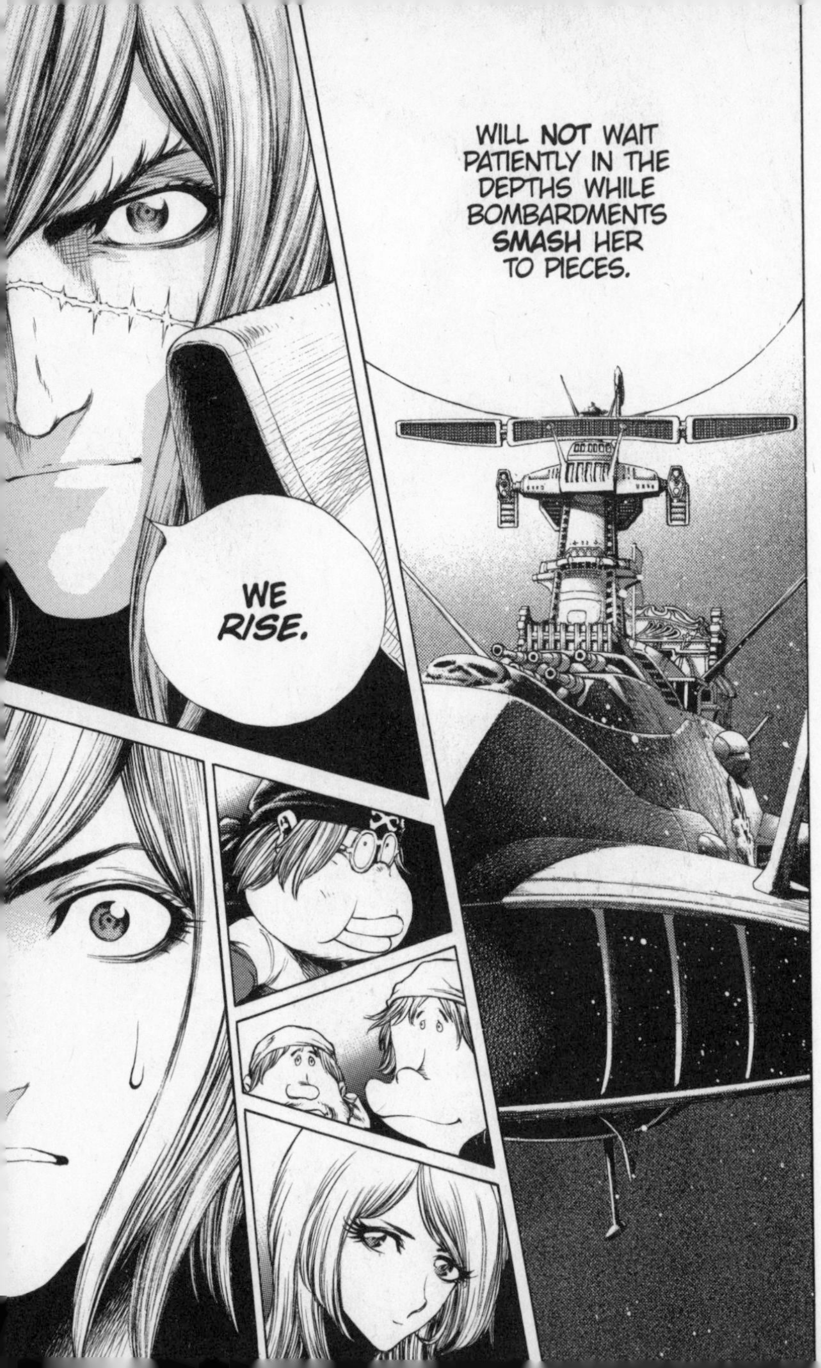
WILL NOT WAIT PATIENTLY IN THE DEPTHS WHILE BOMBARDMENTS SMASH HER TO PIECES.
WE RISE.

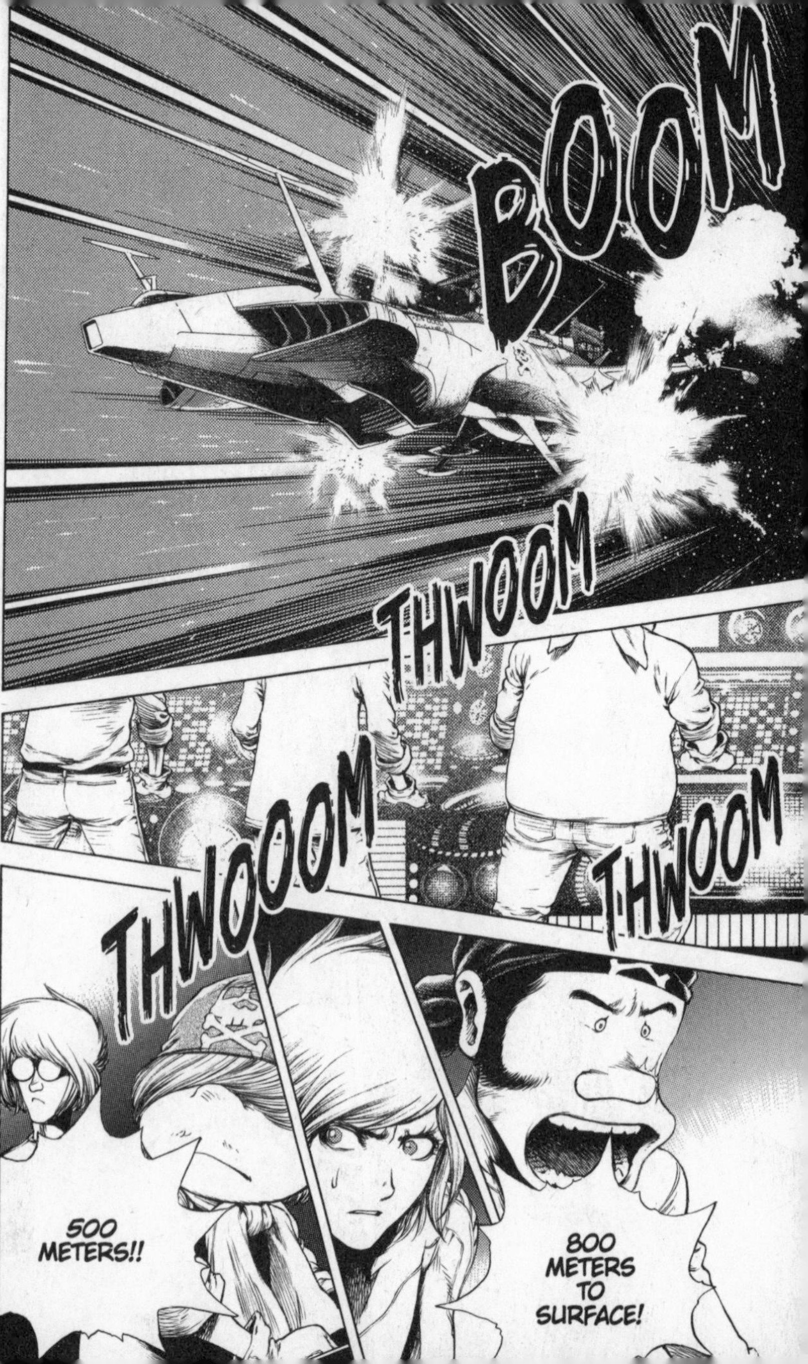
BOOM
THWOOM
THWOOM
THWOOOM
800 METERS TO SURFACE!
500 METERS!!

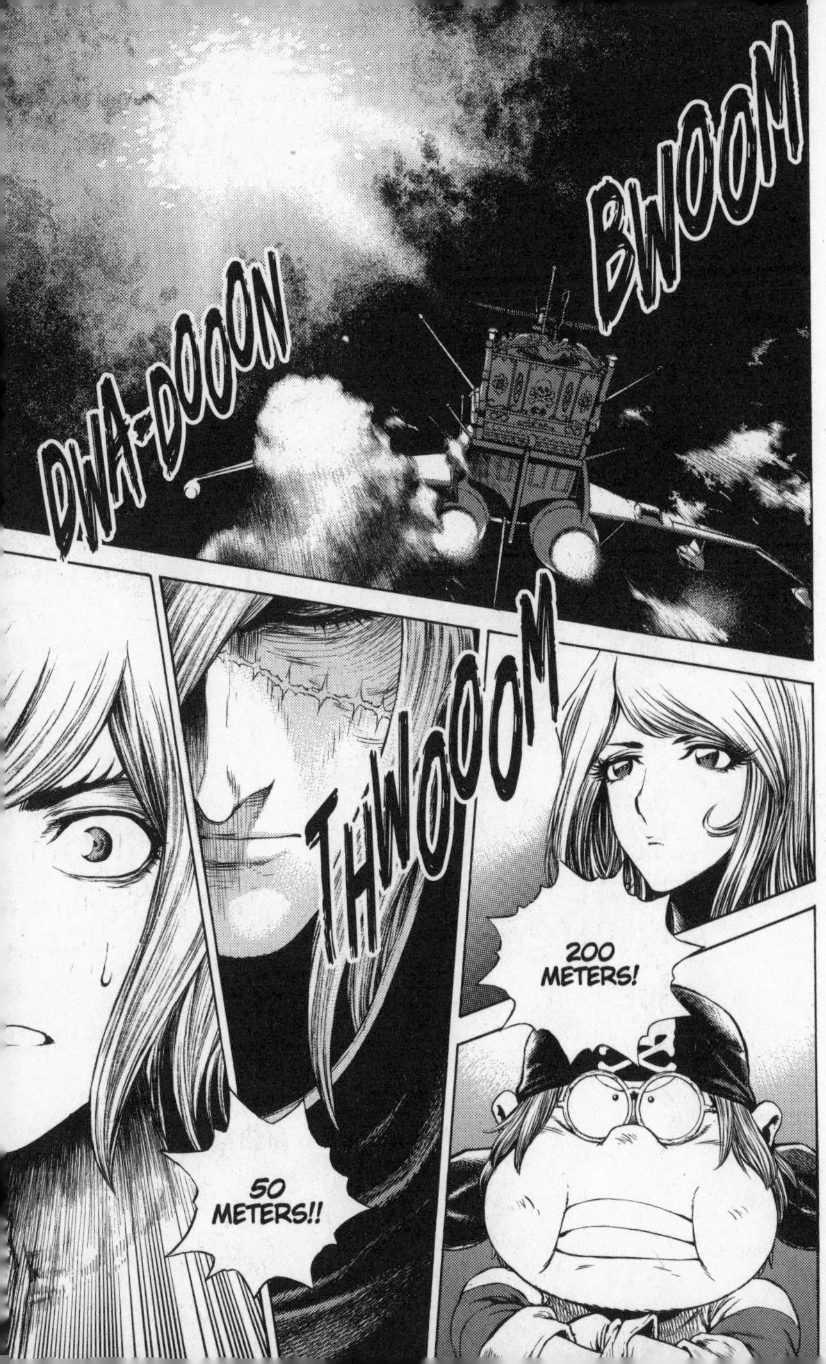
BWOOM
DWA-DOOON
THWOOOM
200 METERS!
50 METERS!!

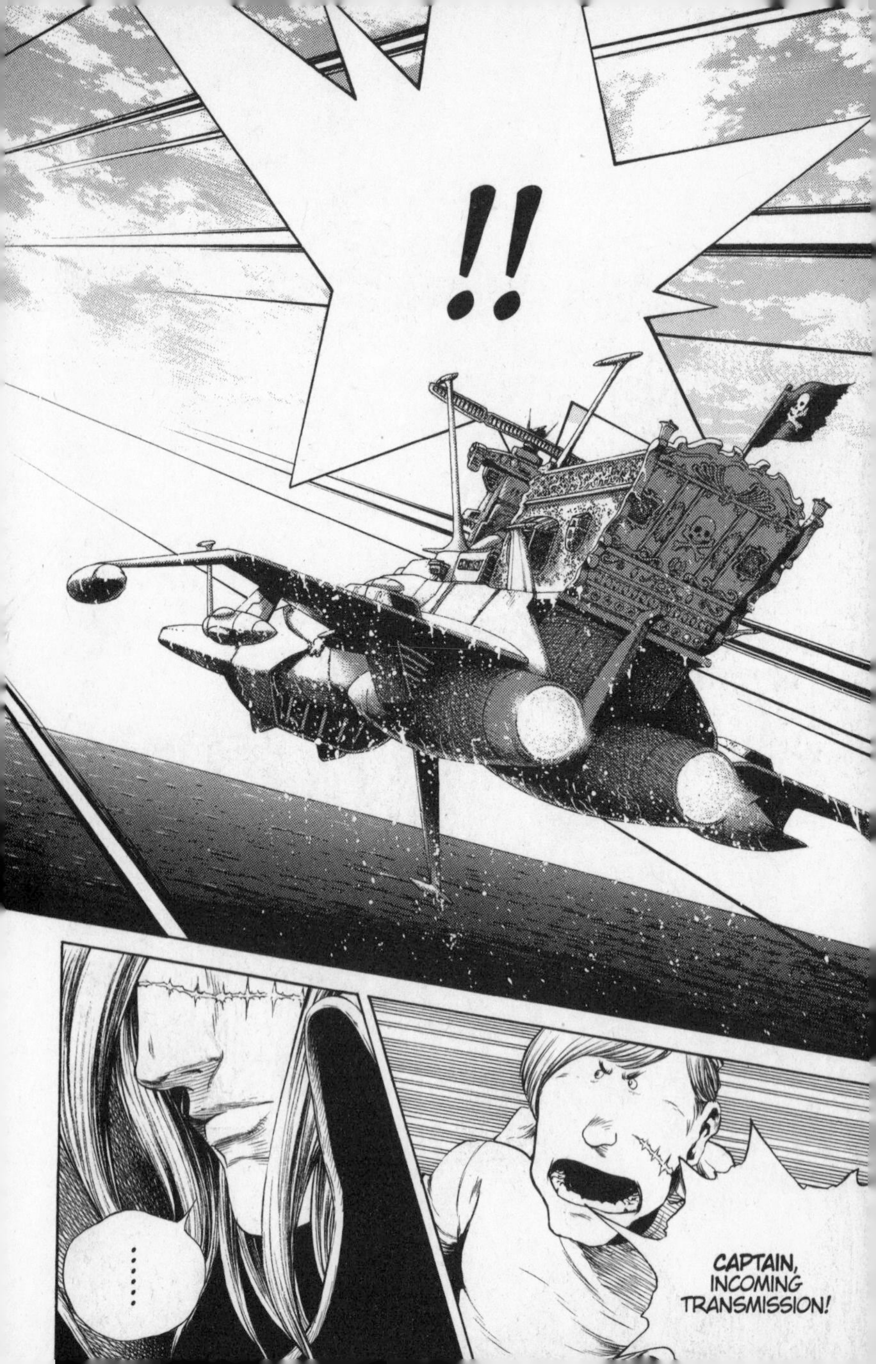
!!
CAPTAIN, INCOMING TRANSMISSION!
......

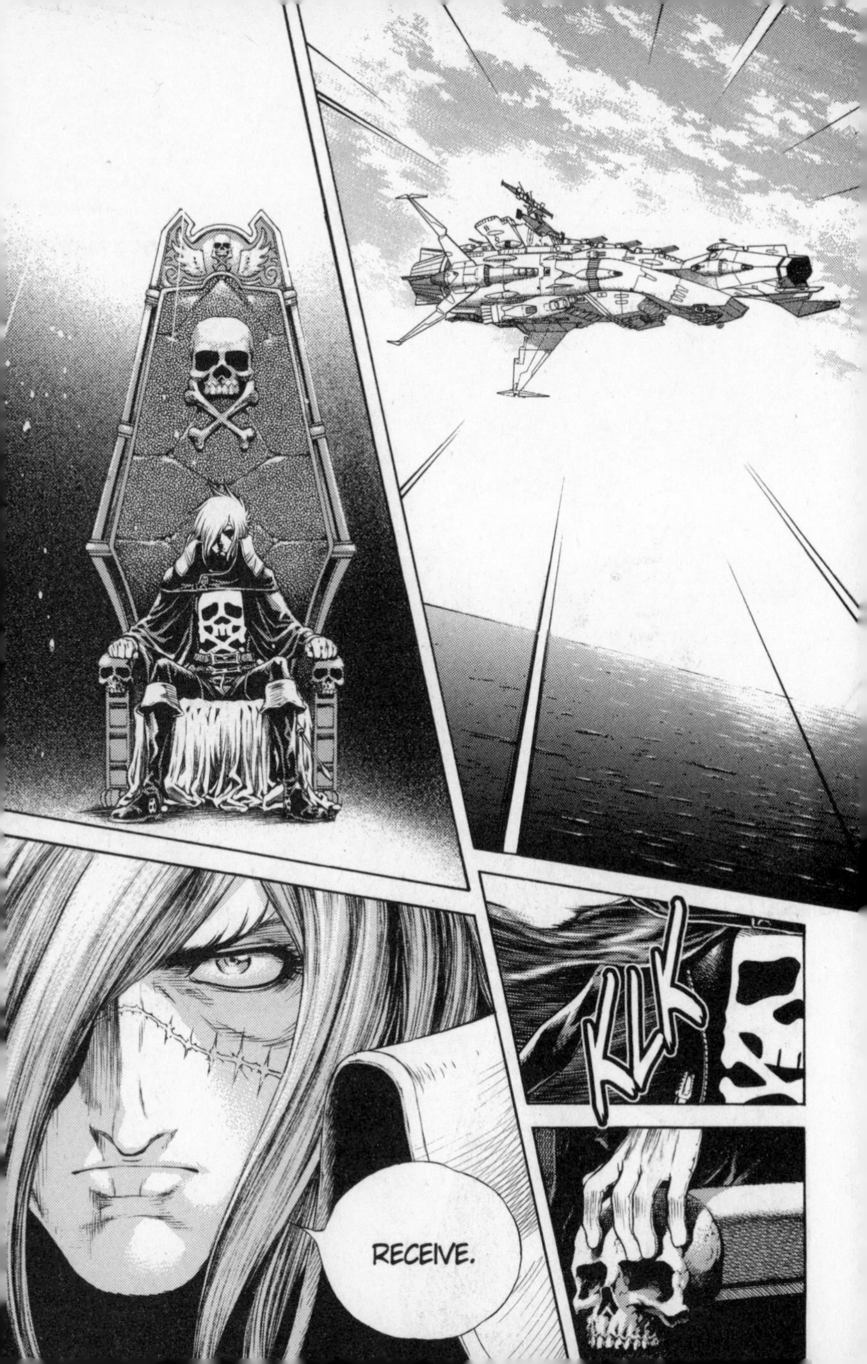
KLIK
RECEIVE.

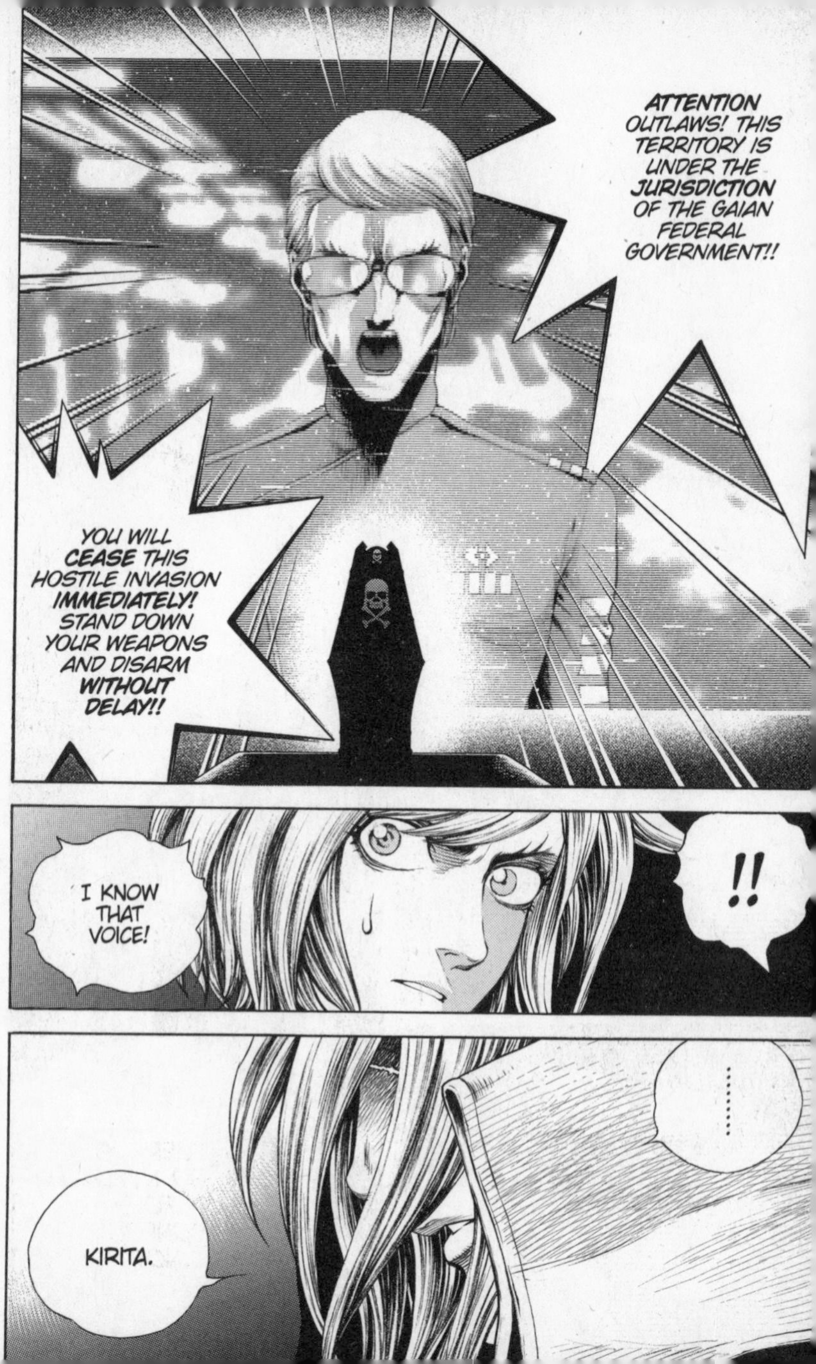
ATTENTION OUTLAWS! THIS TERRITORY IS UNDER THE JURISDICTION OF THE GAIAN FEDERAL GOVERNMENT!!
YOU WILL CEASE THIS HOSTILE INVASION IMMEDIATELY! STAND DOWN YOUR WEAPONS AND DISARM WITHOUT DELAY!!
!!
I KNOW THAT VOICE!
......
KIRITA.

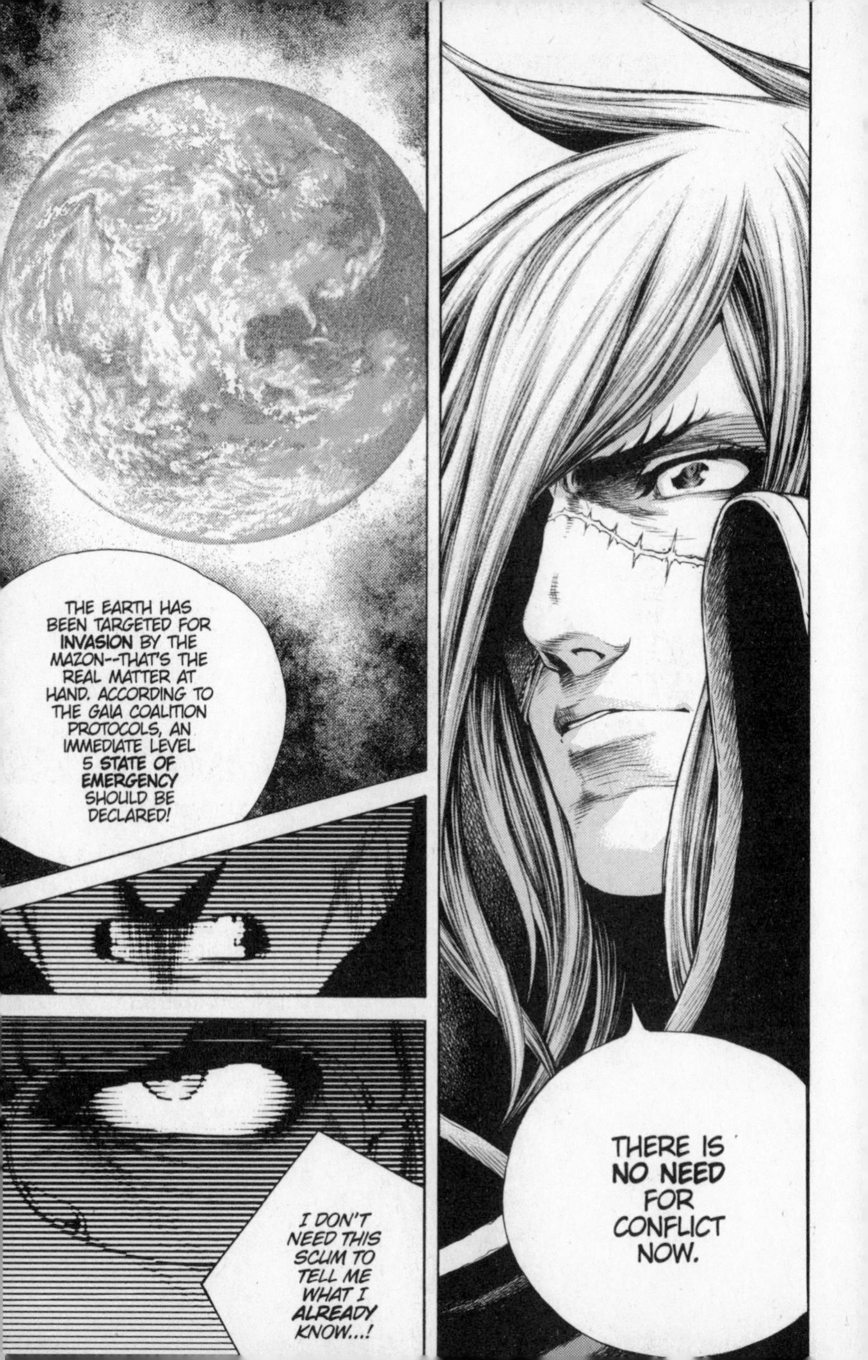
THERE IS NO NEED FOR CONFLICT NOW.
THE EARTH HAS BEEN TARGETED FOR INVASION BY THE MAZON--THAT'S THE REAL MATTER AT HAND. ACCORDING TO THE GAIA COALITION PROTOCOLS, AN IMMEDIATE LEVEL 5 STATE OF EMERGENCY SHOULD BE DECLARED!
I DON'T NEED THIS SCUM TO TELL ME WHAT I ALREADY KNOW...!

BE THAT AS IT MAY, WE REFUSE TO DISREGARD OUR REGULATIONS AND ADMIT RECKLESS OUTLAWS INTO OUR RANKS!!

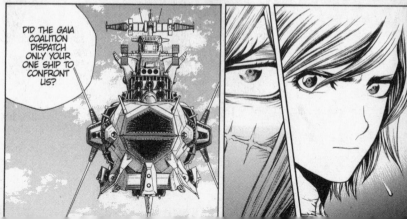

DID THE GAIA COALITION DISPATCH ONLY YOUR ONE SHIP TO CONFRONT US?

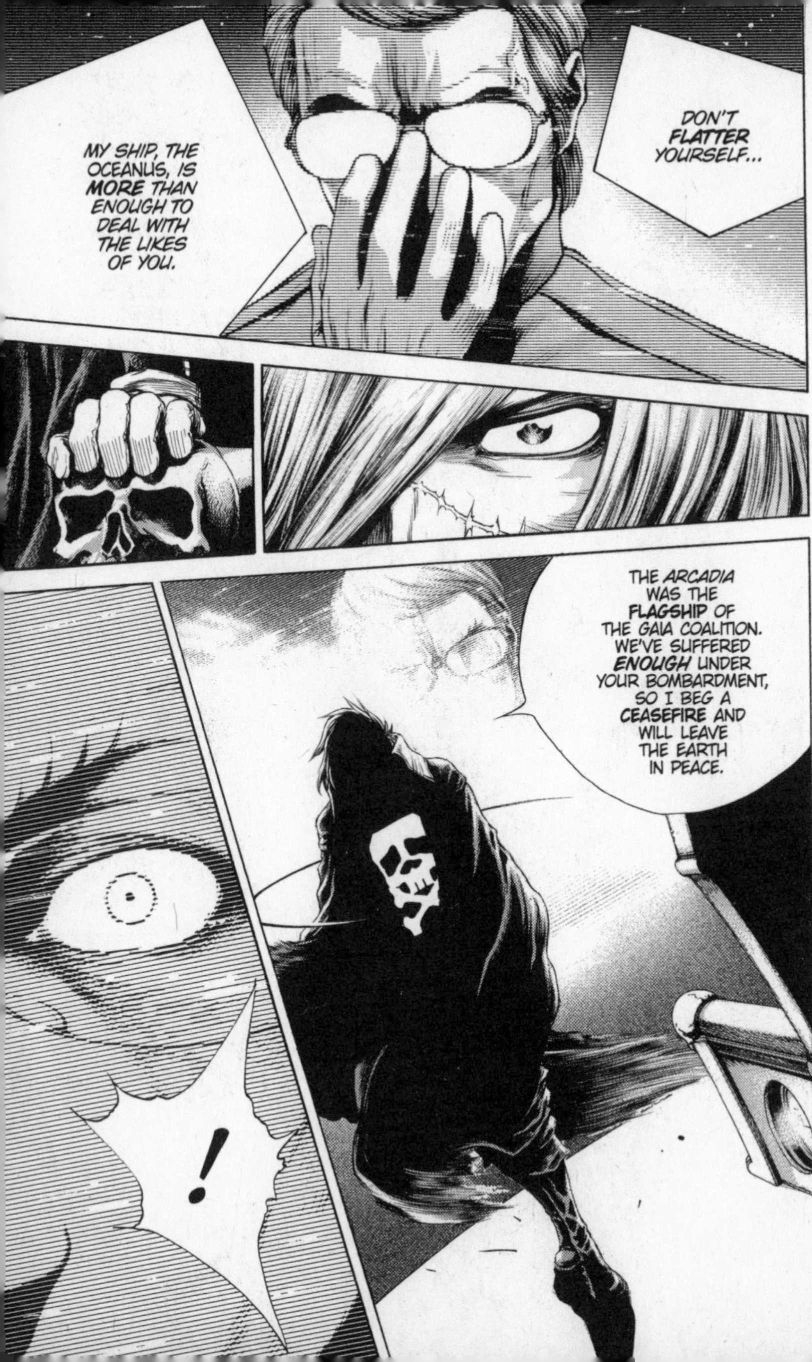
DON'T FLATTER YOURSELF...
MY SHIP, THE OCEANUS, IS MORE THAN ENOUGH TO DEAL WITH THE LIKES OF YOU.
THE ARCADIA WAS THE FLAGSHIP OF THE GAIA COALITION. WE'VE SUFFERED ENOUGH UNDER YOUR BOMBARDMENT, SO I BEG A CEASEFIRE AND WILL LEAVE THE EARTH IN PEACE.
!

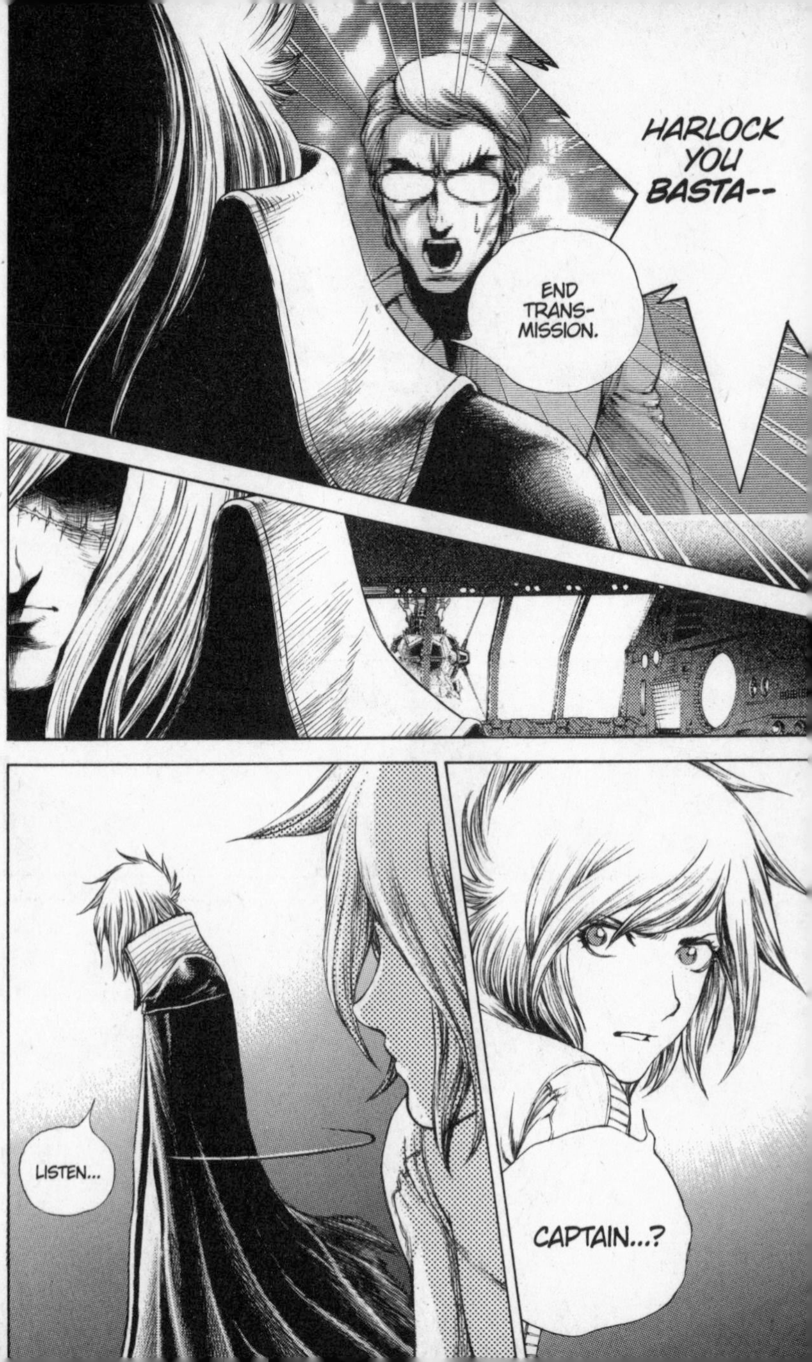
HARLOCK YOU BASTA--
END TRANS-MISSION.
CAPTAIN...?
LISTEN...

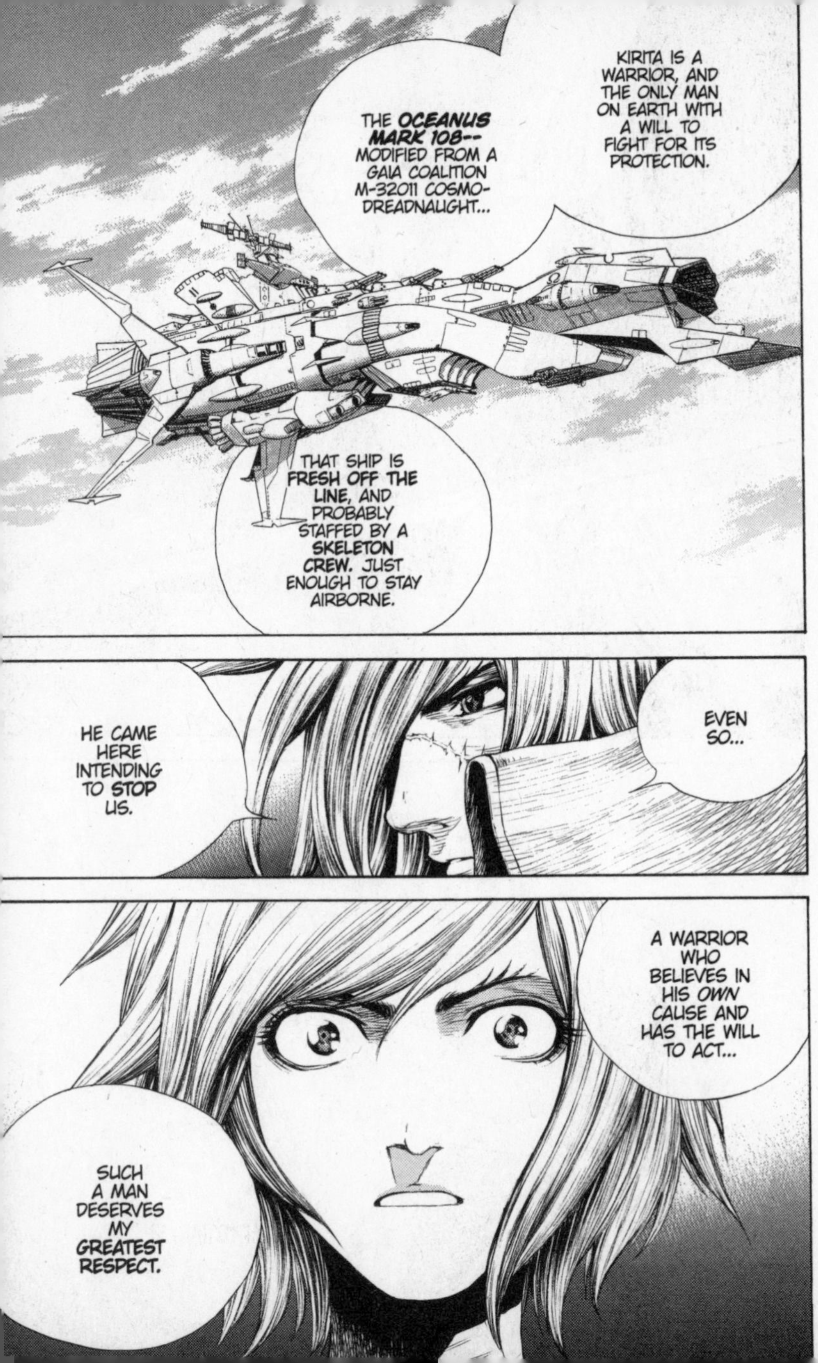
KIRITA IS A WARRIOR, AND THE ONLY MAN ON EARTH WITH A WILL TO FIGHT FOR ITS PROTECTION.
THE ***OCEANUS MARK 108--*** MODIFIED FROM A GAIA COALITION M-32011 COSMO-DREADNAUGHT...
THAT SHIP IS **FRESH OFF THE LINE**, AND PROBABLY STAFFED BY A **SKELETON CREW**. JUST ENOUGH TO STAY AIRBORNE.
EVEN SO...
HE CAME HERE INTENDING TO **STOP** US.
A WARRIOR WHO BELIEVES IN HIS *OWN* CAUSE AND HAS THE WILL TO ACT...
SUCH A MAN DESERVES MY **GREATEST RESPECT.**

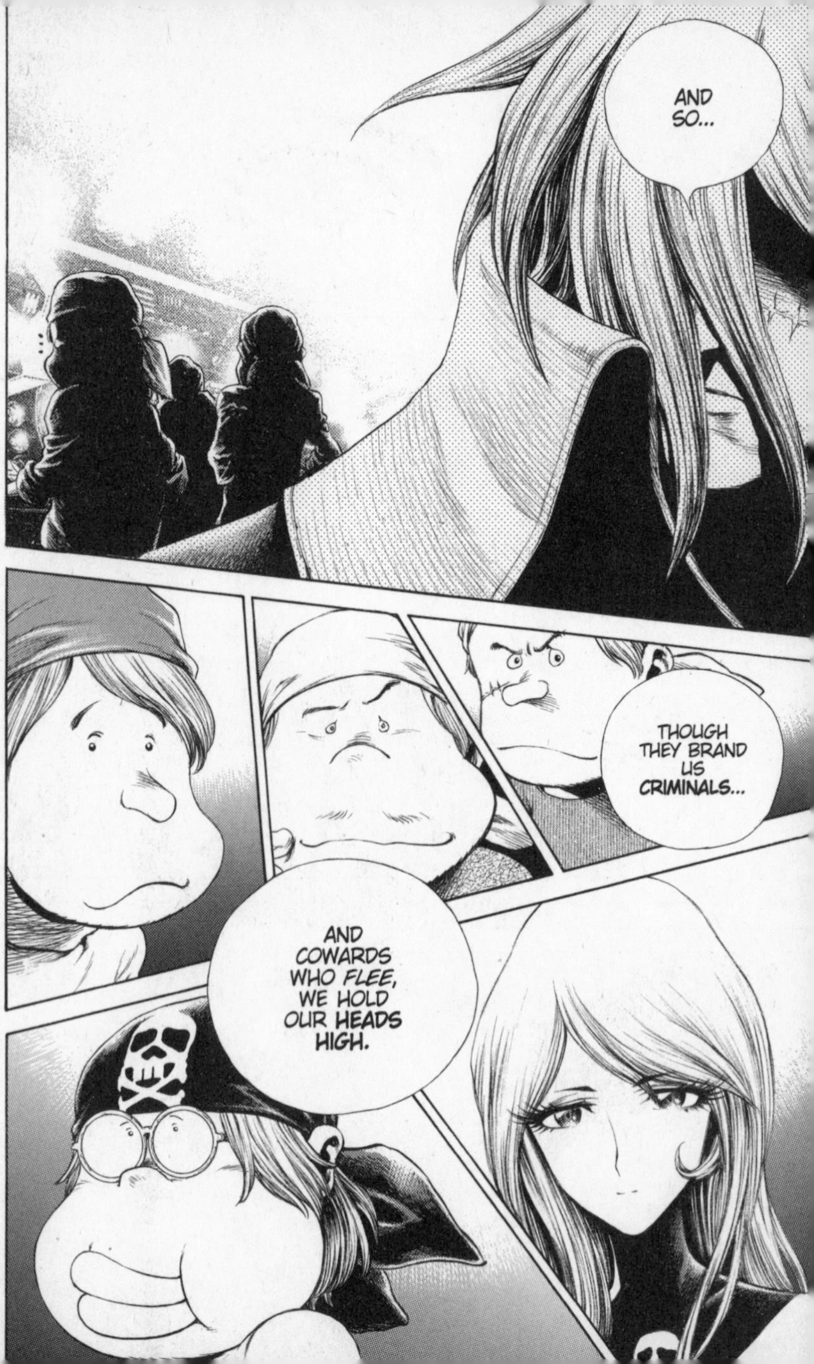
AND SO...
THOUGH THEY BRAND US CRIMINALS...
AND COWARDS WHO *FLEE*, WE HOLD OUR **HEADS HIGH.**

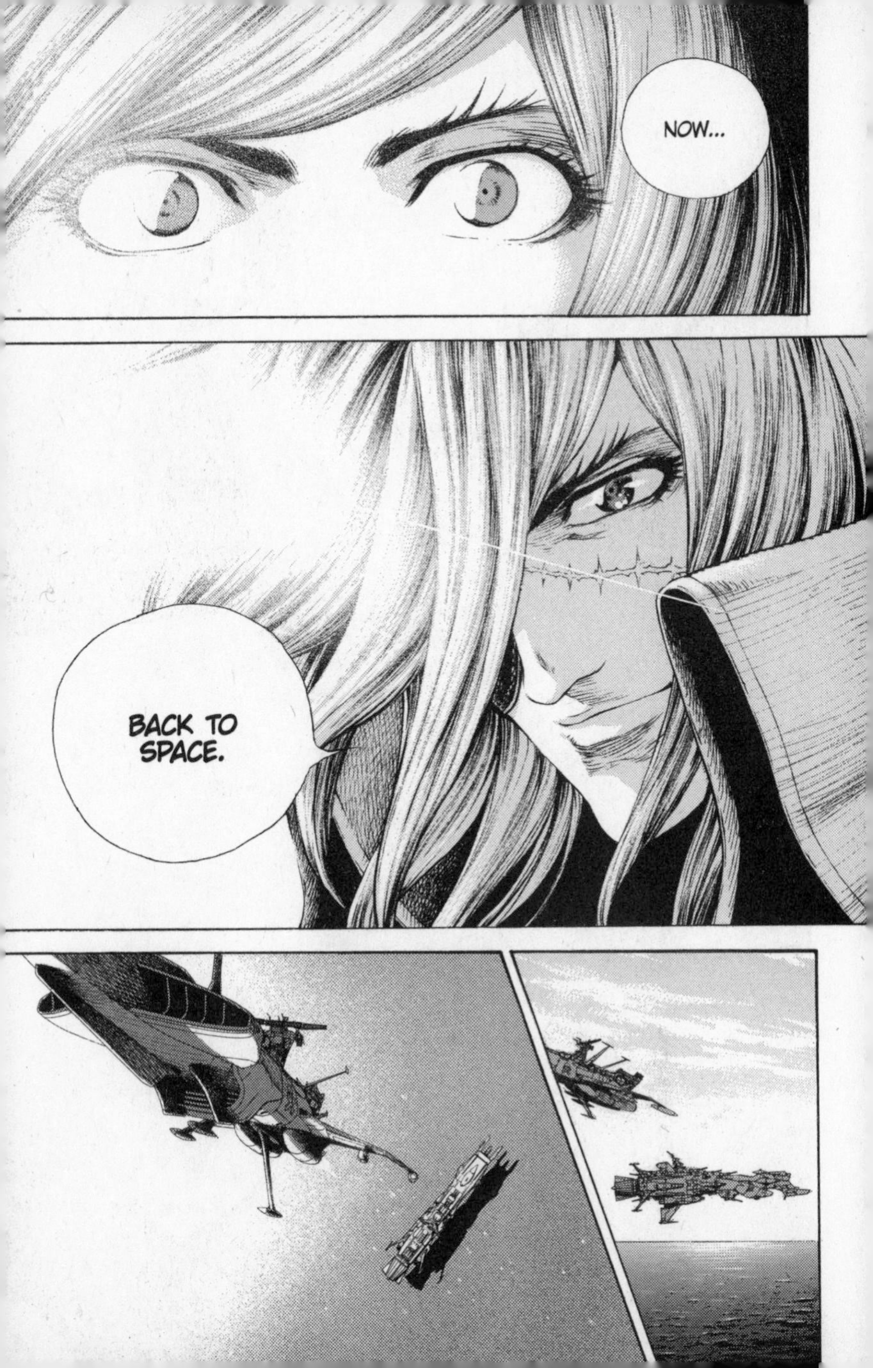
NOW...
BACK TO SPACE.

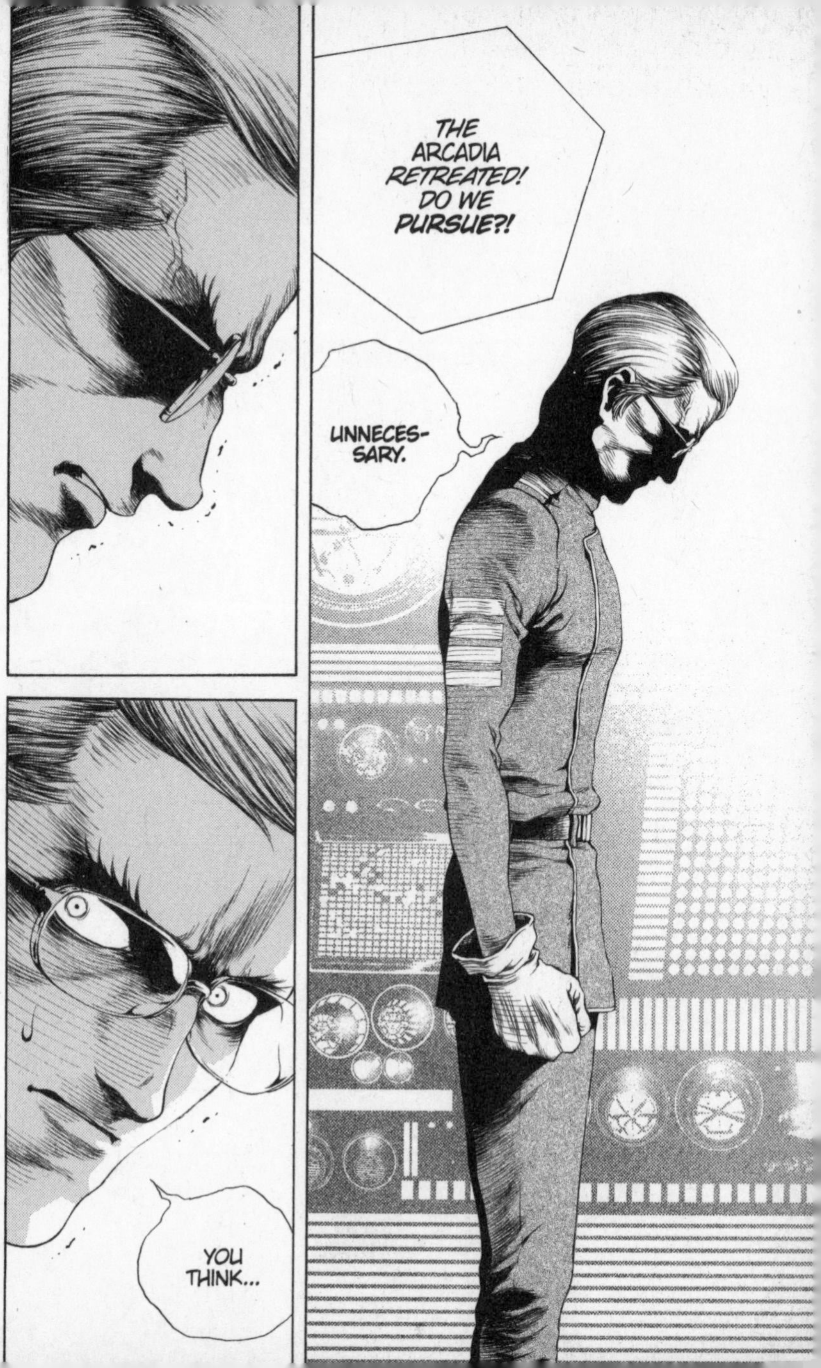
THE ARCADIA RETREATED! DO WE PURSUE?!
UNNECES-SARY.
YOU THINK...

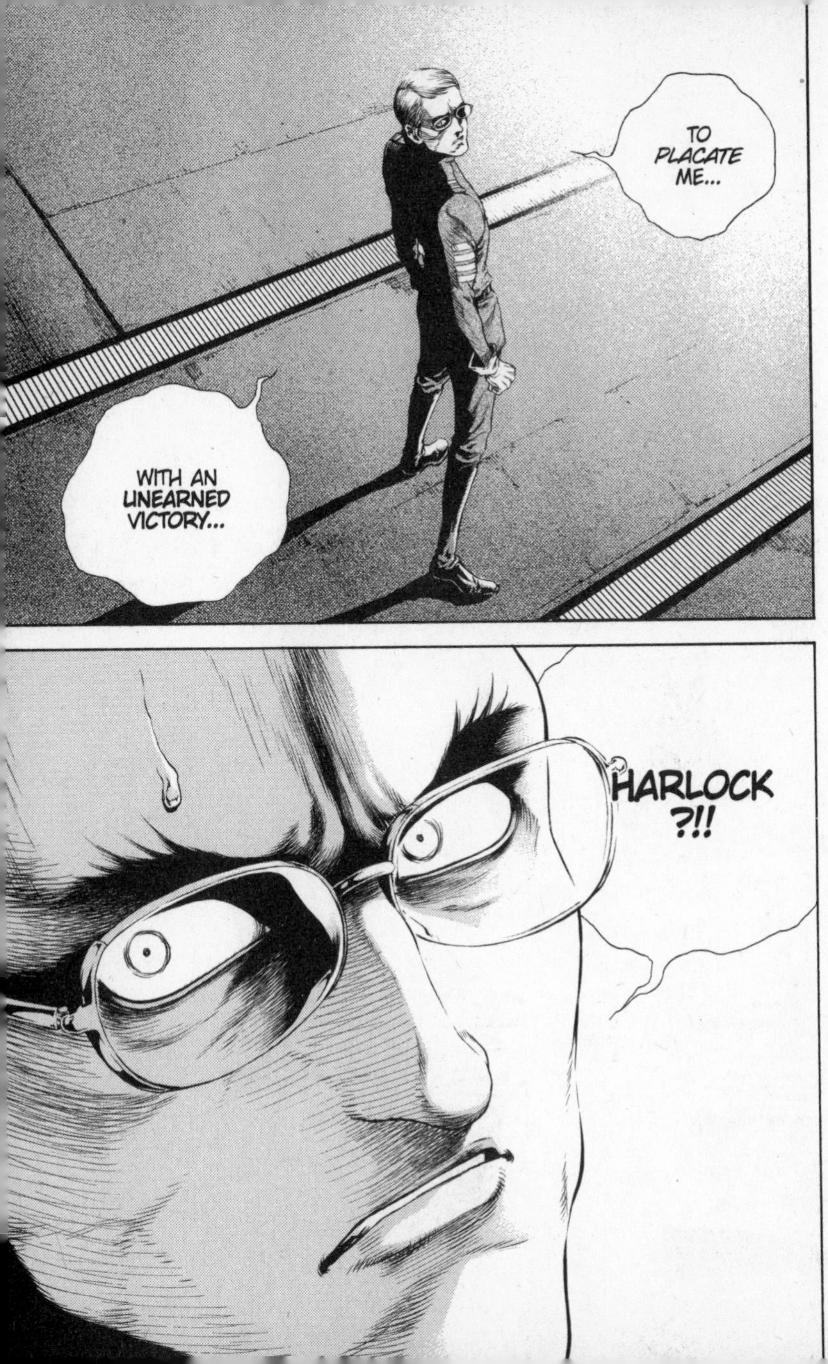
TO PLACATE ME...
WITH AN UNEARNED VICTORY...
HARLOCK ?!!

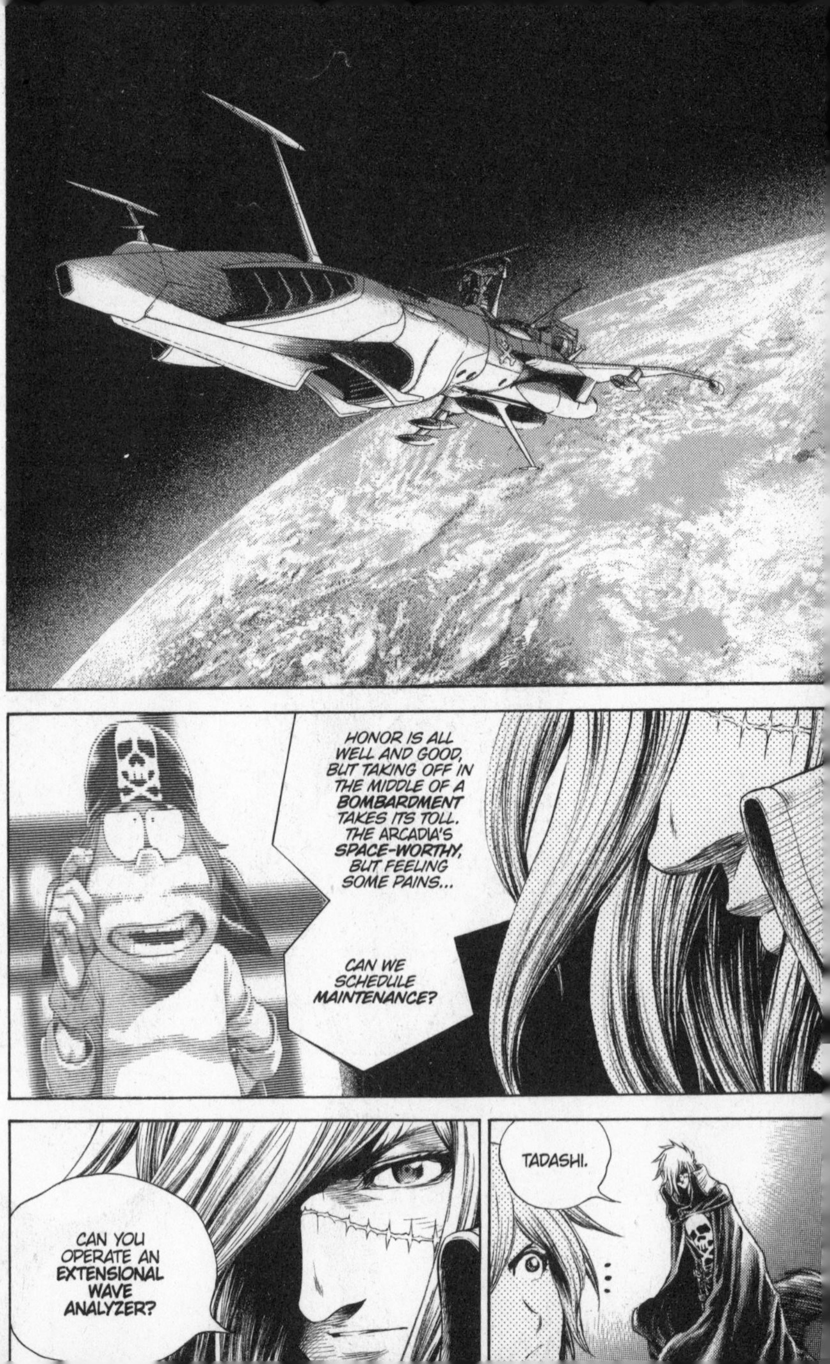
HONOR IS ALL WELL AND GOOD, BUT TAKING OFF IN THE MIDDLE OF A **BOMBARDMENT** TAKES ITS TOLL. THE ARCADIA'S **SPACE-WORTHY,** BUT FEELING SOME PAINS...
CAN WE SCHEDULE **MAINTENANCE?**
TADASHI.
...
CAN YOU OPERATE AN **EXTENSIONAL WAVE ANALYZER?**

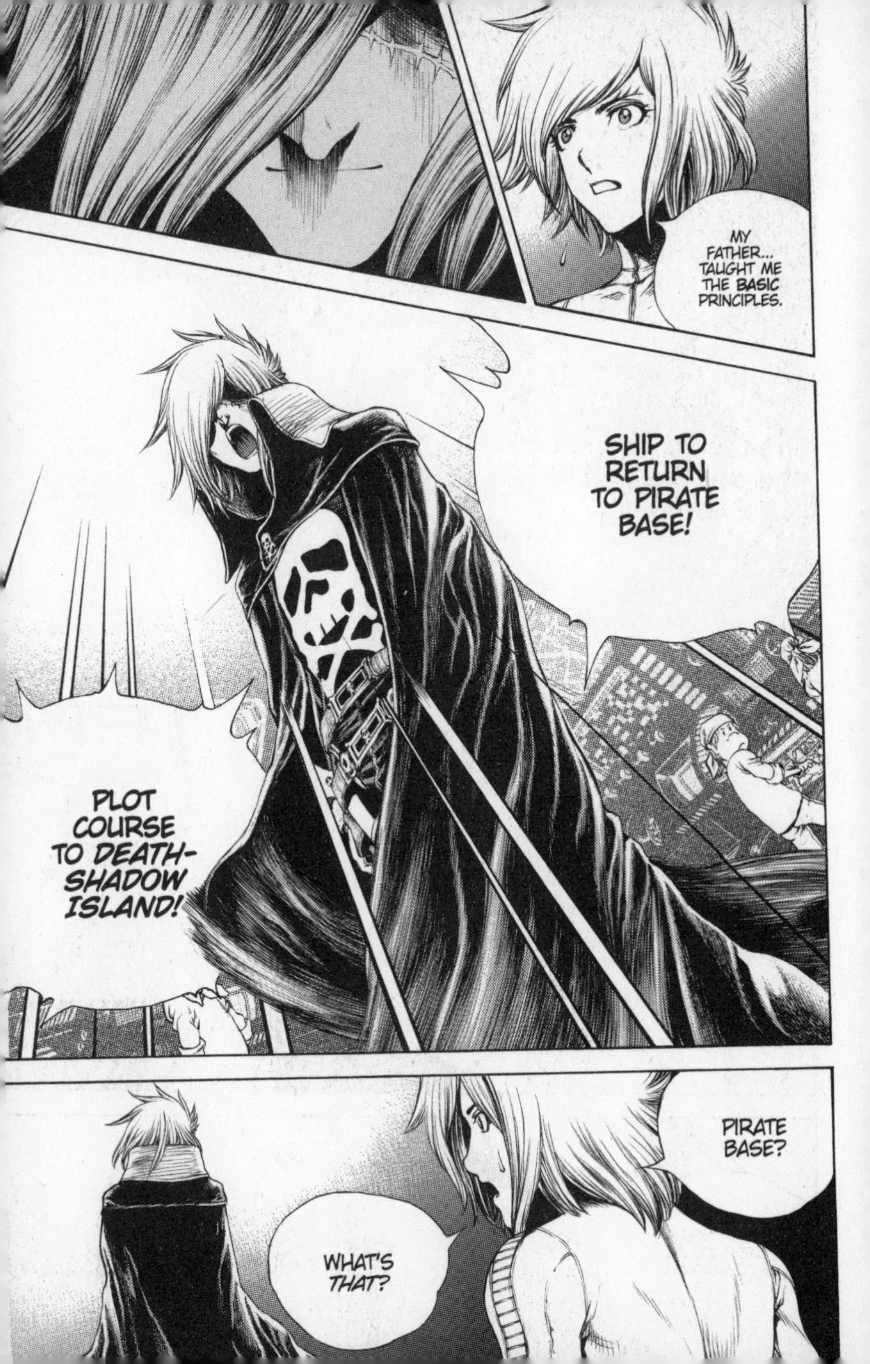
MY FATHER... TAUGHT ME THE BASIC PRINCIPLES.
SHIP TO RETURN TO PIRATE BASE!
PLOT COURSE TO *DEATH-SHADOW ISLAND!*
PIRATE BASE?
WHAT'S *THAT?*

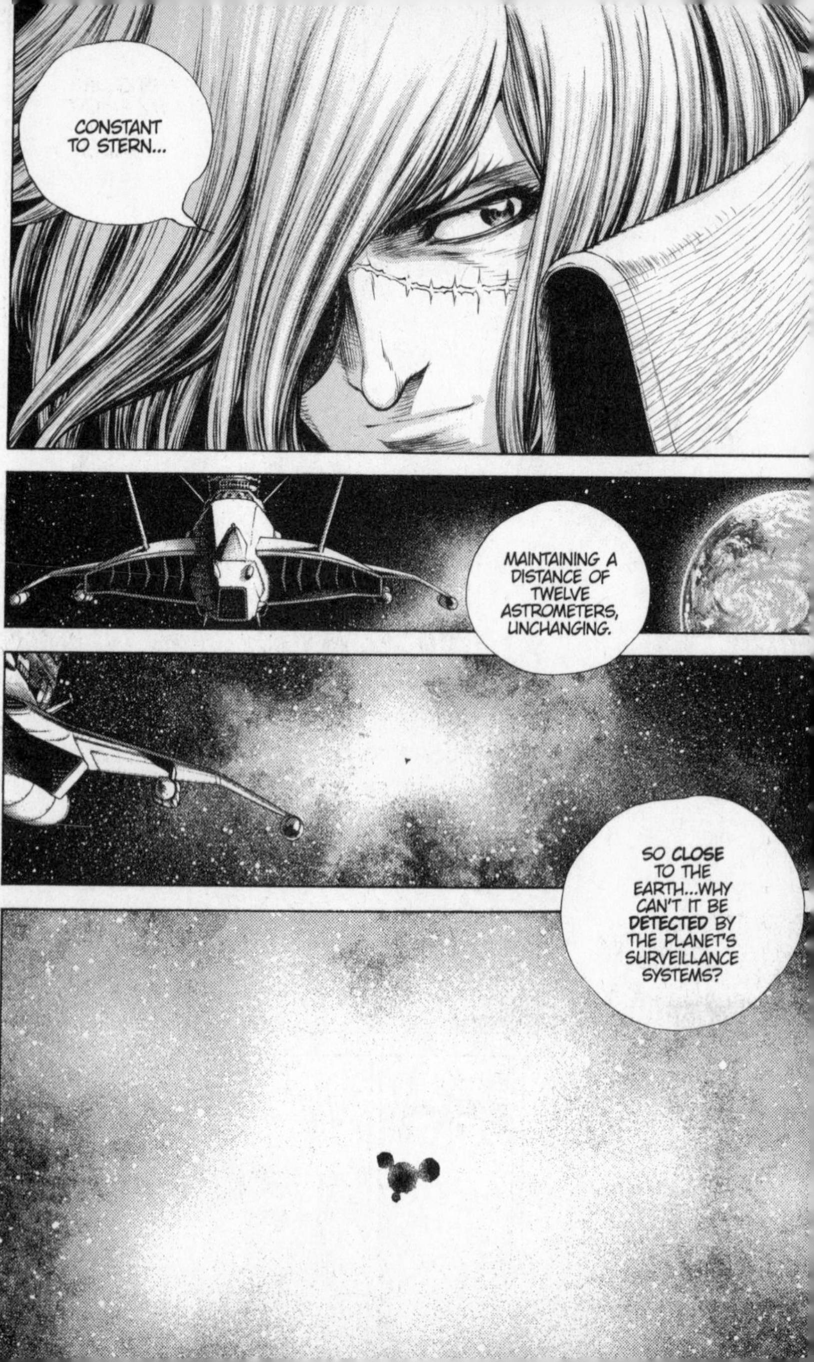
CONSTANT TO STERN...
MAINTAINING A DISTANCE OF TWELVE ASTROMETERS, UNCHANGING.
SO CLOSE TO THE EARTH...WHY CAN'T IT BE DETECTED BY THE PLANET'S SURVEILLANCE SYSTEMS?

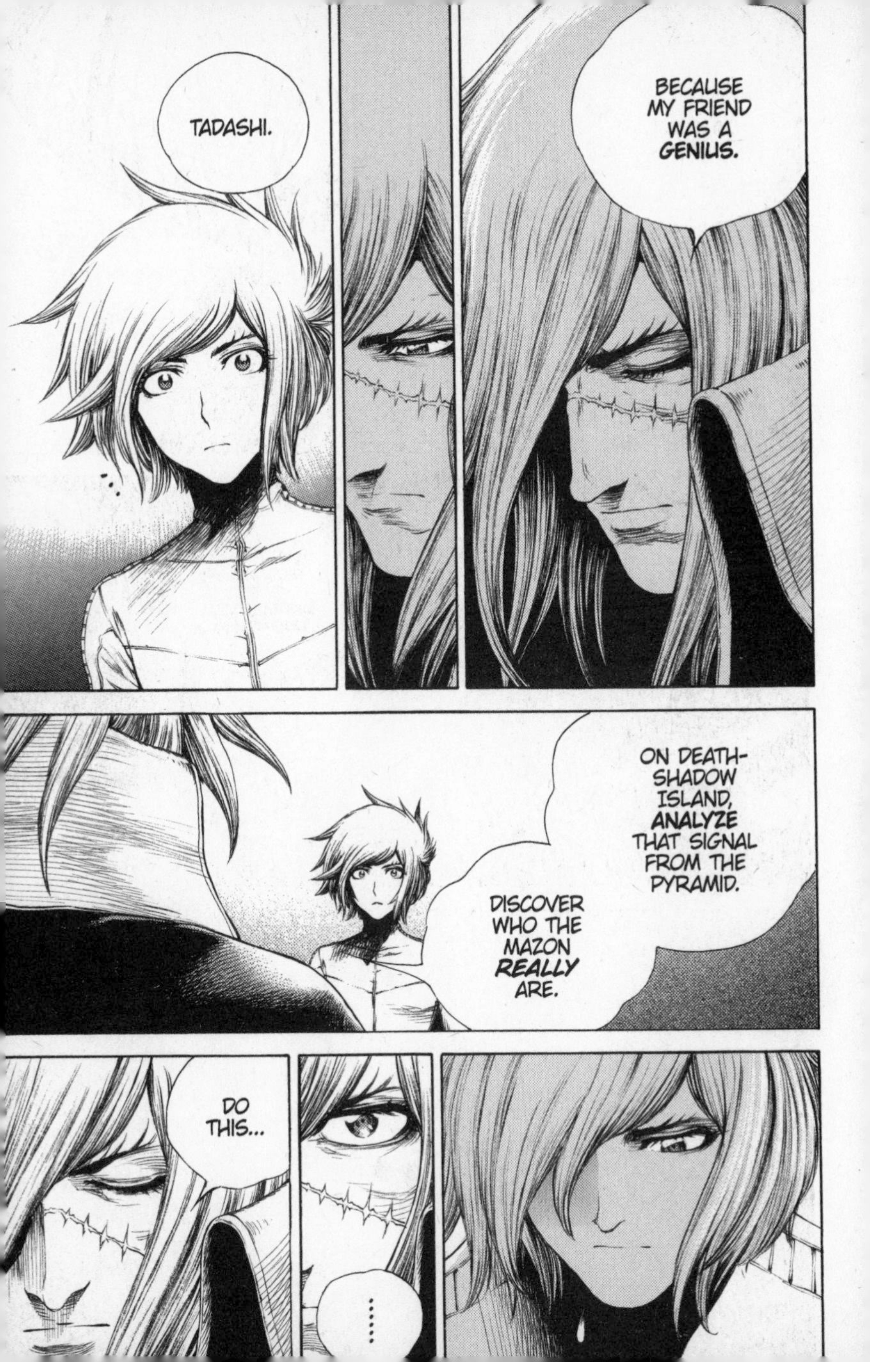
BECAUSE MY FRIEND WAS A GENIUS.
TADASHI.
ON DEATH-SHADOW ISLAND, ANALYZE THAT SIGNAL FROM THE PYRAMID.
DISCOVER WHO THE MAZON REALLY ARE.
DO THIS...
......

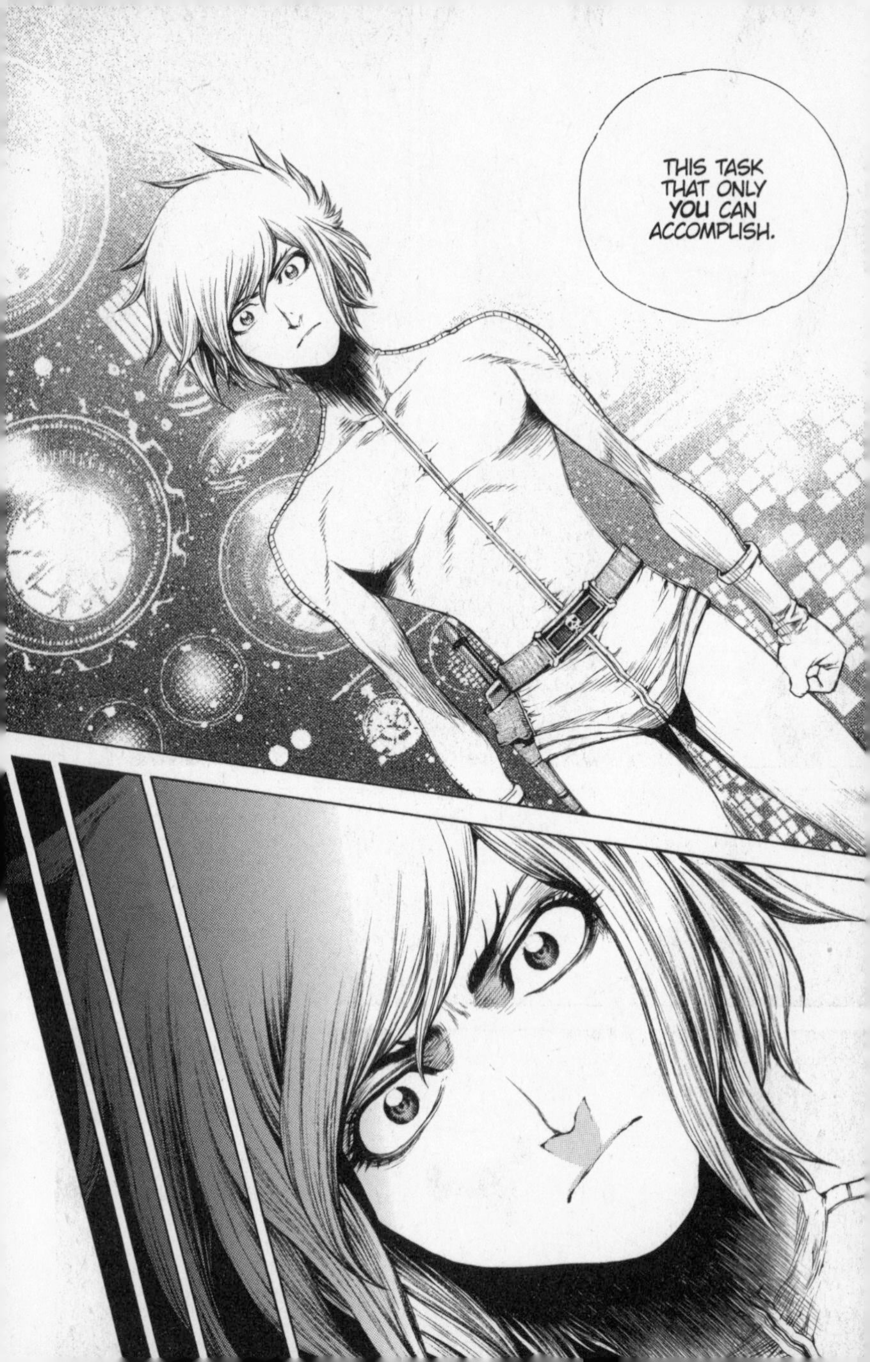
THIS TASK THAT ONLY YOU CAN ACCOMPLISH.

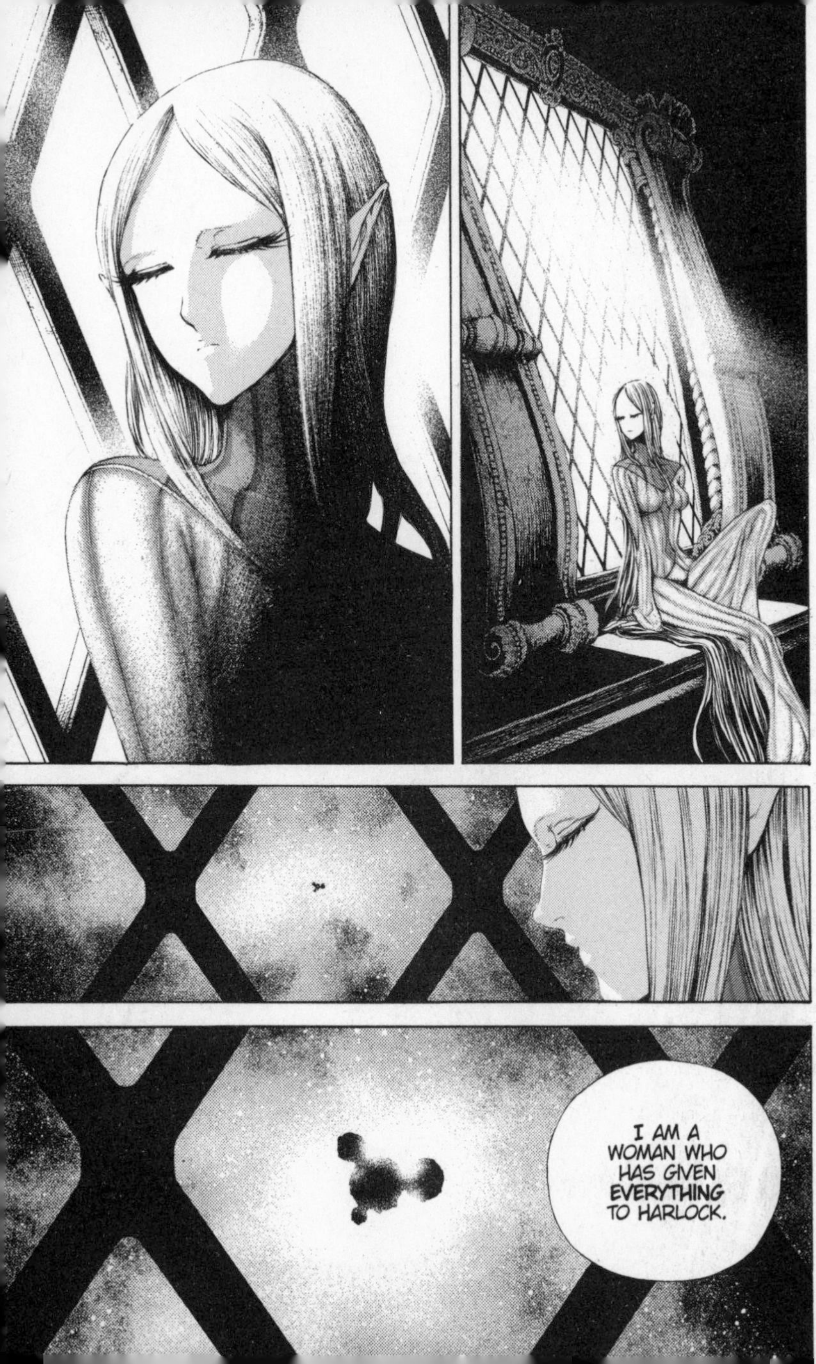
I AM A WOMAN WHO HAS GIVEN EVERYTHING TO HARLOCK.

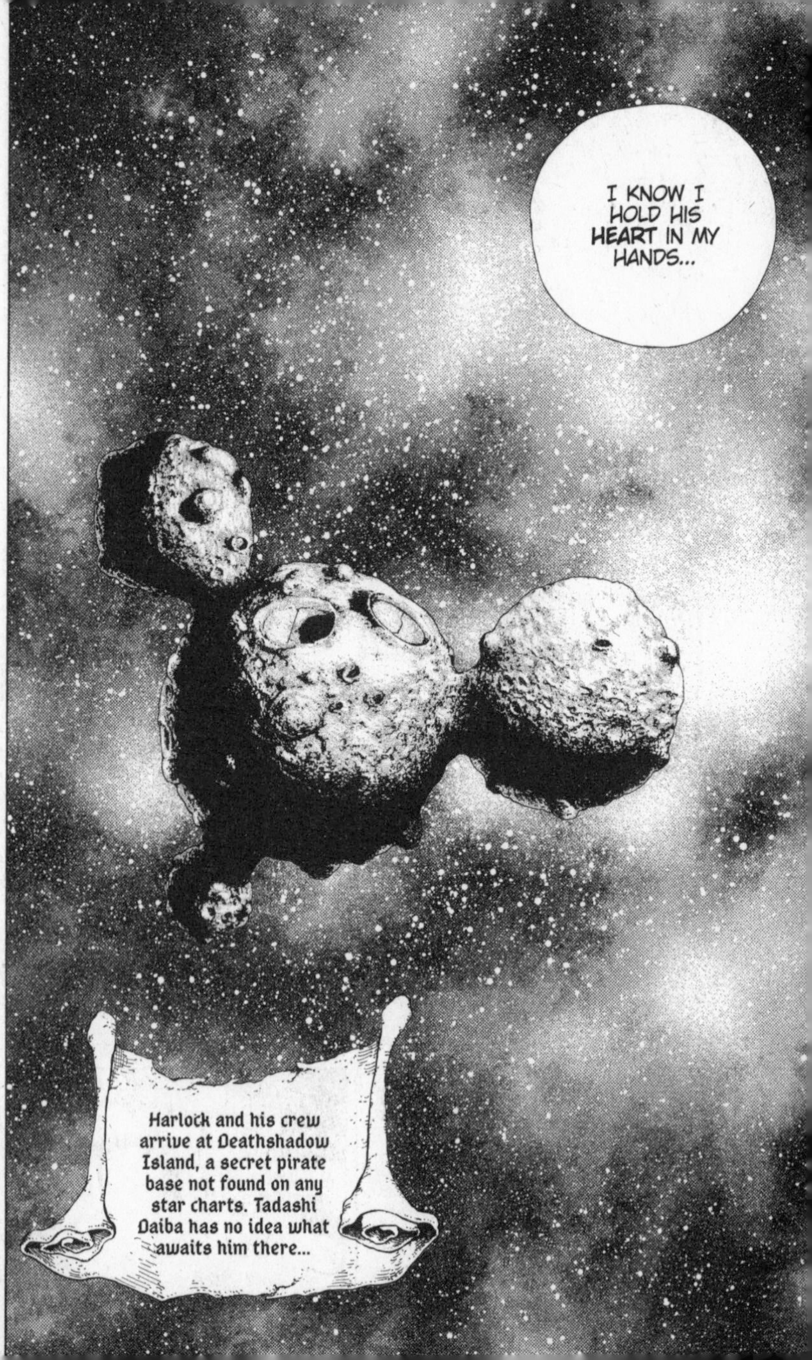
I KNOW I HOLD HIS HEART IN MY HANDS...
Harlock and his crew arrive at Deathshadow Island, a secret pirate base not found on any star charts. Tadashi Daiba has no idea what awaits him there...

MEGALOPOLIS HAS LONG BEEN WELL GOVERNED, UNDER YOUR PRIME MINISTER!

BUT NOW THIS VOLKA ZANDAR ANNOUNCES HIS CANDIDACY!

CHAPTER 12 ☠ ZERO

VOLKA ZANDAR TAKES HIS ORDERS FROM THE WEALTHY AND THE MACHINE PEOPLE!

HE'S OUR ENEMY--!!

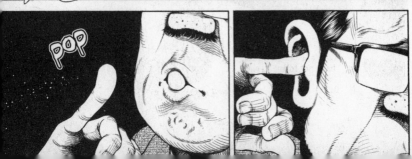

POP

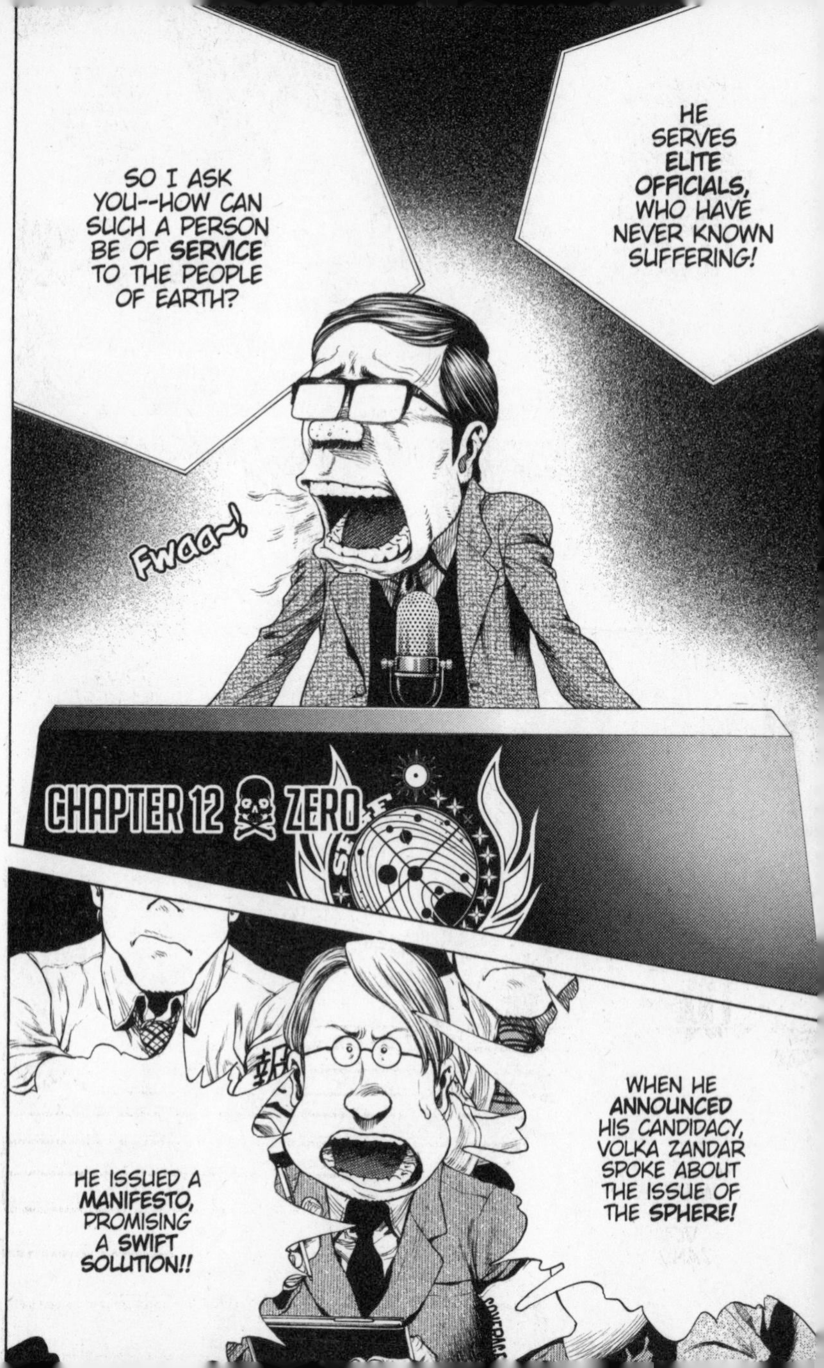
HE SERVES ELITE OFFICIALS, WHO HAVE NEVER KNOWN SUFFERING!
SO I ASK YOU--HOW CAN SUCH A PERSON BE OF SERVICE TO THE PEOPLE OF EARTH?
Fwaa~!
CHAPTER 12 ZERO
WHEN HE ANNOUNCED HIS CANDIDACY, VOLKA ZANDAR SPOKE ABOUT THE ISSUE OF THE SPHERE!
HE ISSUED A MANIFESTO, PROMISING A SWIFT SOLUTION!!

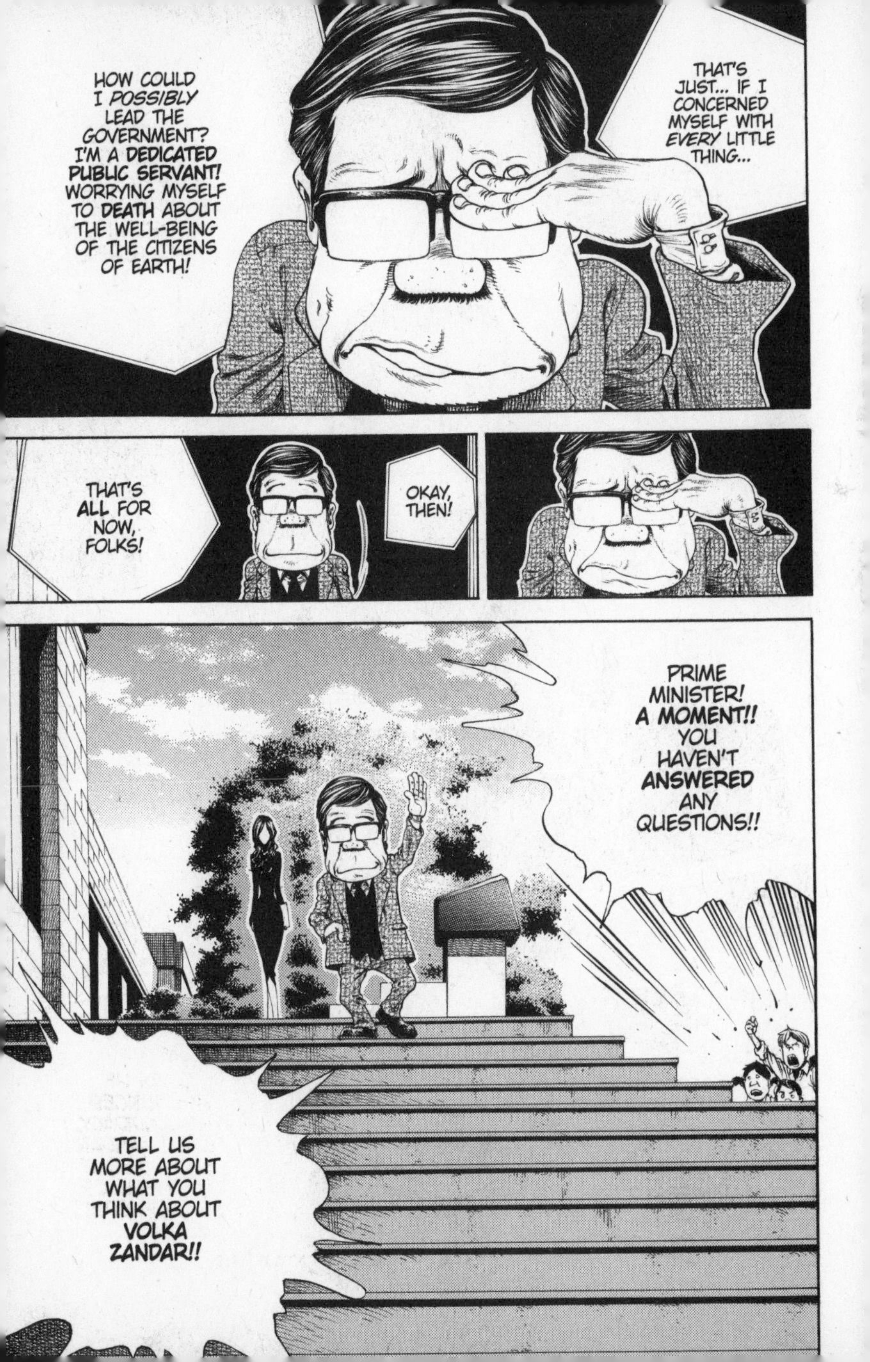
THAT'S JUST... IF I CONCERNED MYSELF WITH EVERY LITTLE THING...
HOW COULD I POSSIBLY LEAD THE GOVERNMENT? I'M A DEDICATED PUBLIC SERVANT! WORRYING MYSELF TO DEATH ABOUT THE WELL-BEING OF THE CITIZENS OF EARTH!
OKAY, THEN!
THAT'S ALL FOR NOW, FOLKS!
PRIME MINISTER! A MOMENT!! YOU HAVEN'T ANSWERED ANY QUESTIONS!!
TELL US MORE ABOUT WHAT YOU THINK ABOUT VOLKA ZANDAR!!

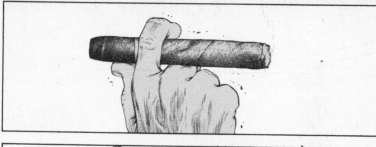

KRNCH

WHY?!

WHY
NOW?!!

png

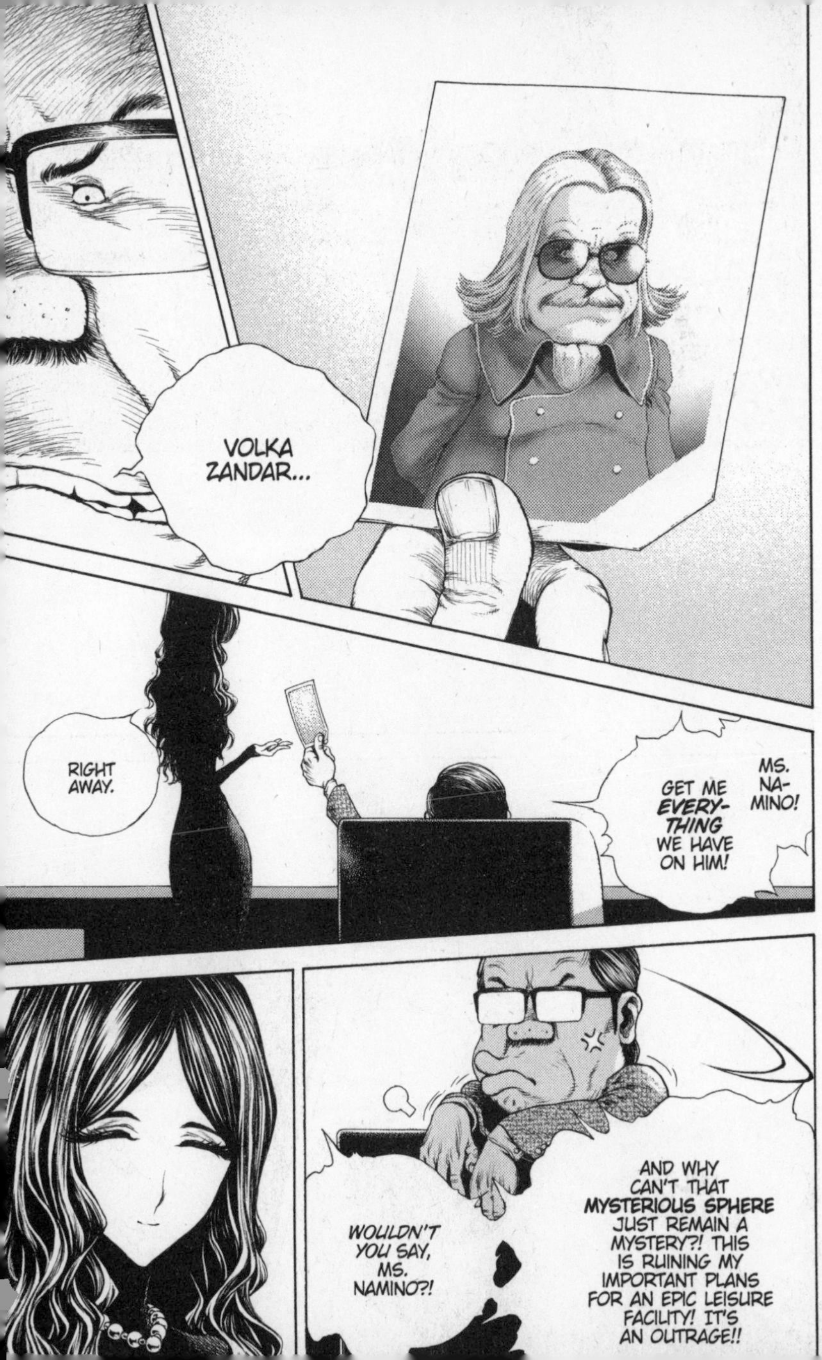
VOLKA ZANDAR...
MS. NAMINO!
GET ME EVERYTHING WE HAVE ON HIM!
RIGHT AWAY.
AND WHY CAN'T THAT MYSTERIOUS SPHERE JUST REMAIN A MYSTERY?! THIS IS RUINING MY IMPORTANT PLANS FOR AN EPIC LEISURE FACILITY! IT'S AN OUTRAGE!!
WOULDN'T YOU SAY, MS. NAMINO?!

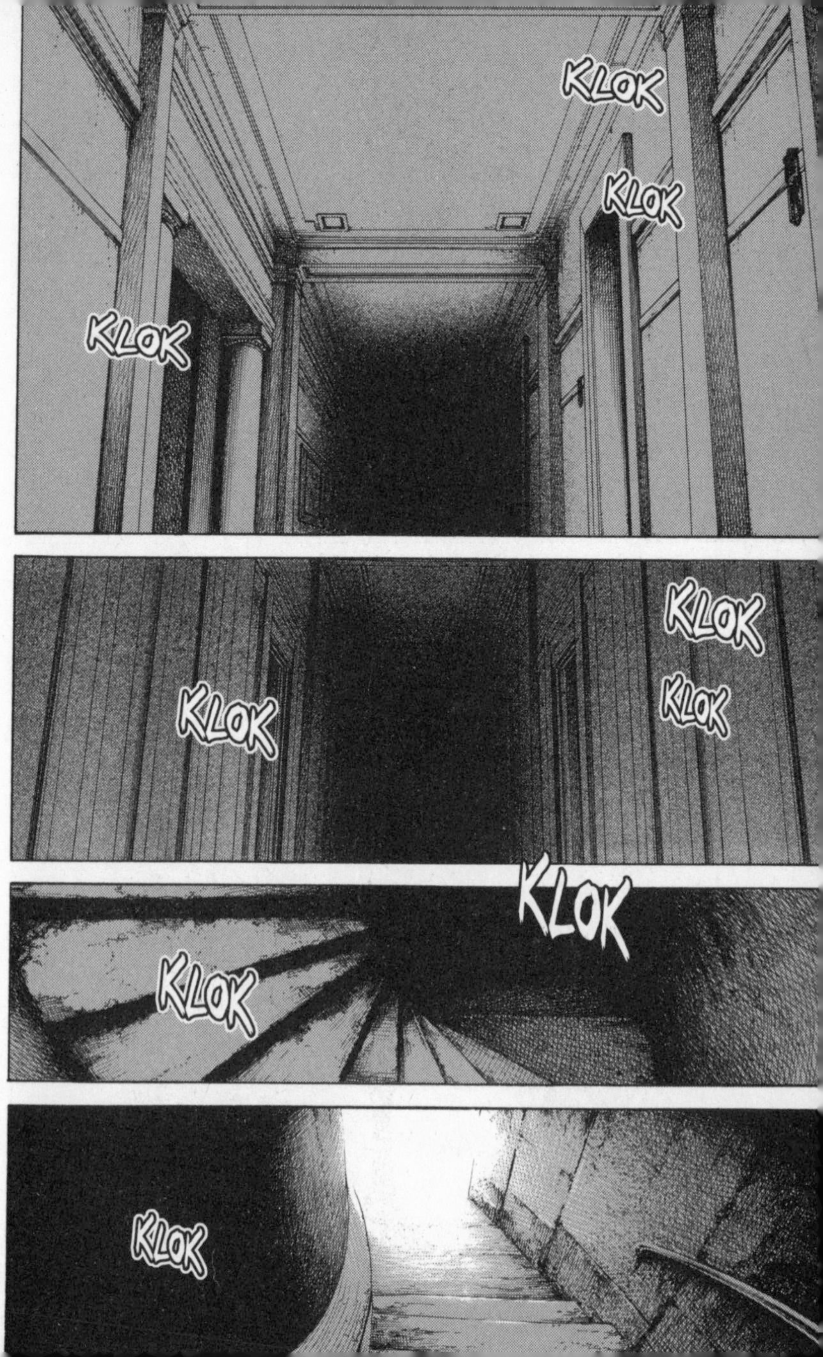
KLOK
KLOK
KLOK
KLOK
KLOK
KLOK
KLOK
KLOK
KLOK

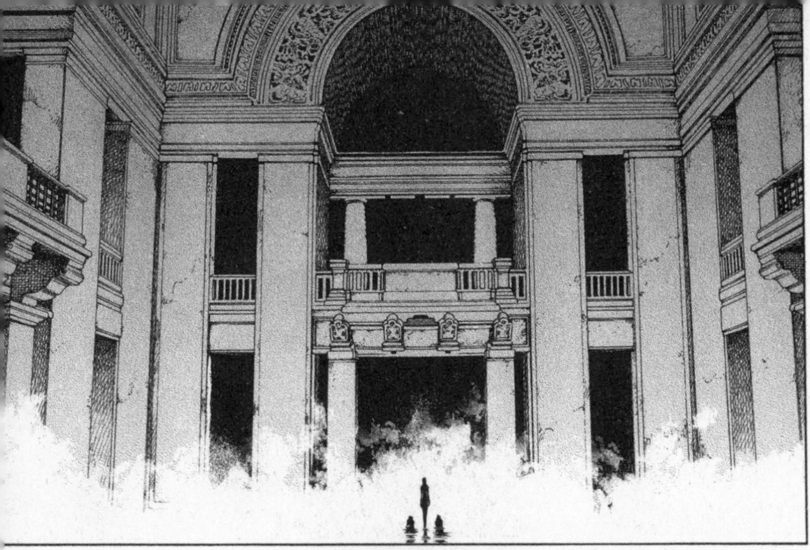

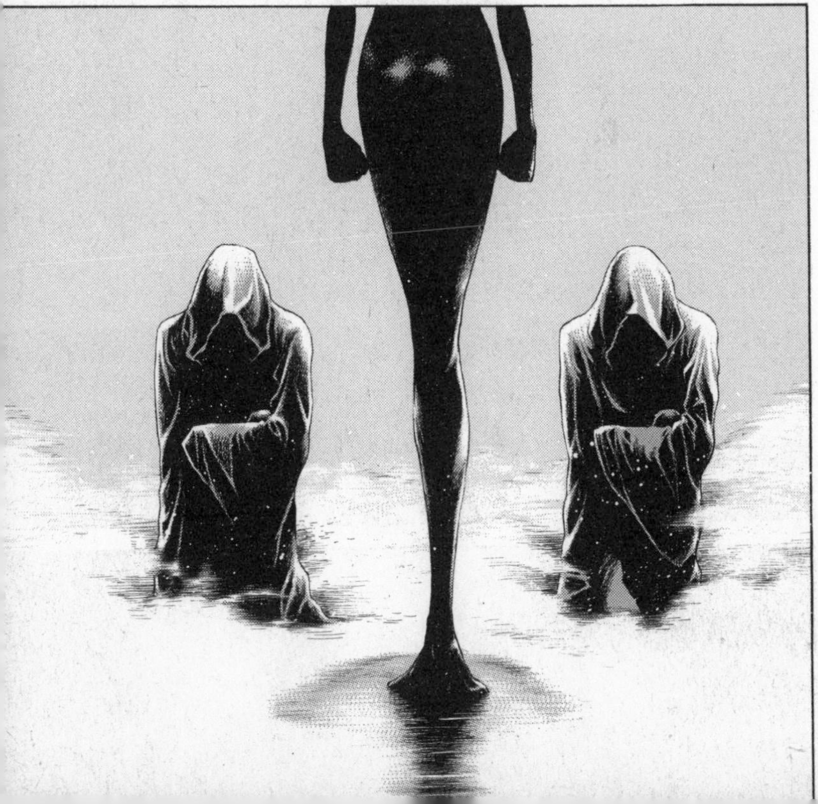

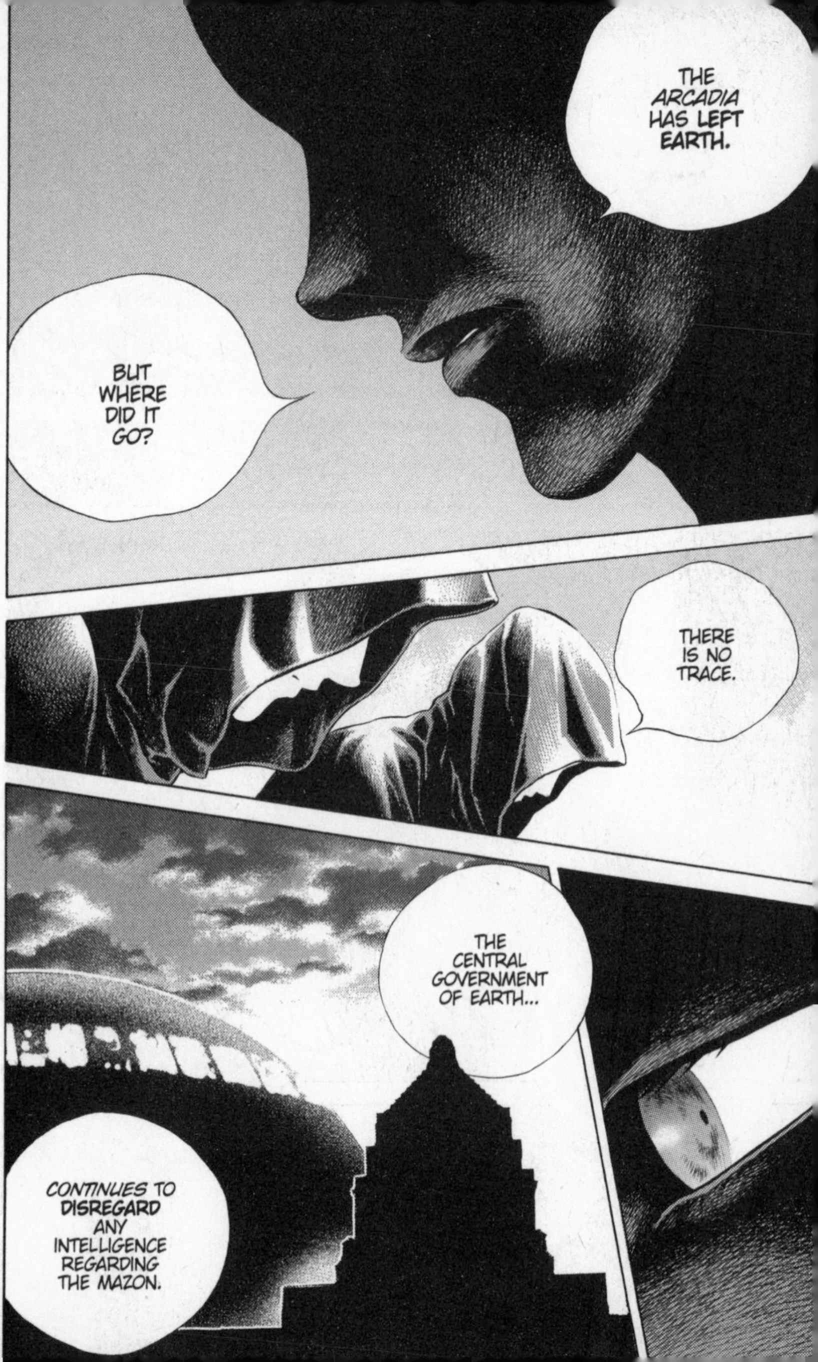
THE *ARCADIA* HAS LEFT EARTH.
BUT WHERE DID IT GO?
THERE IS NO TRACE.
THE CENTRAL GOVERNMENT OF EARTH...
CONTINUES TO **DISREGARD** ANY INTELLIGENCE REGARDING THE MAZON.

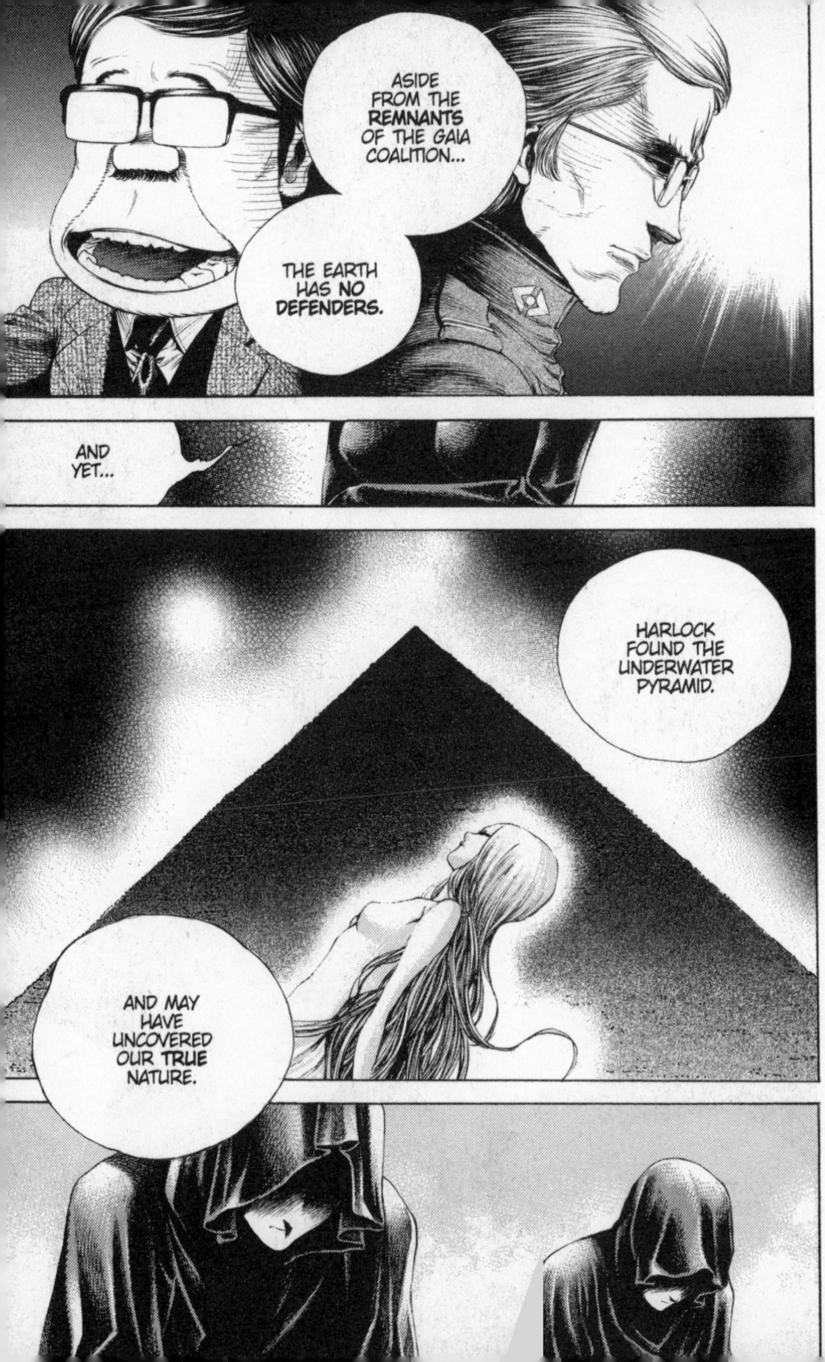
ASIDE FROM THE REMNANTS OF THE GAIA COALITION...
THE EARTH HAS NO DEFENDERS.
AND YET...
HARLOCK FOUND THE UNDERWATER PYRAMID.
AND MAY HAVE UNCOVERED OUR TRUE NATURE.

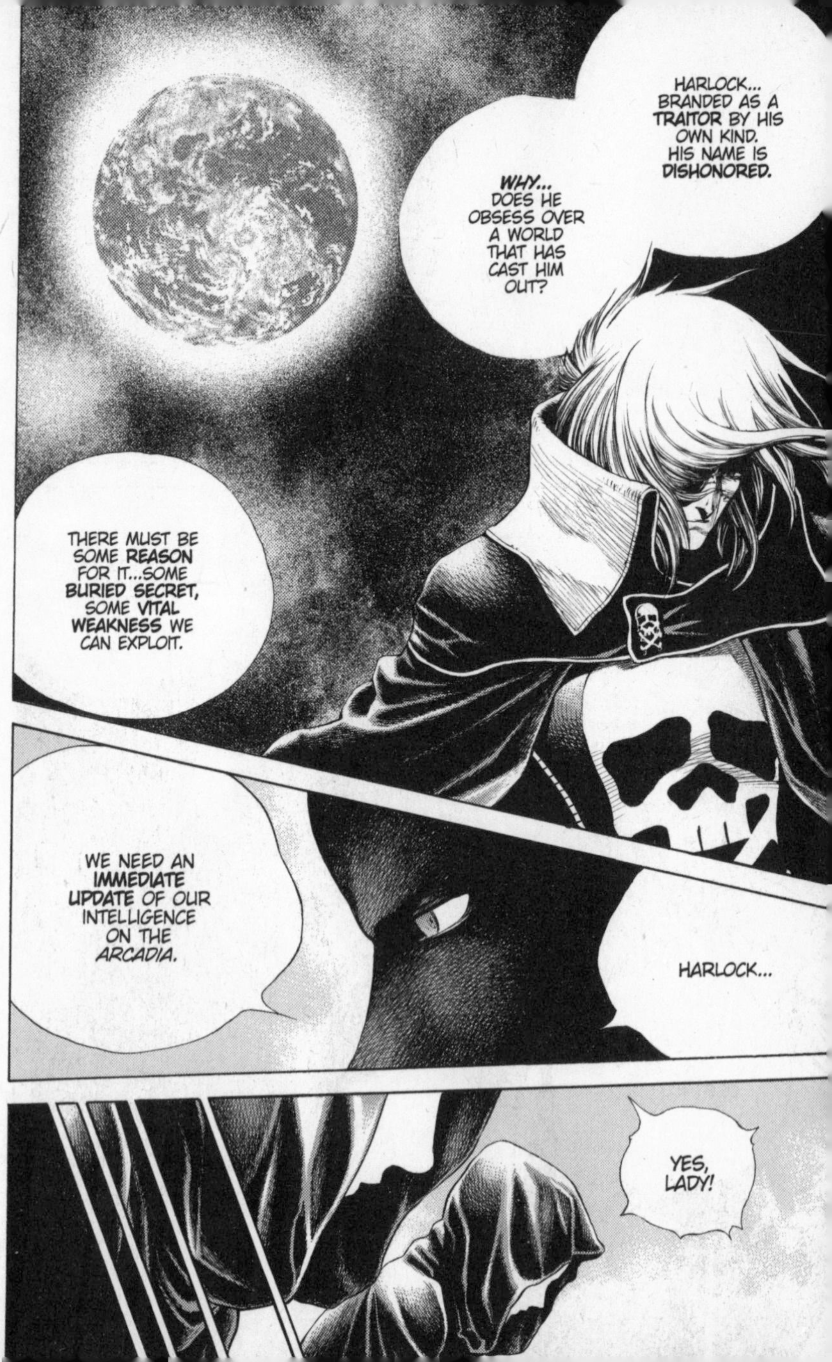
HARLOCK... BRANDED AS A **TRAITOR** BY HIS OWN KIND. HIS NAME IS **DISHONORED.**
WHY... DOES HE OBSESS OVER A WORLD THAT HAS CAST HIM OUT?
THERE MUST BE SOME **REASON** FOR IT...SOME **BURIED SECRET,** SOME **VITAL WEAKNESS** WE CAN EXPLOIT.
HARLOCK...
WE NEED AN **IMMEDIATE UPDATE** OF OUR INTELLIGENCE ON THE *ARCADIA.*
YES, LADY!

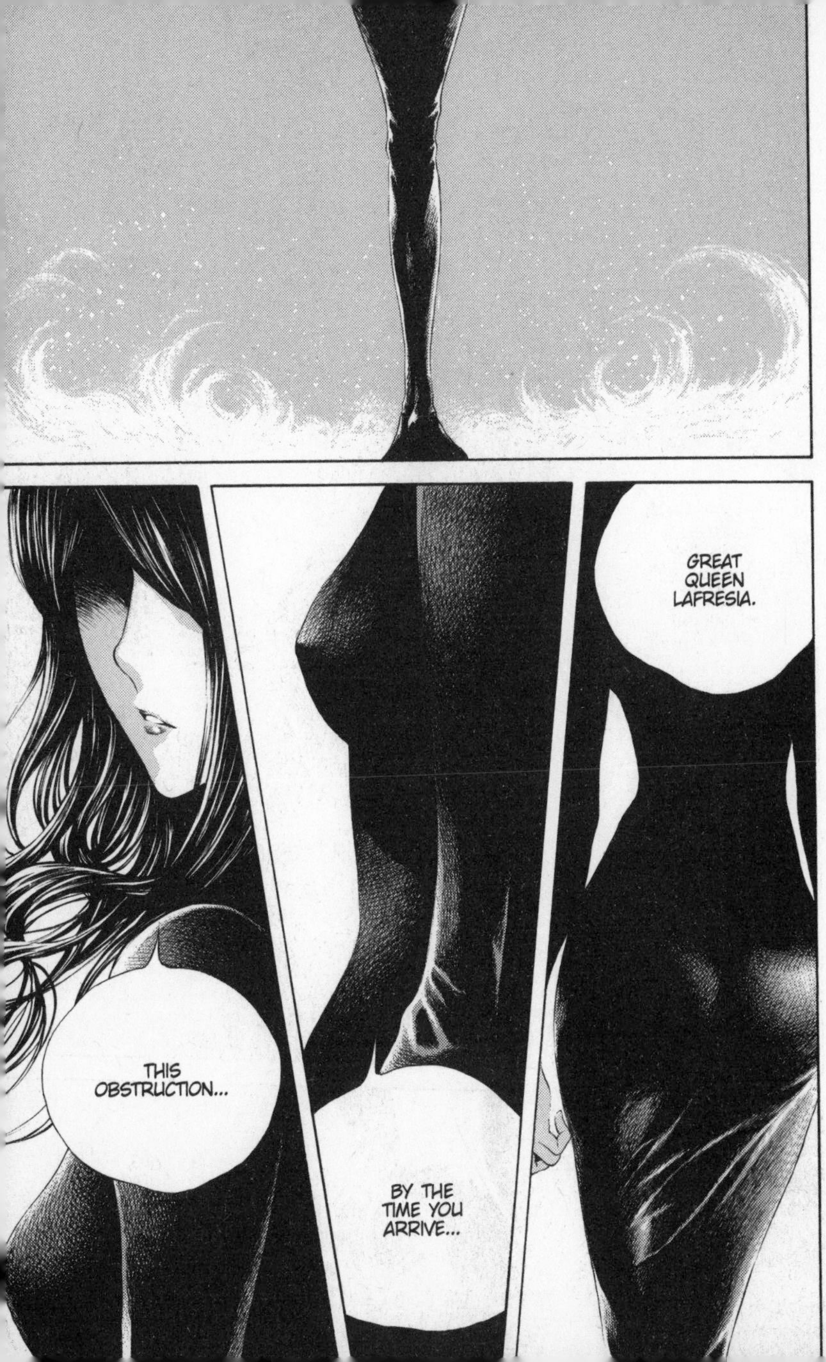
GREAT QUEEN LAFRESIA.
BY THE TIME YOU ARRIVE...
THIS OBSTRUCTION...

SHALL BE
REMOVED!

ANALYTICS

INCREDIBLE.

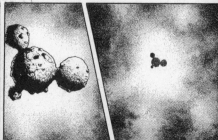

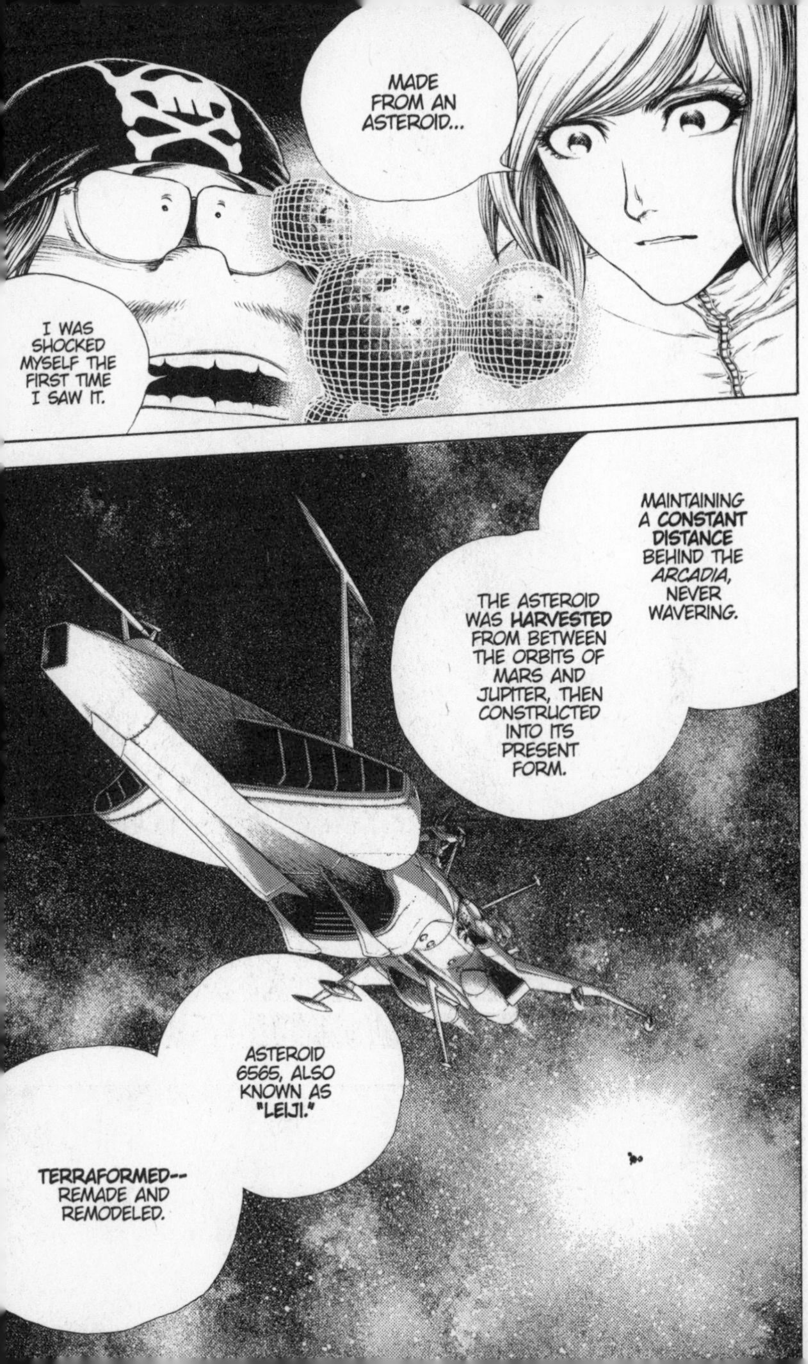
MADE FROM AN ASTEROID...
I WAS SHOCKED MYSELF THE FIRST TIME I SAW IT.
MAINTAINING A CONSTANT DISTANCE BEHIND THE ARCADIA, NEVER WAVERING.
THE ASTEROID WAS HARVESTED FROM BETWEEN THE ORBITS OF MARS AND JUPITER, THEN CONSTRUCTED INTO ITS PRESENT FORM.
ASTEROID 6565, ALSO KNOWN AS "LEIJI."
TERRAFORMED-- REMADE AND REMODELED.

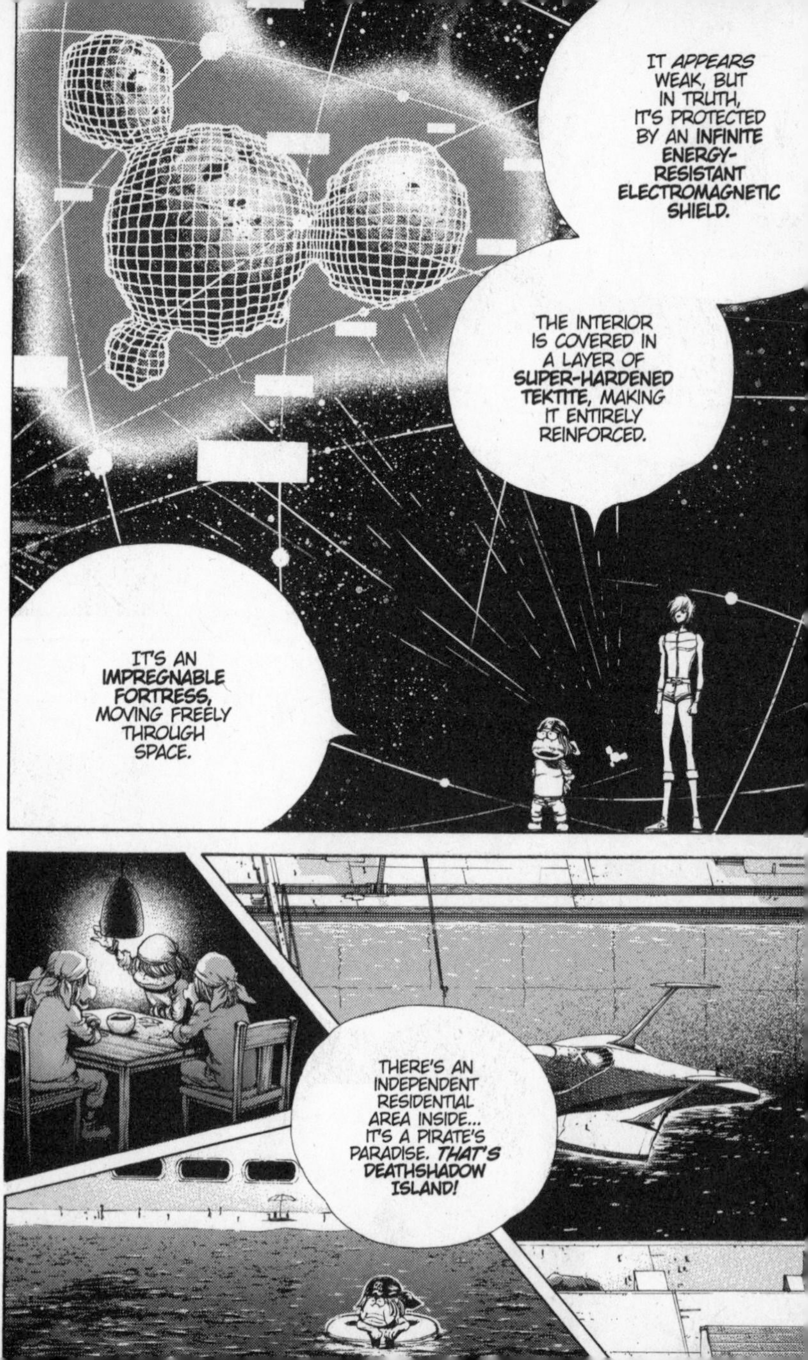
IT APPEARS WEAK, BUT IN TRUTH, IT'S PROTECTED BY AN INFINITE ENERGY-RESISTANT ELECTROMAGNETIC SHIELD.
THE INTERIOR IS COVERED IN A LAYER OF SUPER-HARDENED TEKTITE, MAKING IT ENTIRELY REINFORCED.
IT'S AN IMPREGNABLE FORTRESS, MOVING FREELY THROUGH SPACE.
THERE'S AN INDEPENDENT RESIDENTIAL AREA INSIDE... IT'S A PIRATE'S PARADISE. THAT'S DEATHSHADOW ISLAND!

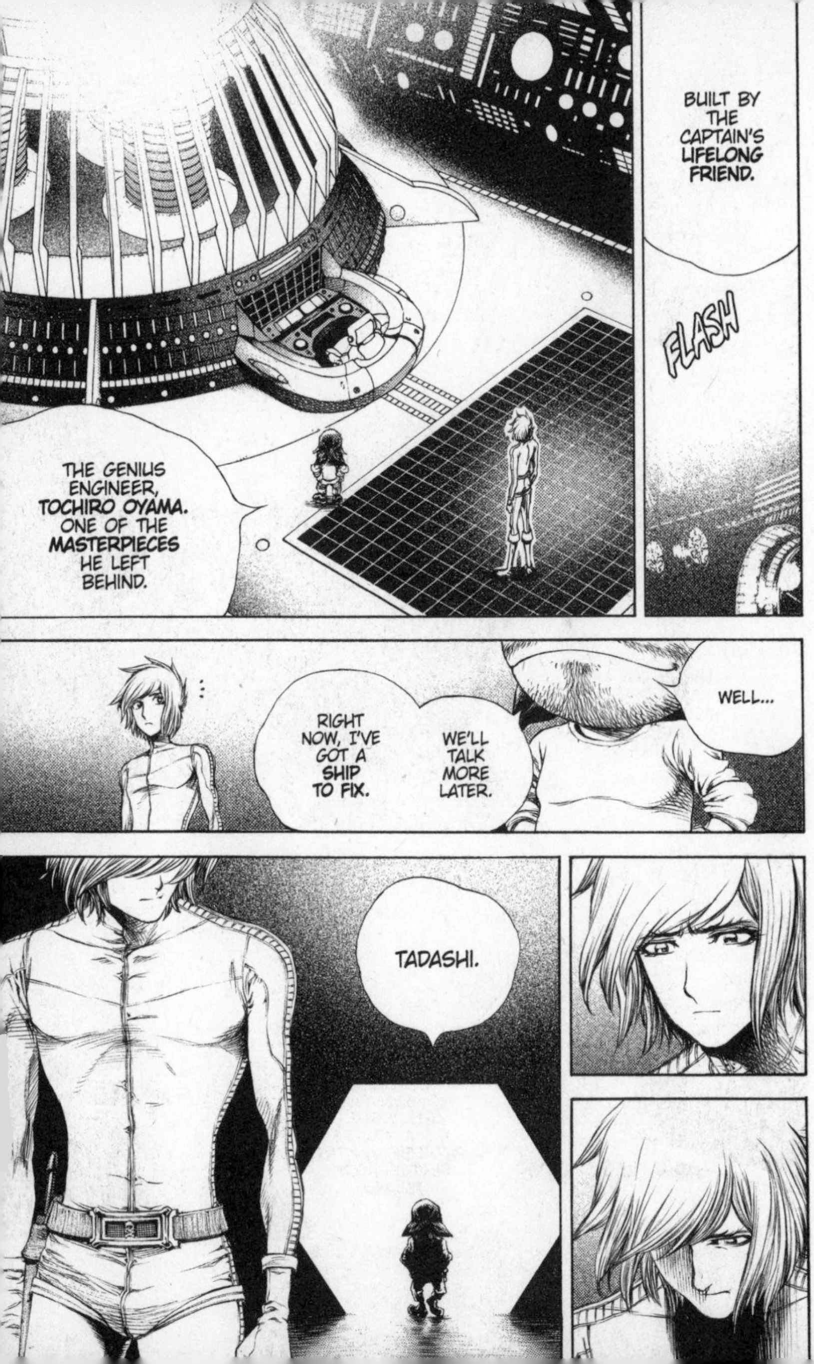
BUILT BY THE CAPTAIN'S LIFELONG FRIEND.
FLASH
THE GENIUS ENGINEER, TOCHIRO OYAMA. ONE OF THE MASTERPIECES HE LEFT BEHIND.
WELL...
WE'LL TALK MORE LATER.
RIGHT NOW, I'VE GOT A SHIP TO FIX.
...
TADASHI.

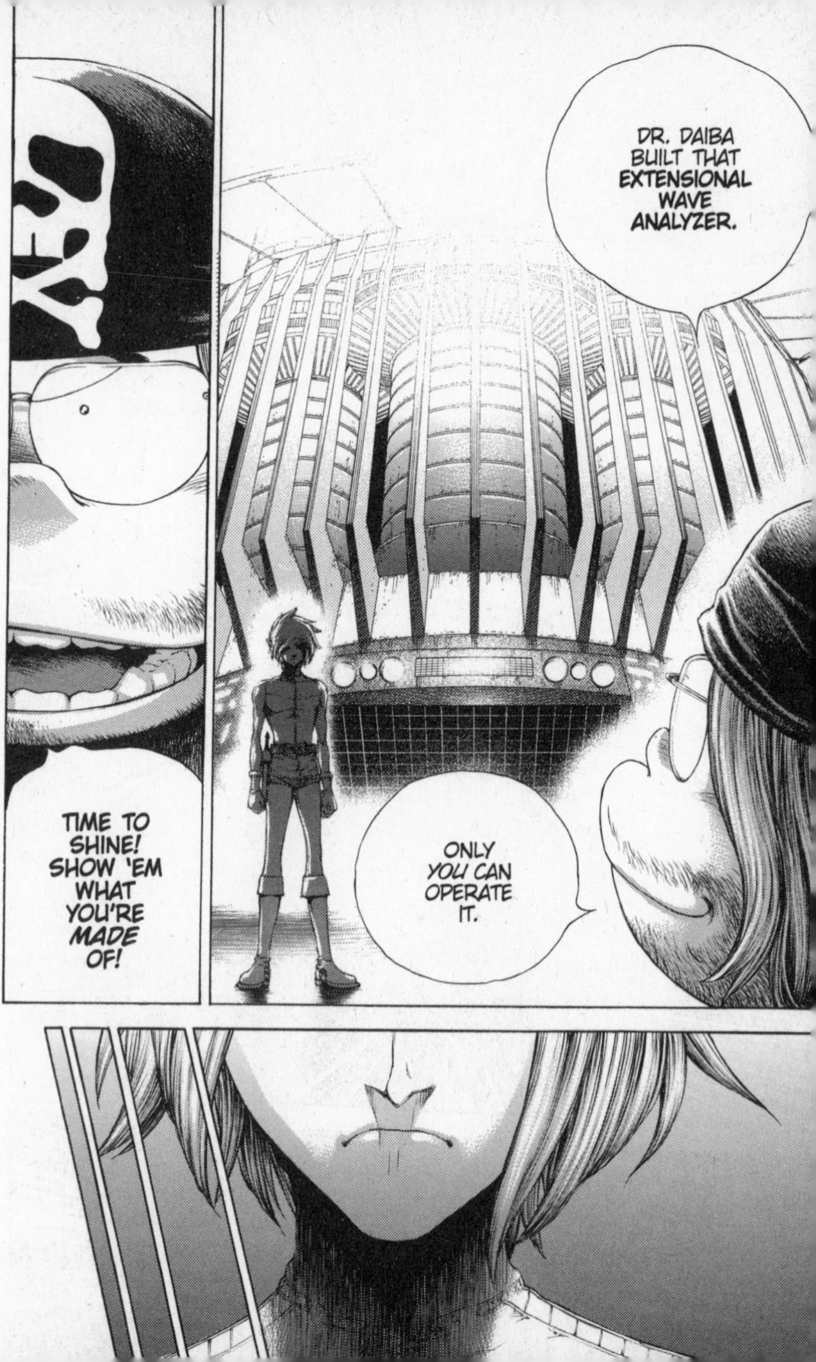
DR. DAIBA BUILT THAT EXTENSIONAL WAVE ANALYZER.
ONLY *YOU* CAN OPERATE IT.
TIME TO SHINE! SHOW 'EM WHAT YOU'RE *MADE* OF!

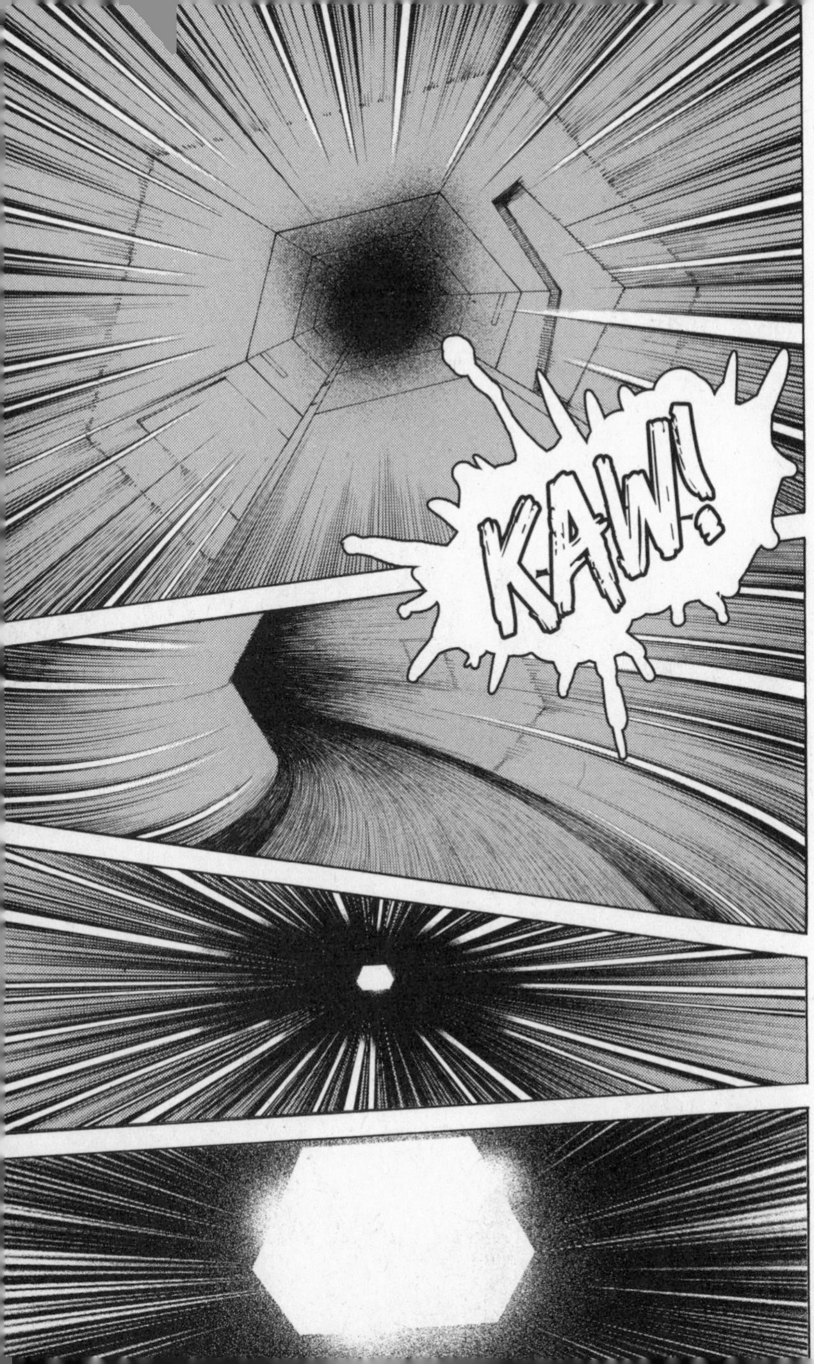
KAW!

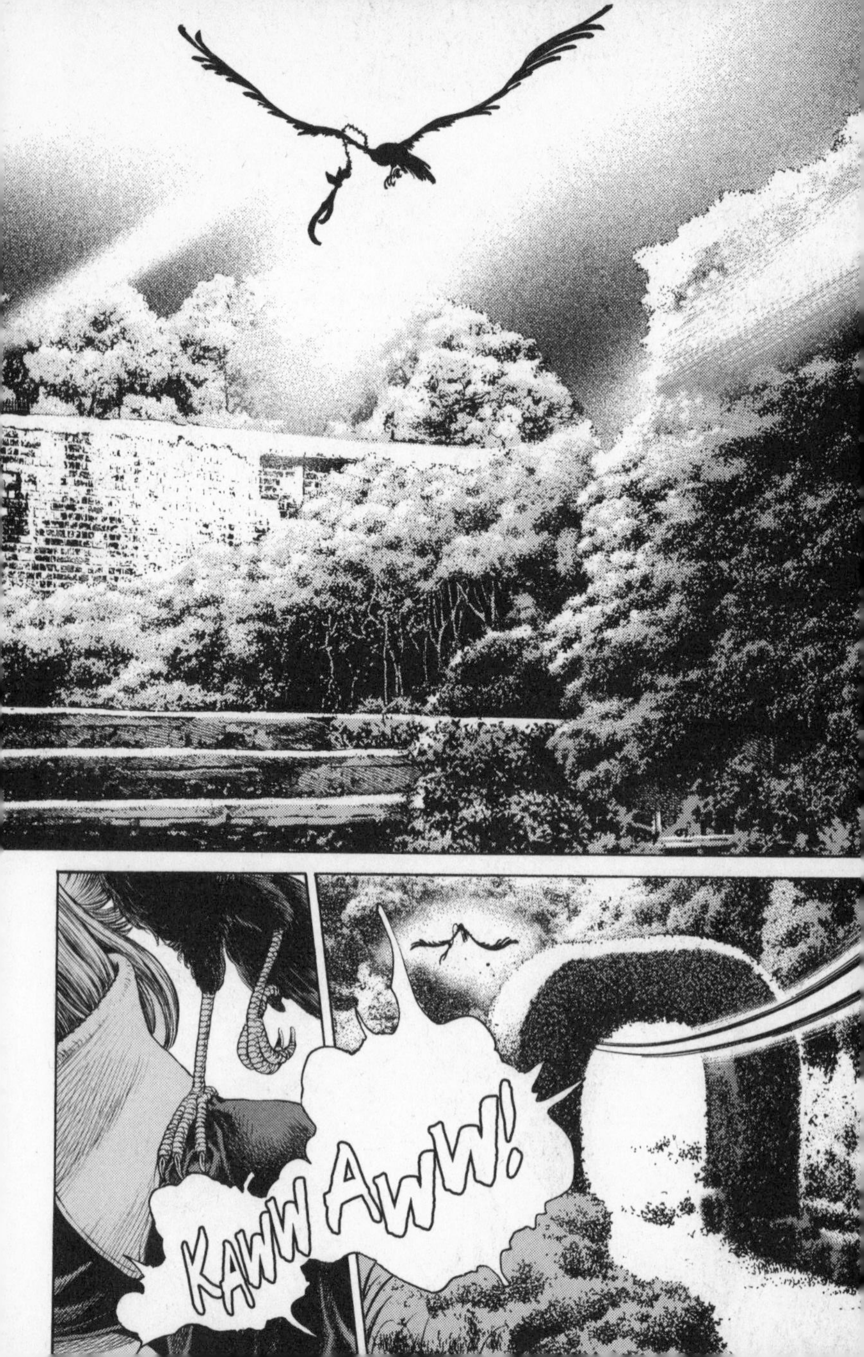
KAWW AWW!

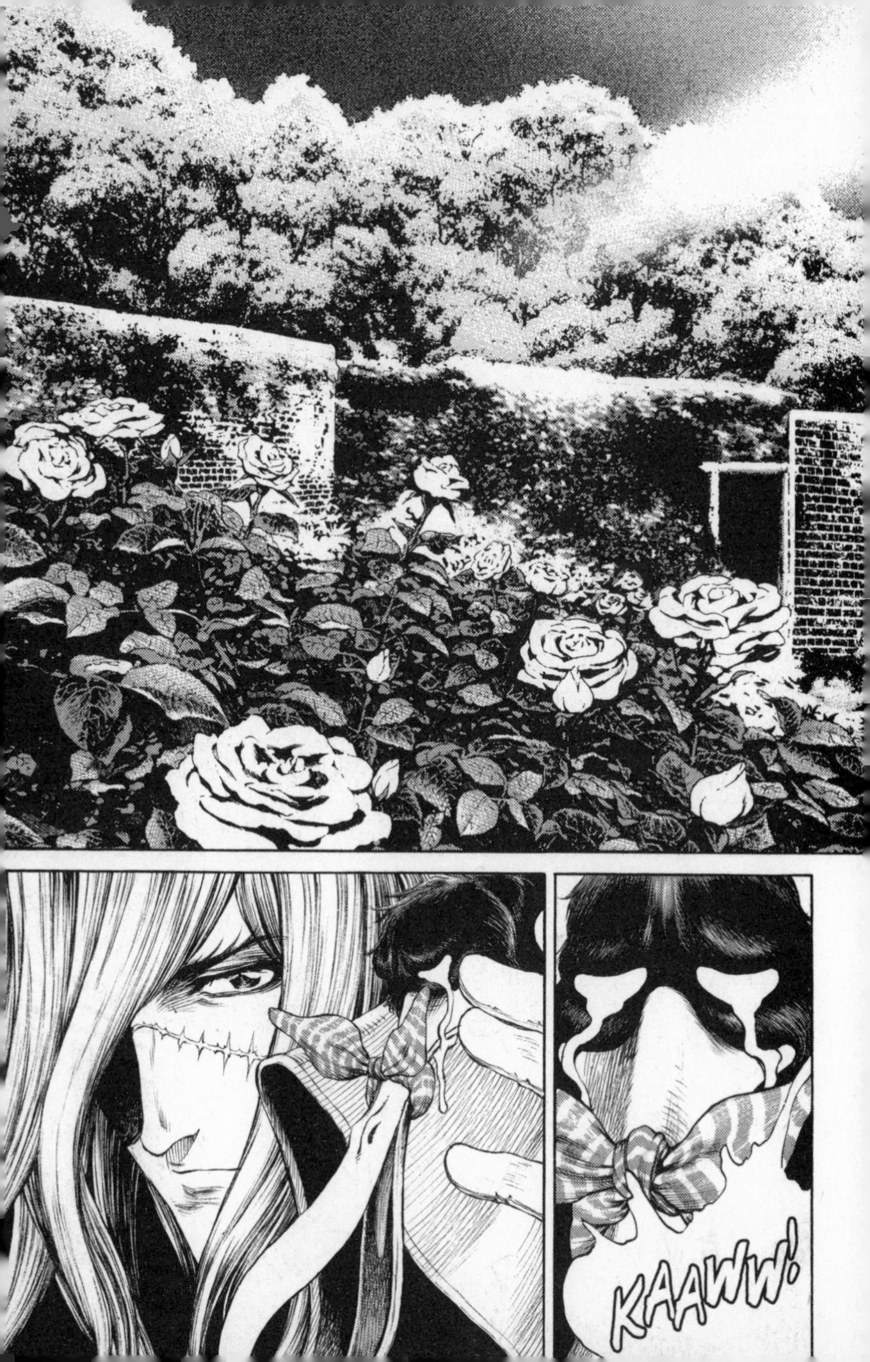
KAAWW!

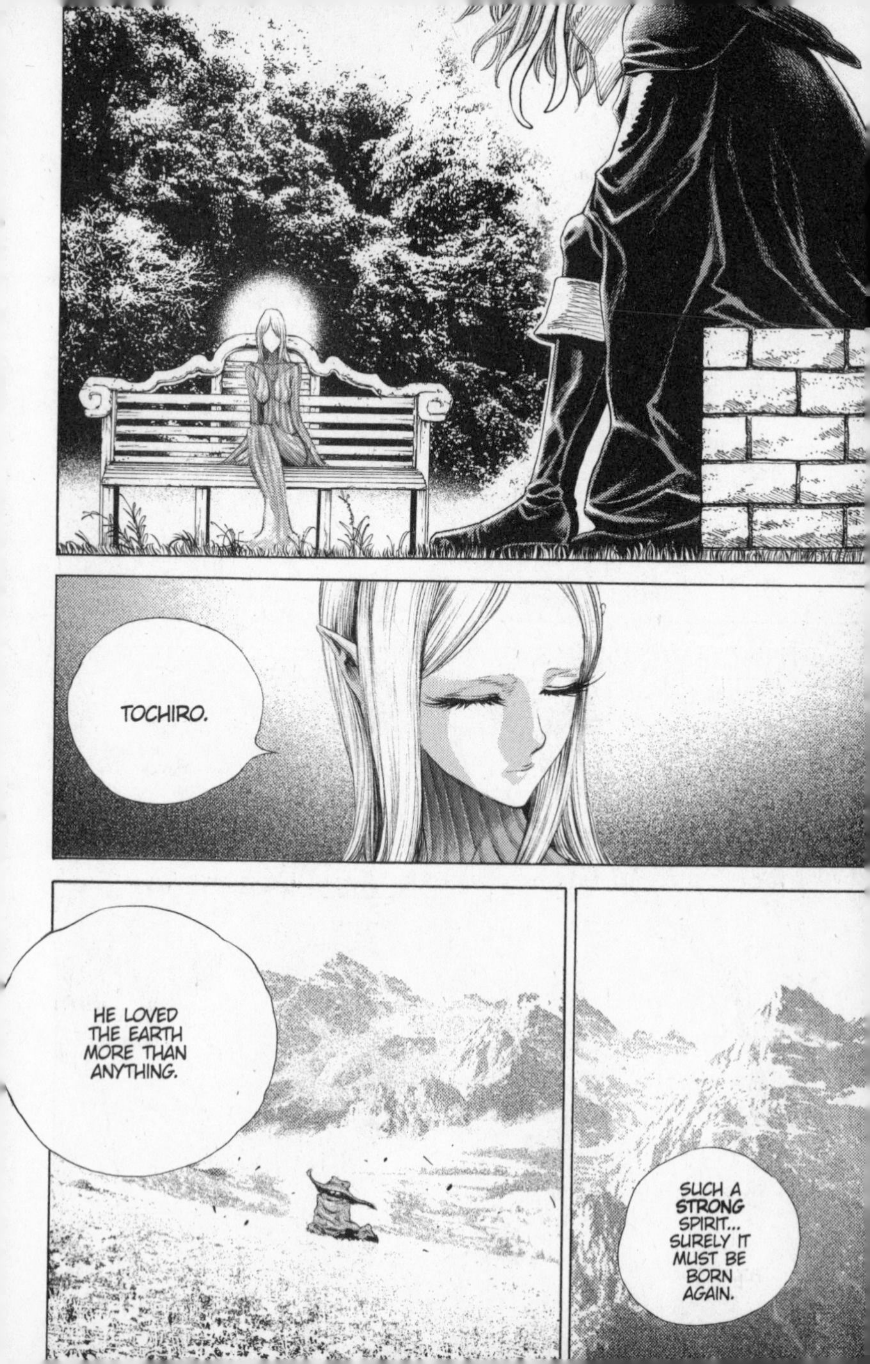
TOCHIRO.
HE LOVED THE EARTH MORE THAN ANYTHING.
SUCH A STRONG SPIRIT... SURELY IT MUST BE BORN AGAIN.

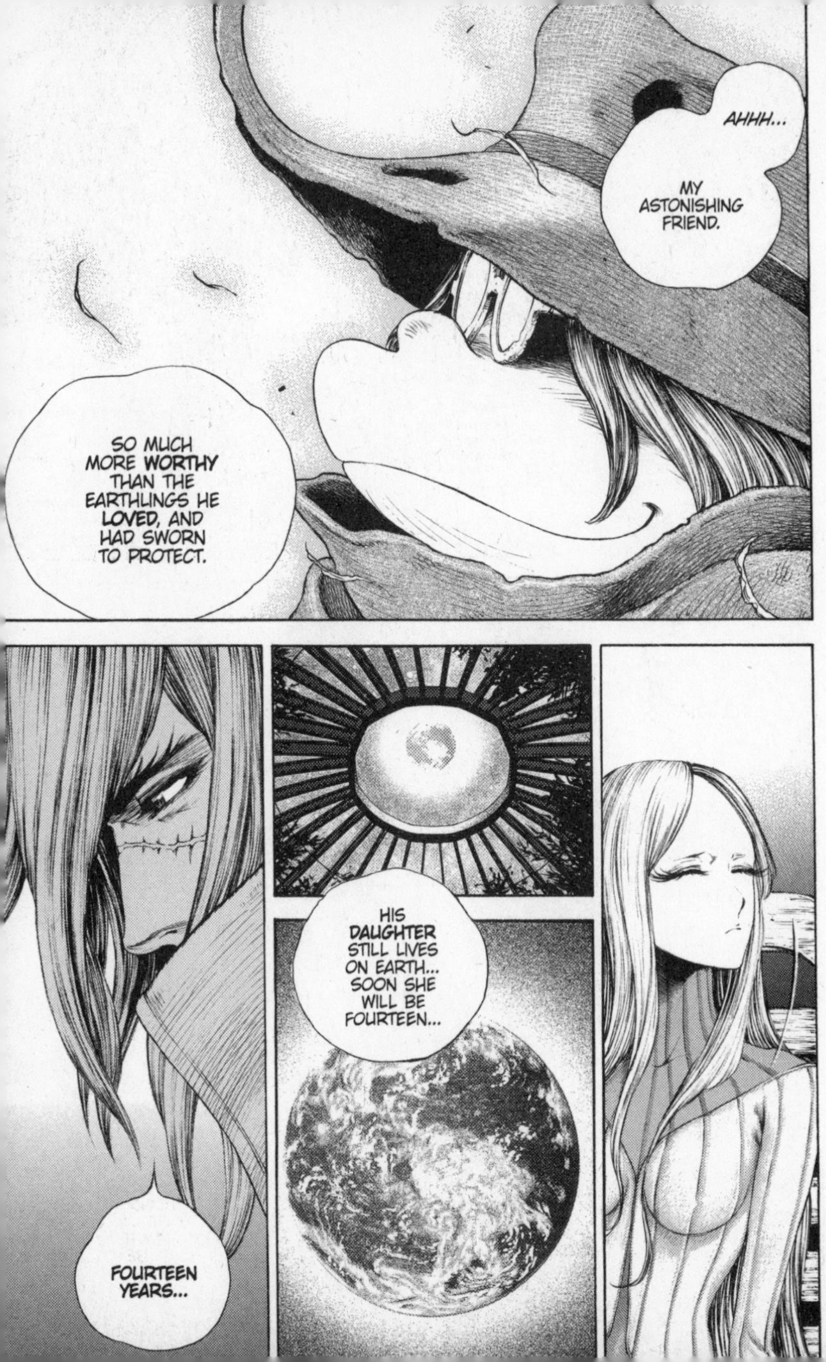
AHHH...
MY ASTONISHING FRIEND.
SO MUCH MORE WORTHY THAN THE EARTHLINGS HE LOVED, AND HAD SWORN TO PROTECT.
HIS DAUGHTER STILL LIVES ON EARTH... SOON SHE WILL BE FOURTEEN...
FOURTEEN YEARS...

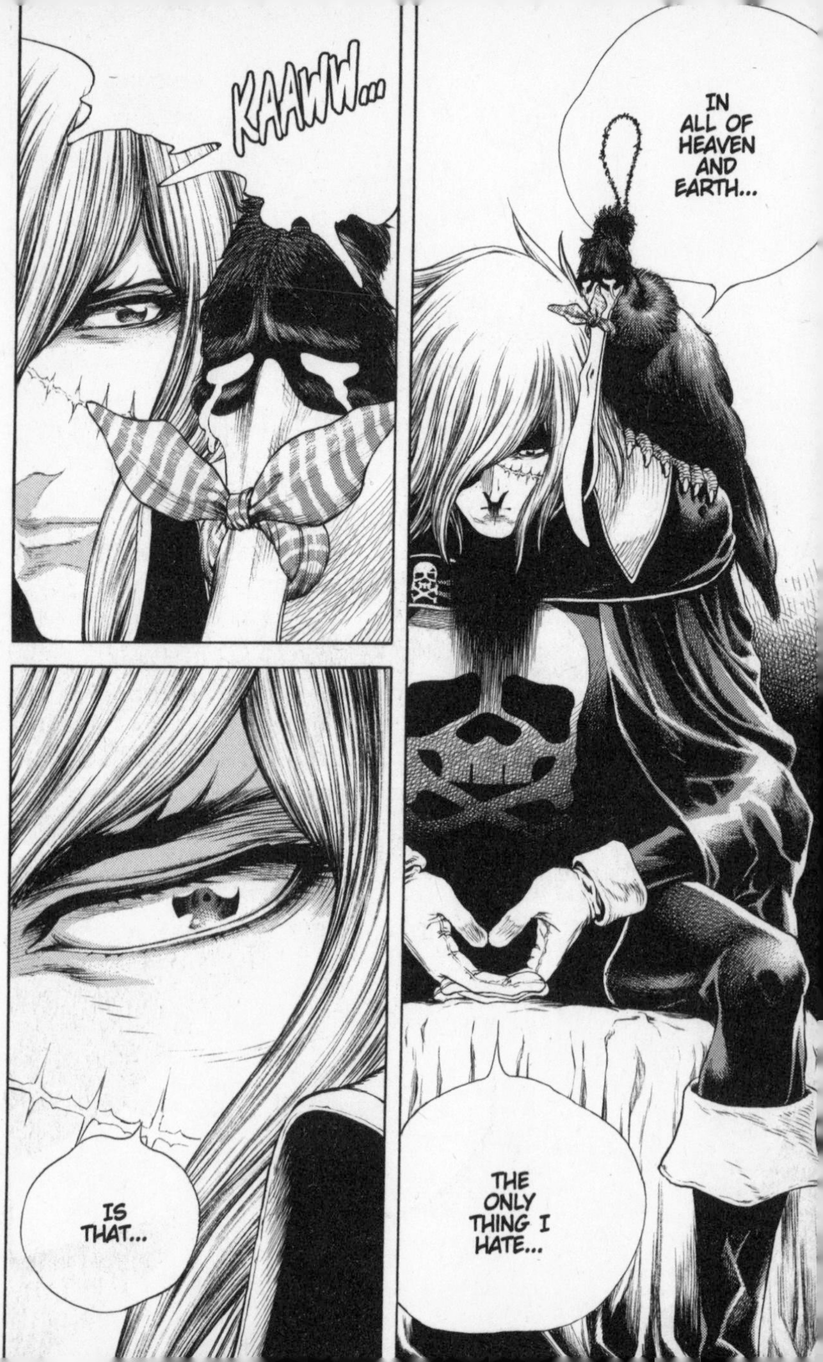
IN ALL OF HEAVEN AND EARTH...
THE ONLY THING I HATE...
KAAWW...
IS THAT...

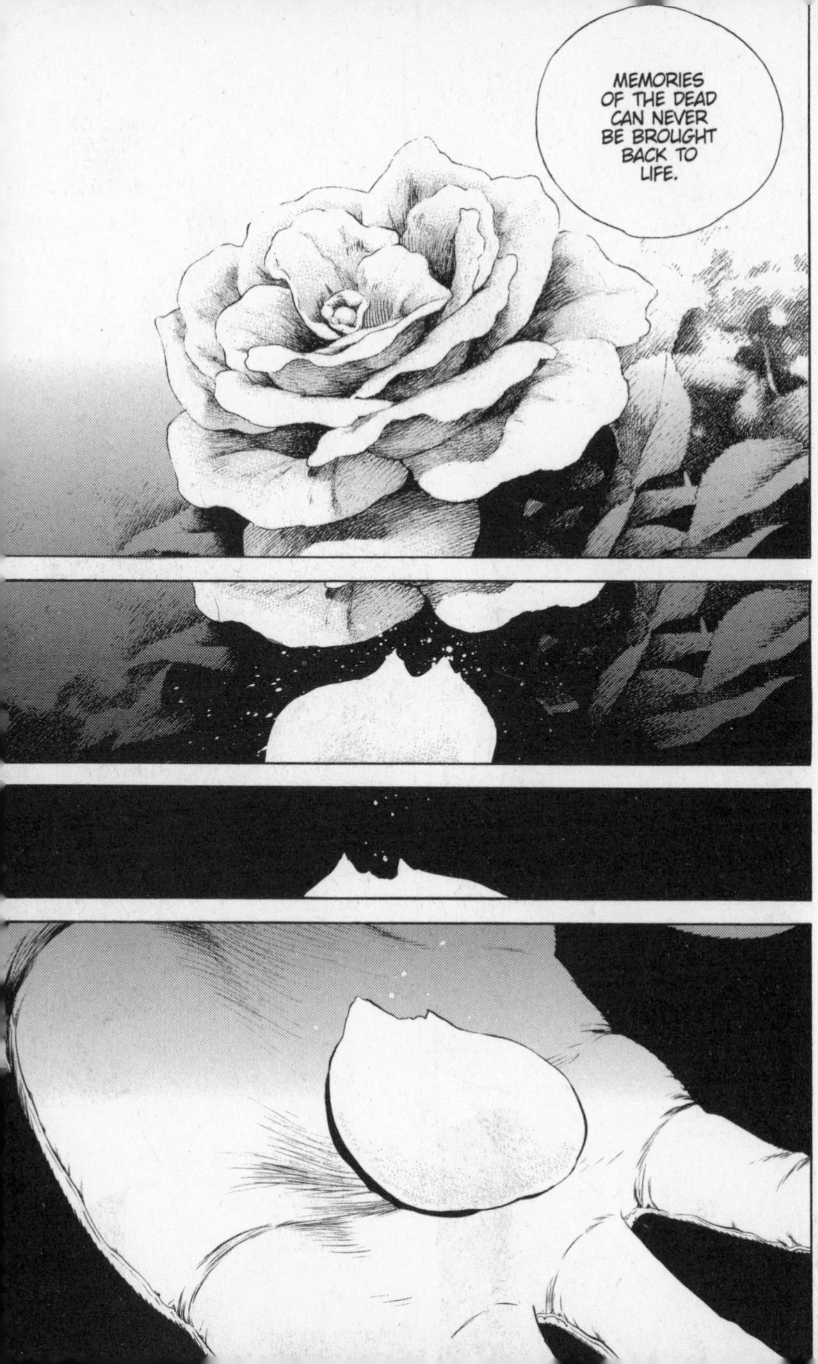
MEMORIES OF THE DEAD CAN NEVER BE BROUGHT BACK TO LIFE.

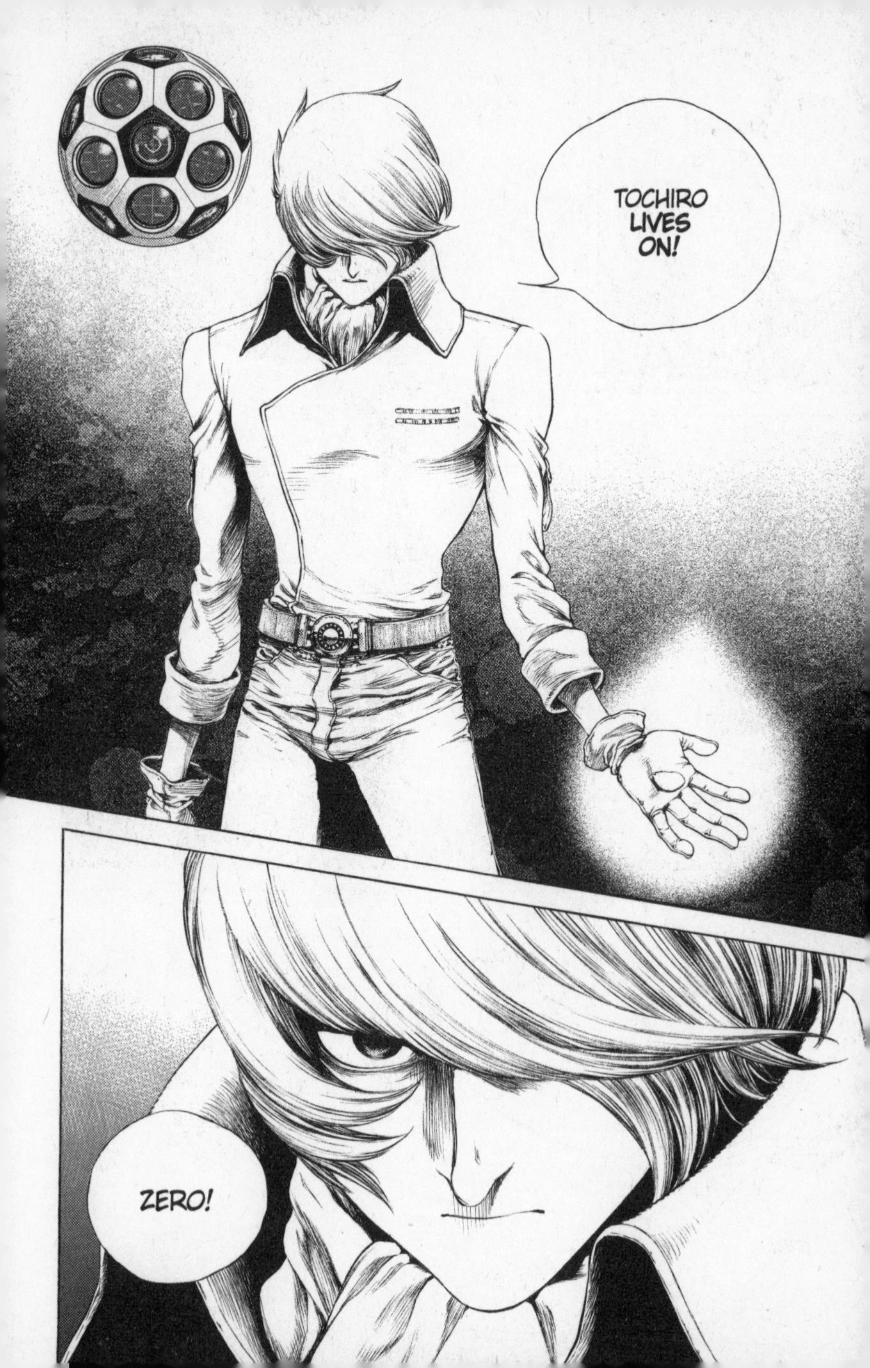
TOCHIRO LIVES ON!
ZERO!

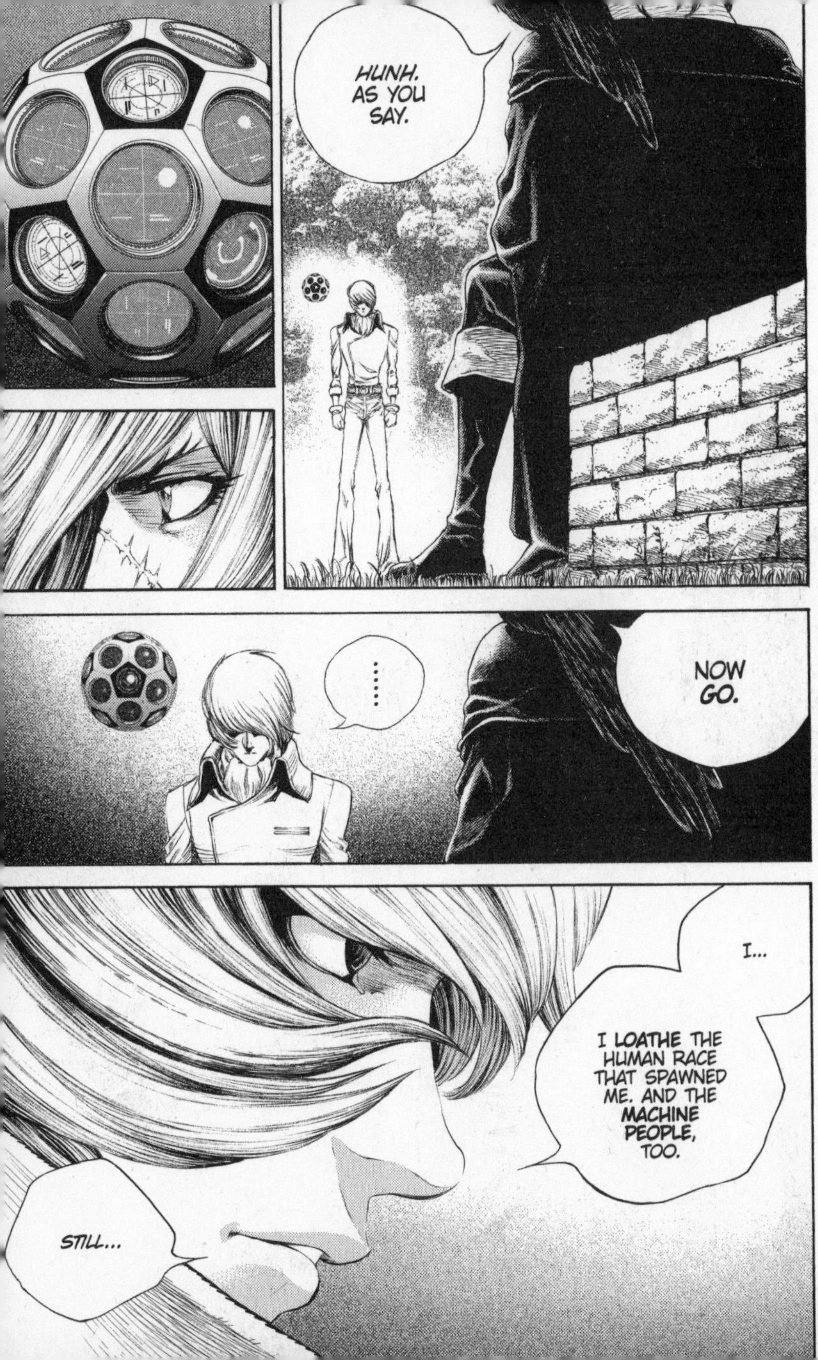
HUNH. AS YOU SAY.
NOW GO.
......
I...
I LOATHE THE HUMAN RACE THAT SPAWNED ME. AND THE MACHINE PEOPLE, TOO.
STILL...

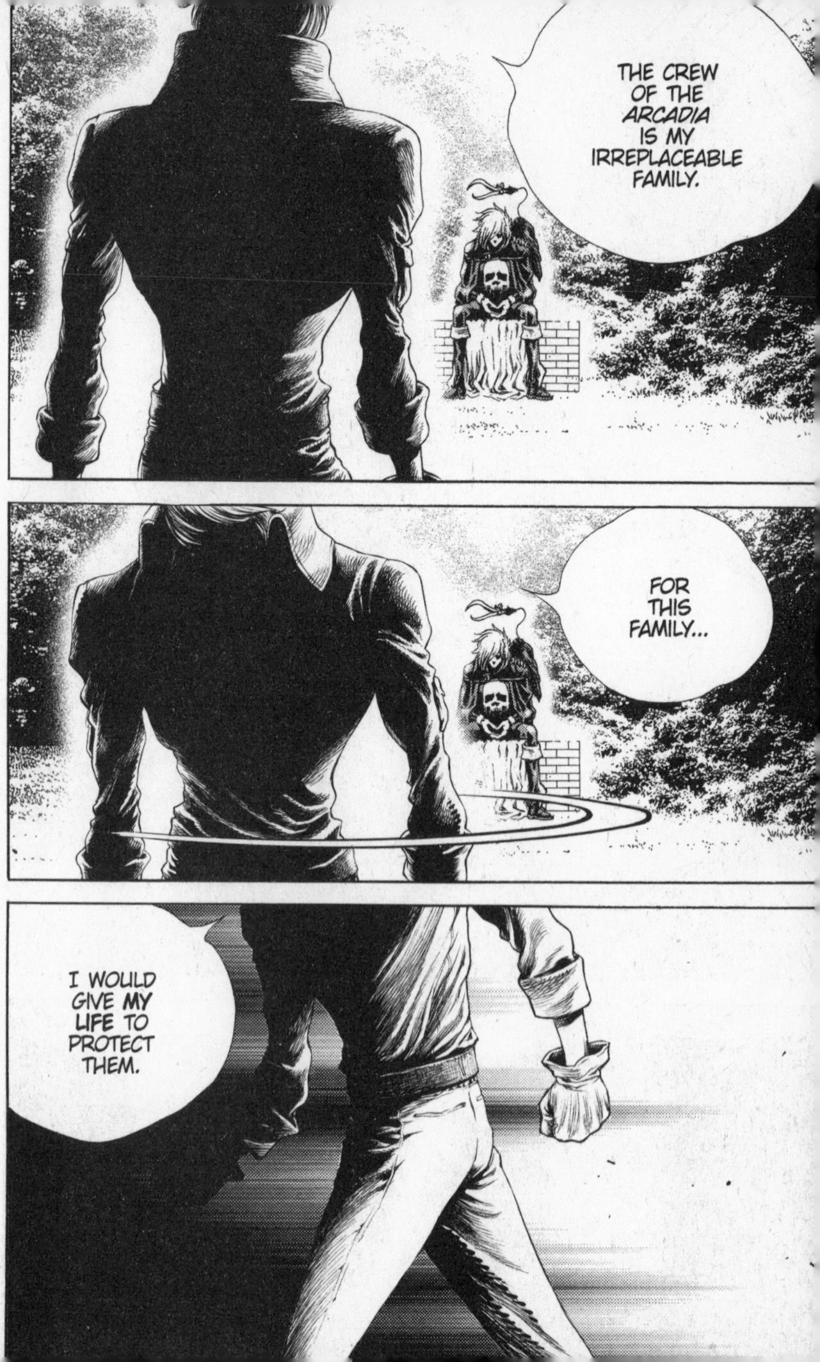
THE CREW OF THE *ARCADIA* IS MY IRREPLACEABLE FAMILY.
FOR THIS FAMILY...
I WOULD GIVE MY LIFE TO PROTECT THEM.

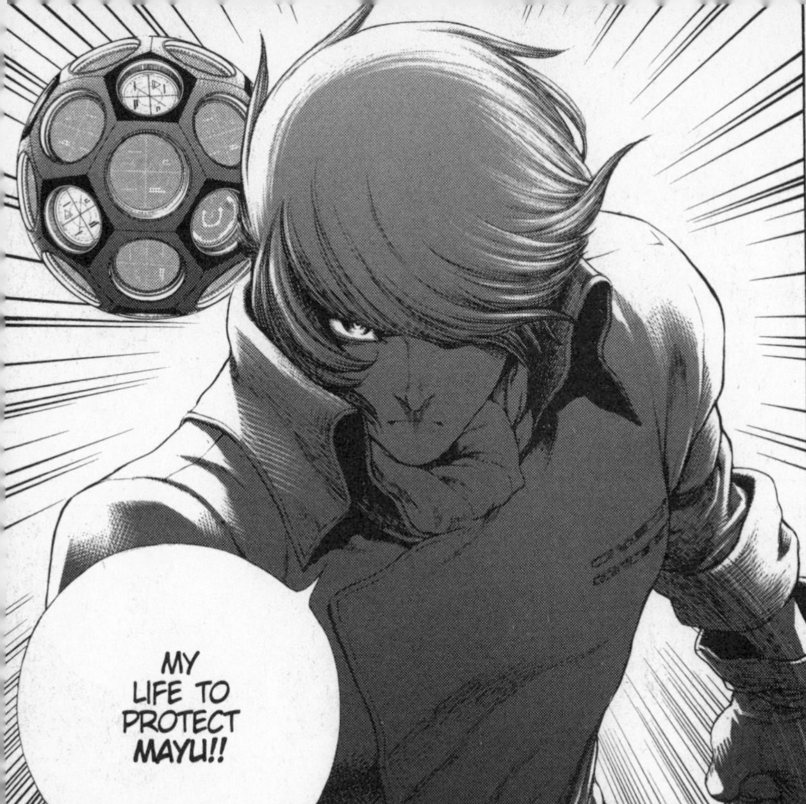
MY LIFE TO PROTECT MAYU!!
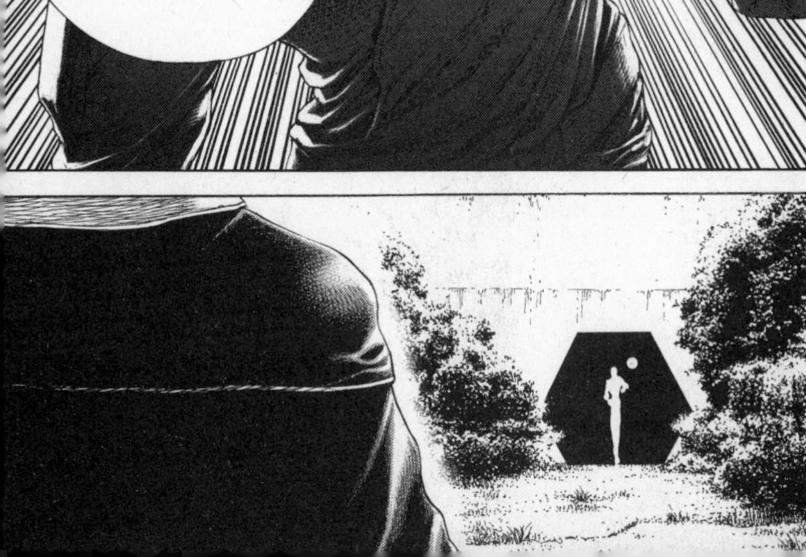

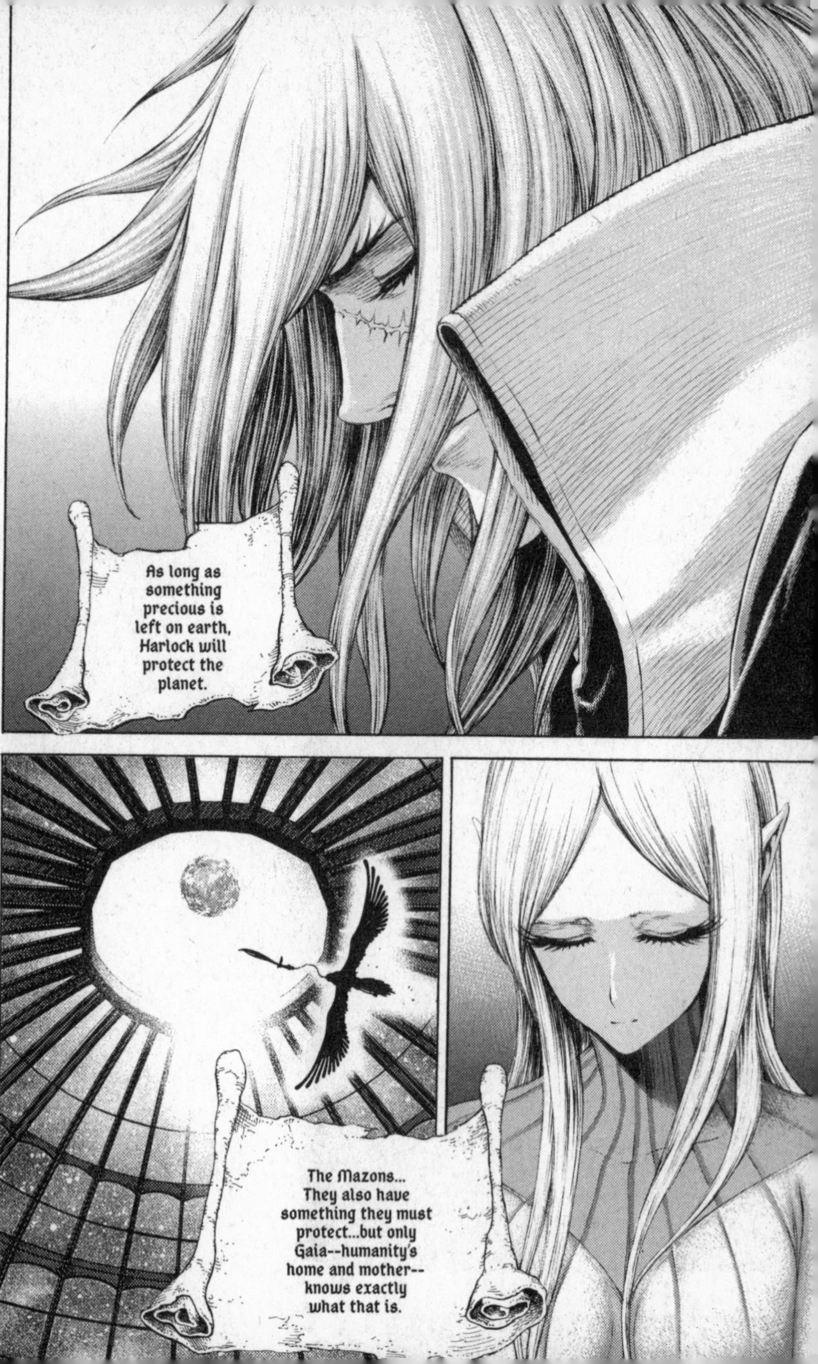
As long as something precious is left on earth, Harlock will protect the planet.
The Mazons... They also have something they must protect...but only Gaia--humanity's home and mother--knows exactly what that is.

CAPTAIN HARLOCK 3
SPACE PIRATE DIMENSIONAL VOYAGE

CAPTAIN HARLOCK 3
SPACE PIRATE DIMENSIONAL VOYAGE

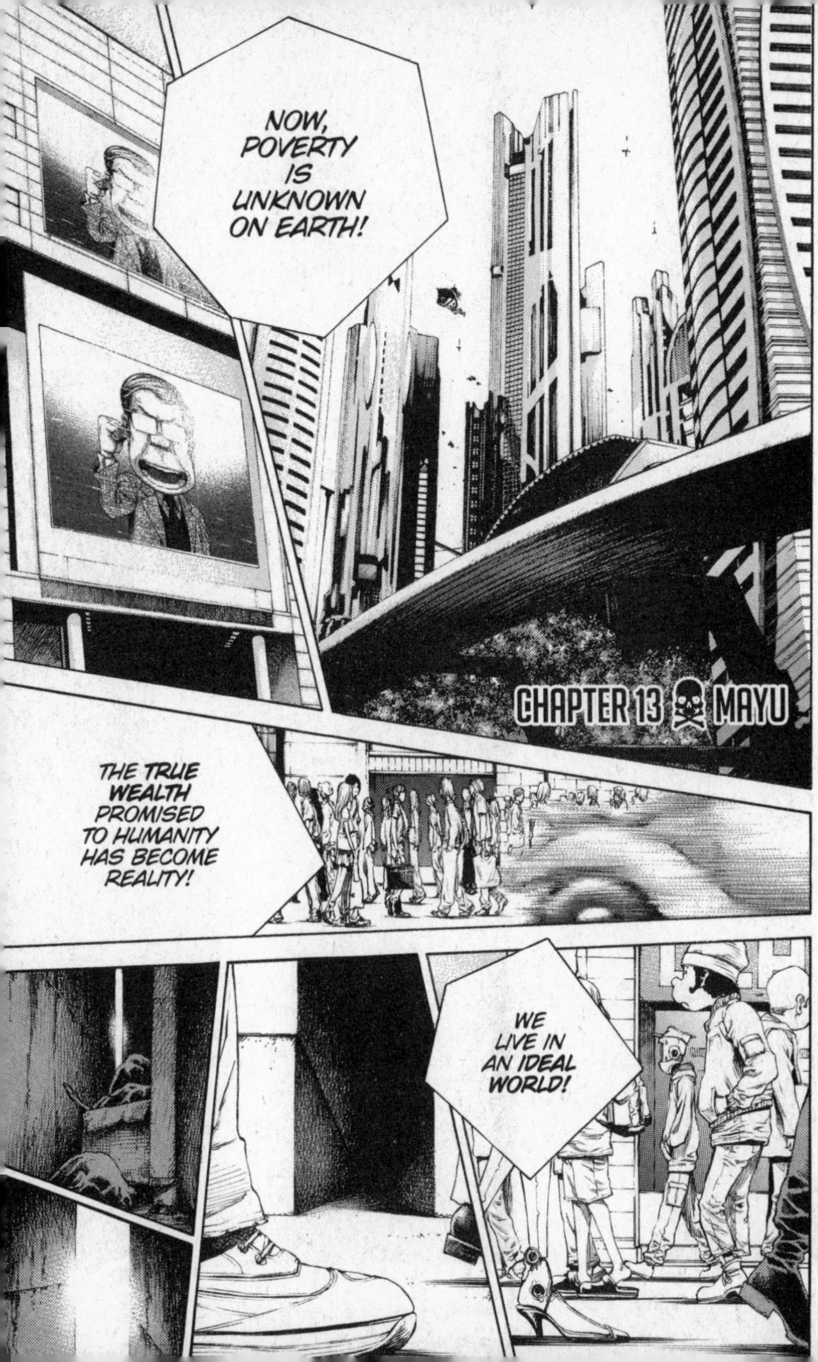
CHAPTER 13 MAYU
NOW, POVERTY IS UNKNOWN ON EARTH!
THE TRUE WEALTH PROMISED TO HUMANITY HAS BECOME REALITY!
WE LIVE IN AN IDEAL WORLD!

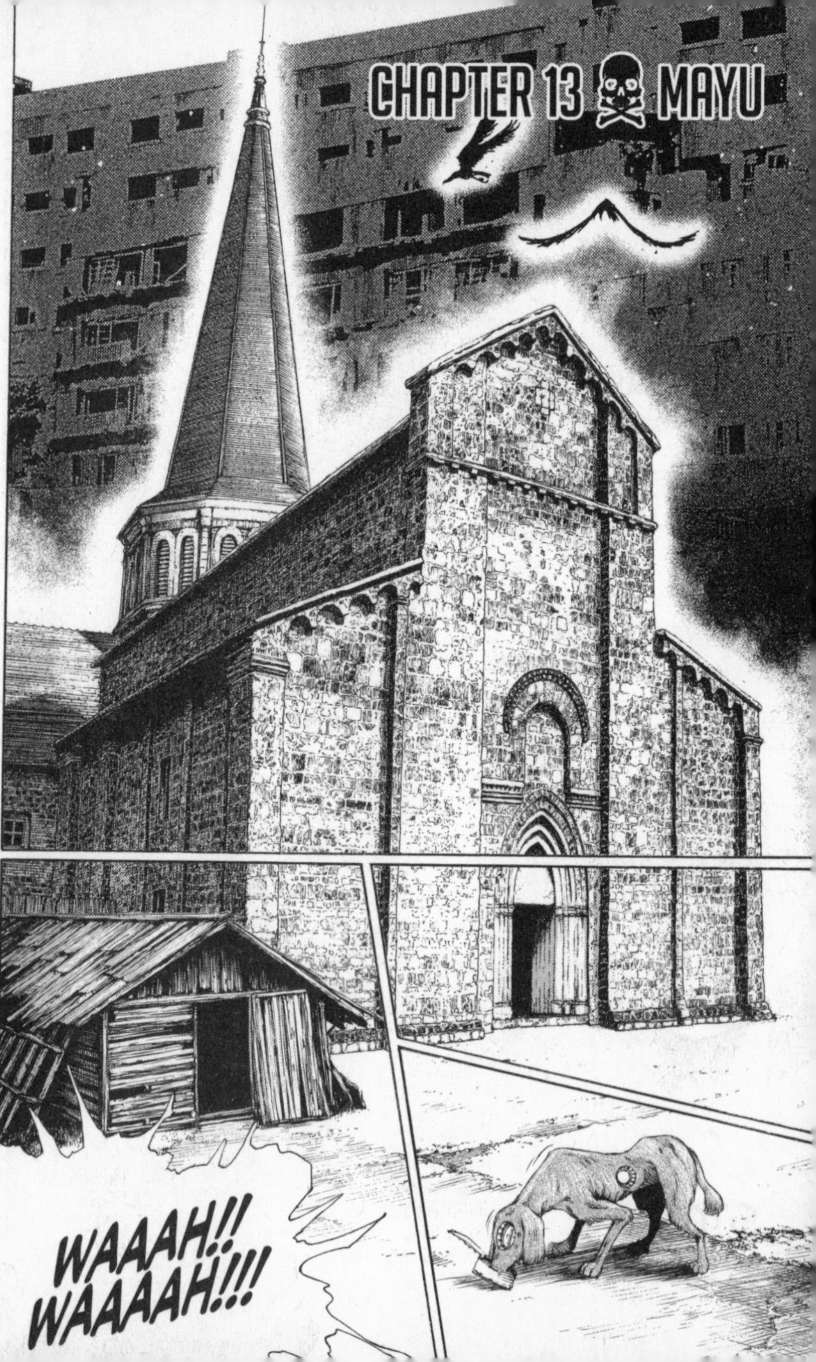
CHAPTER 13 MAYU
WAAAH!! WAAAAH!!!

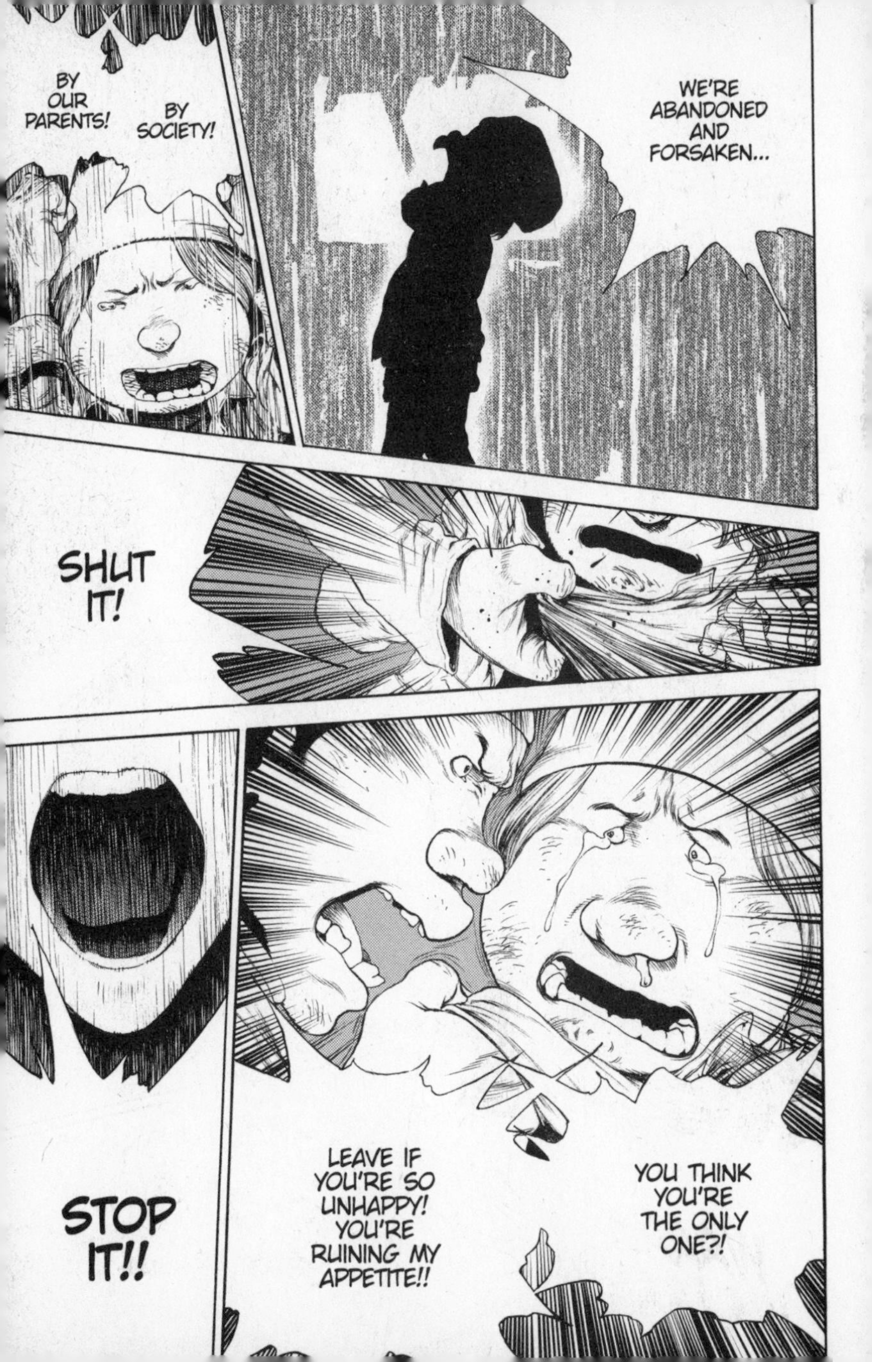
WE'RE ABANDONED AND FORSAKEN...
BY OUR PARENTS!
BY SOCIETY!
SHUT IT!
YOU THINK YOU'RE THE ONLY ONE?!
LEAVE IF YOU'RE SO UNHAPPY! YOU'RE RUINING MY APPETITE!!
STOP IT!!

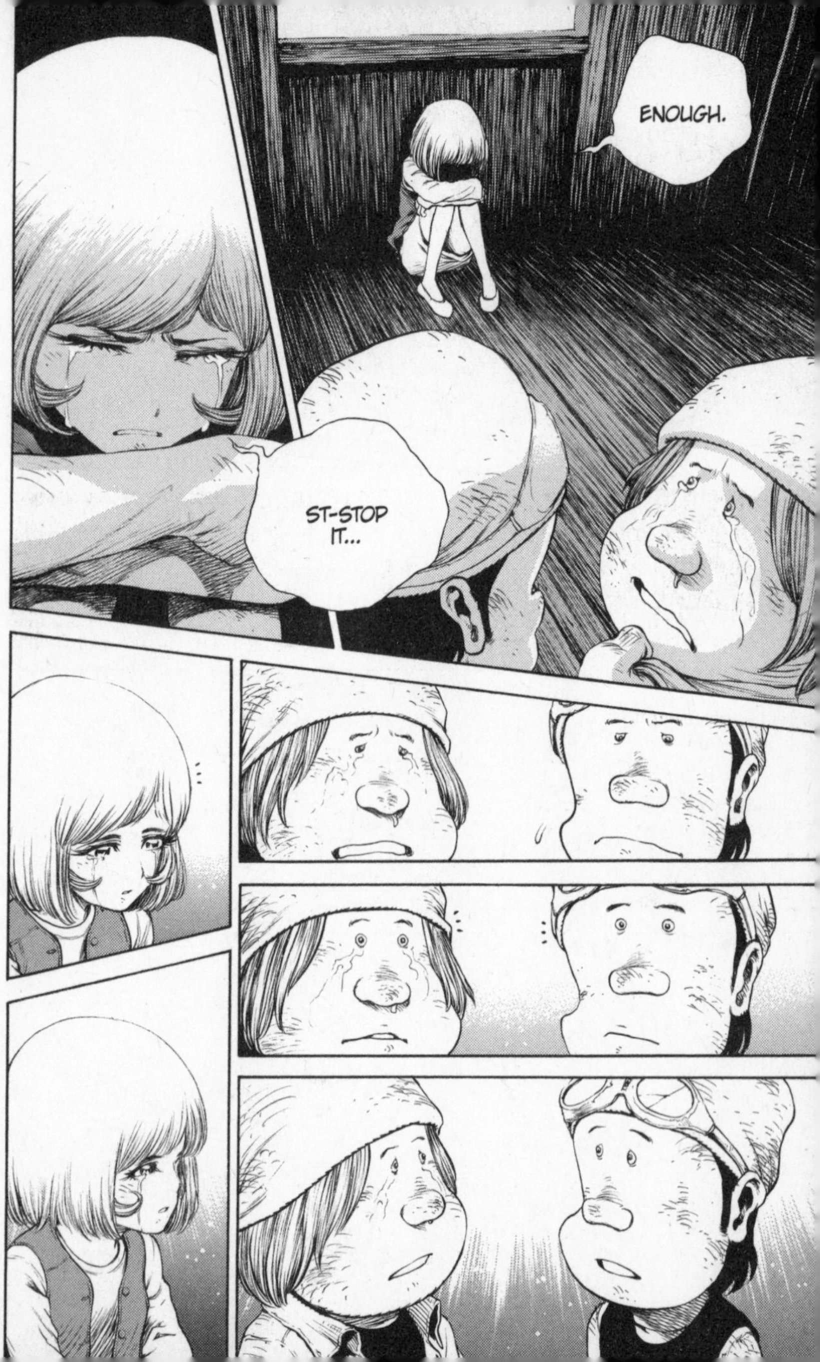
ENOUGH.
ST-STOP IT...

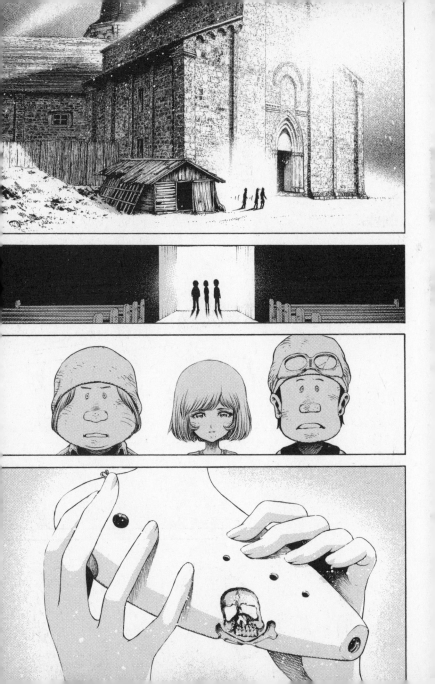

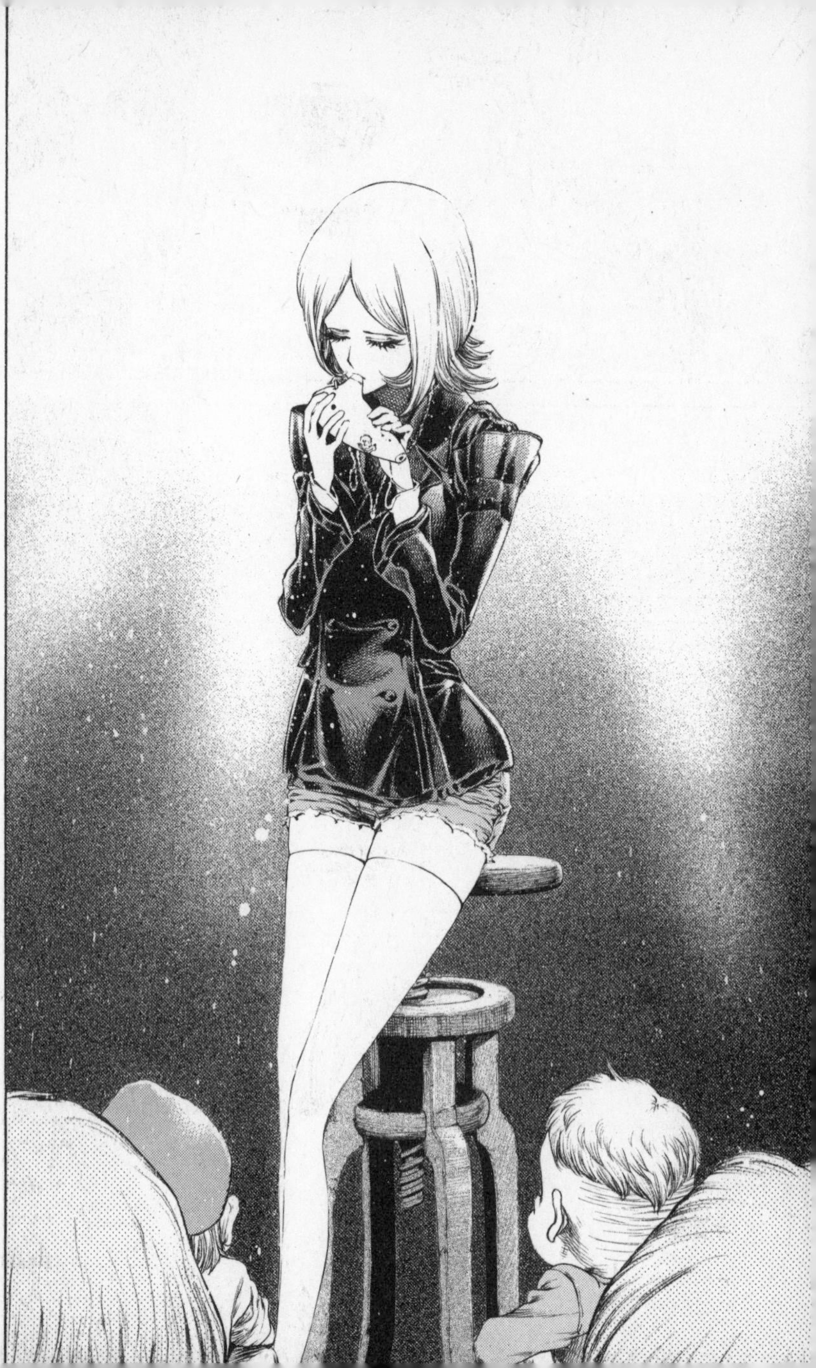

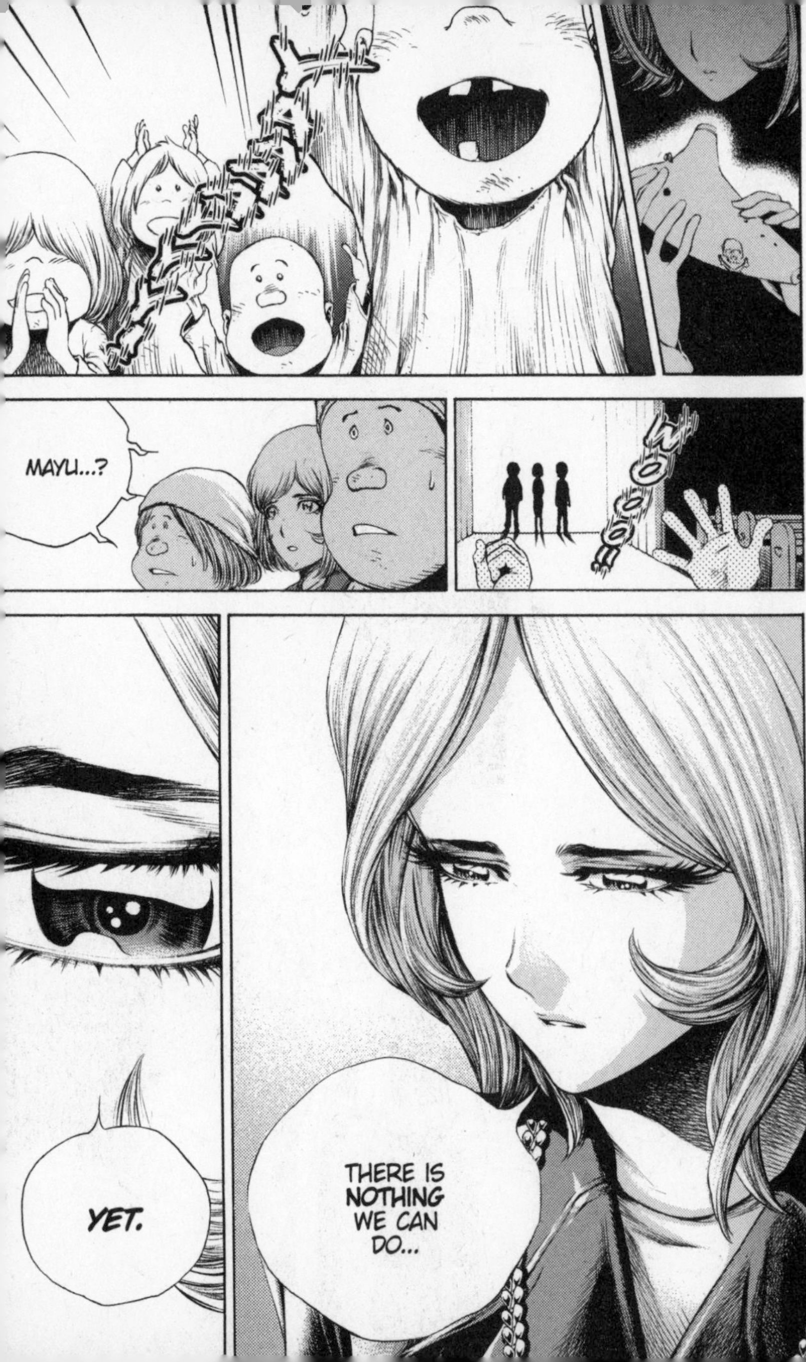
MAYU...?
THERE IS NOTHING WE CAN DO...
YET.

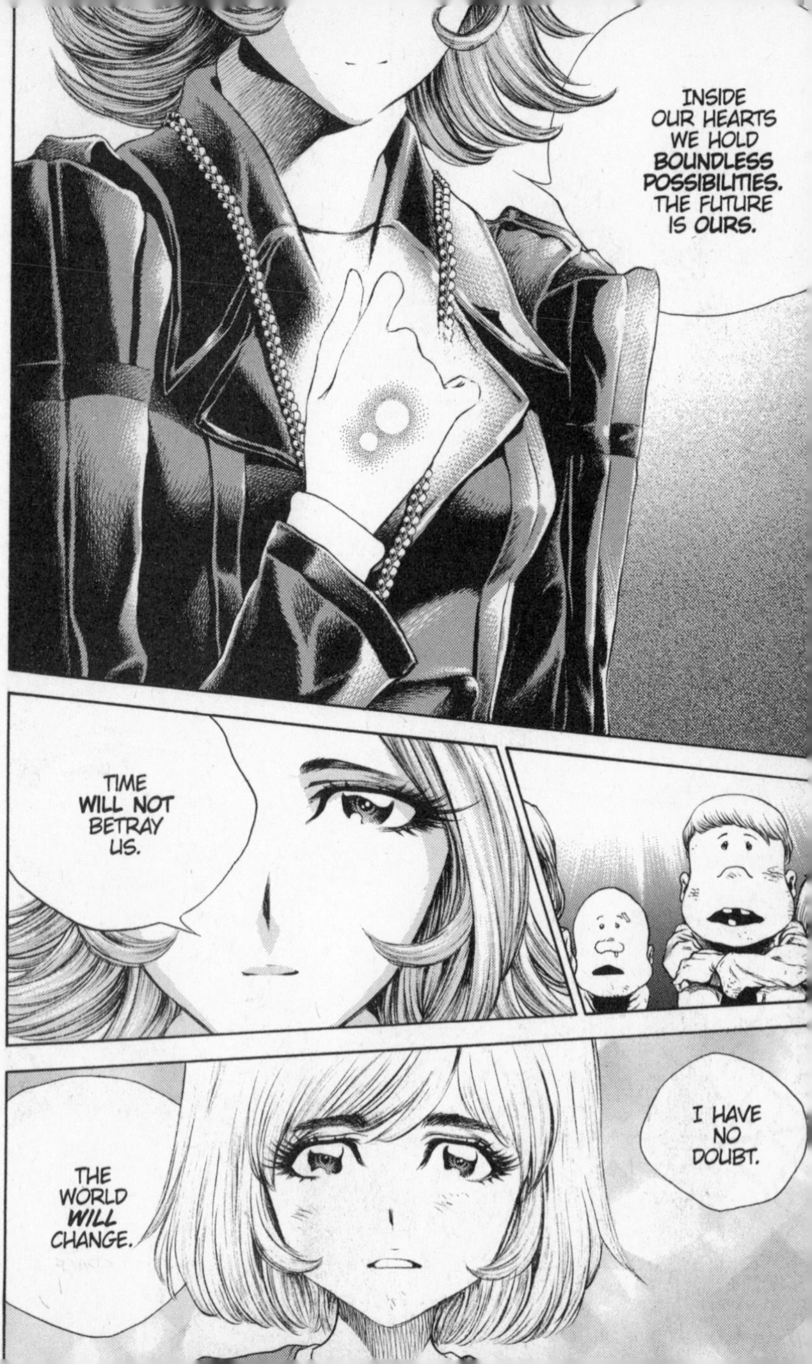
INSIDE OUR HEARTS WE HOLD BOUNDLESS POSSIBILITIES. THE FUTURE IS OURS.
TIME WILL NOT BETRAY US.
I HAVE NO DOUBT.
THE WORLD WILL CHANGE.

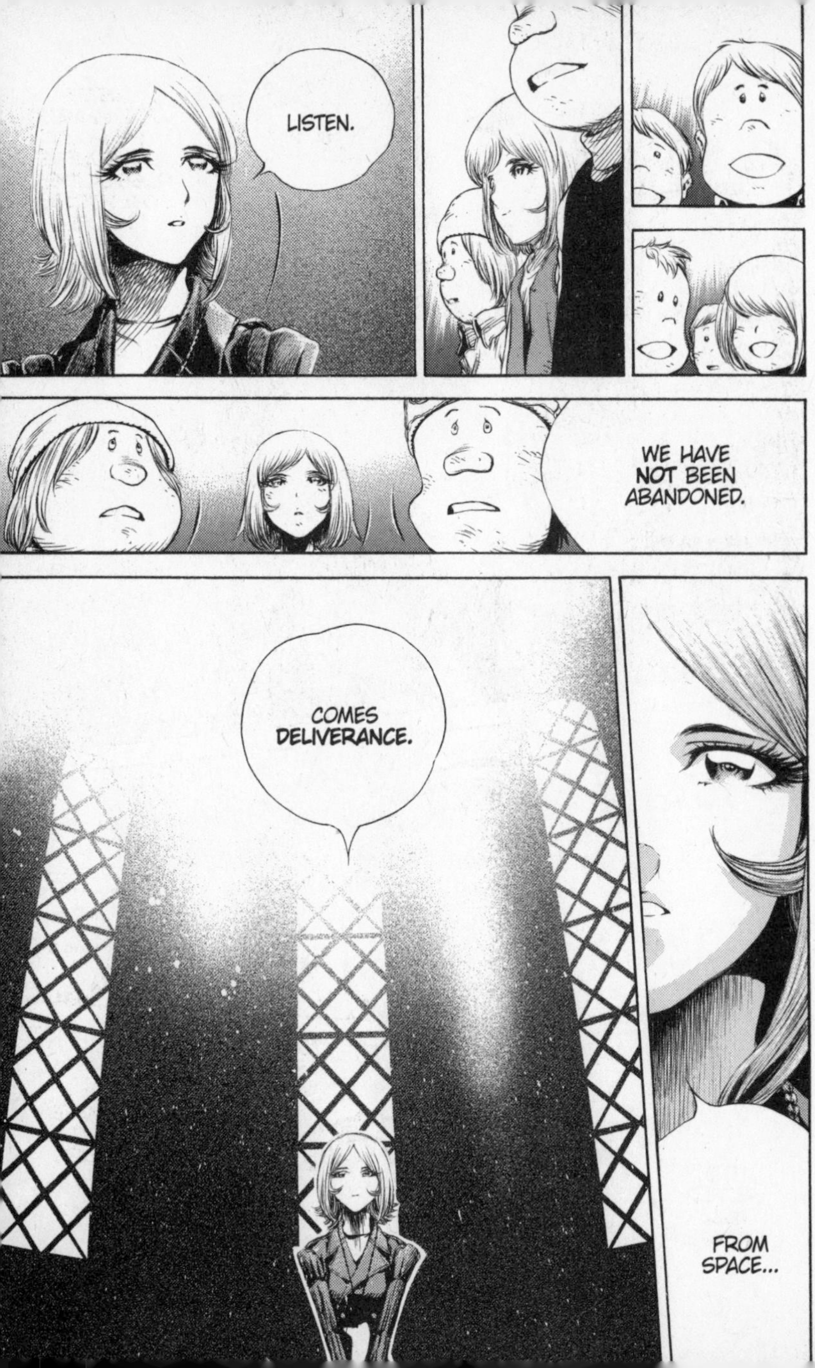
LISTEN.
WE HAVE NOT BEEN ABANDONED.
FROM SPACE...
COMES DELIVERANCE.

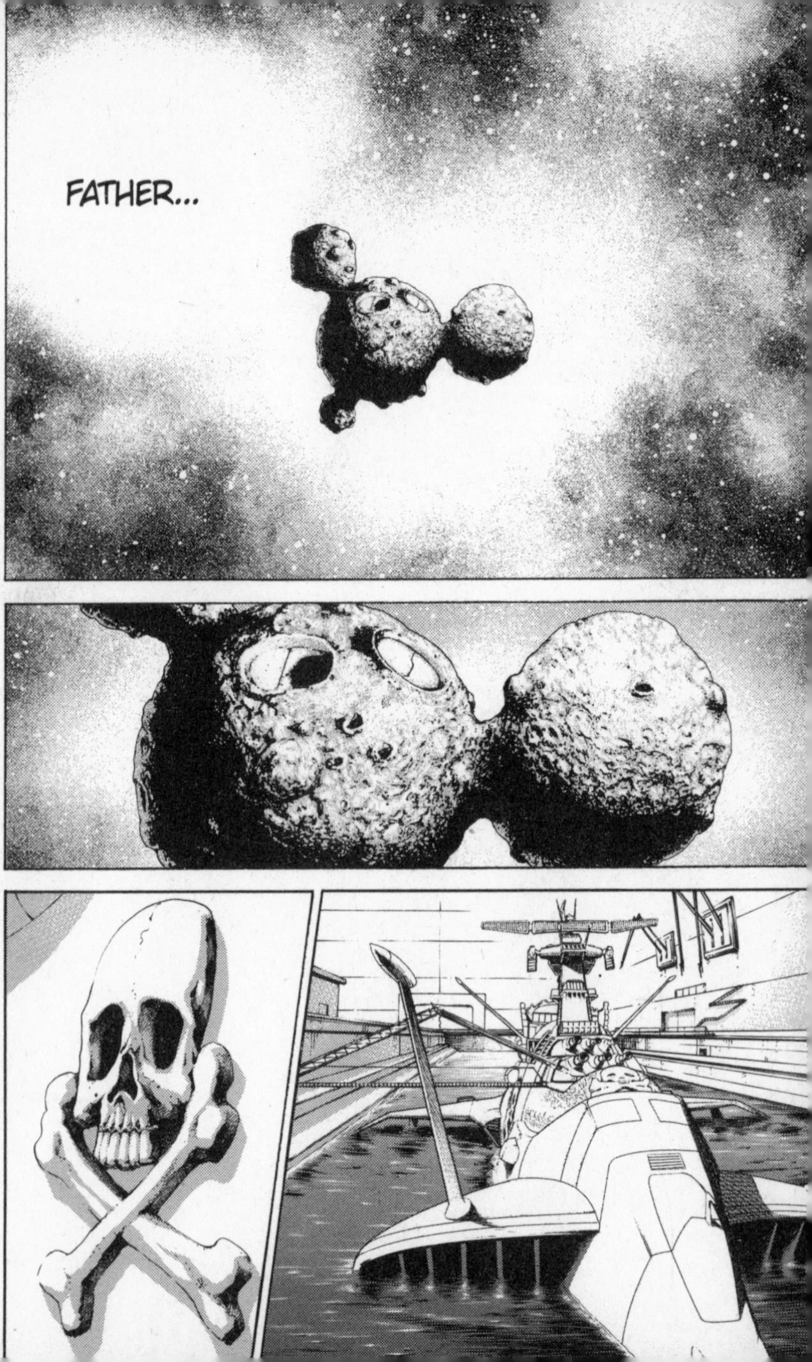
FATHER...

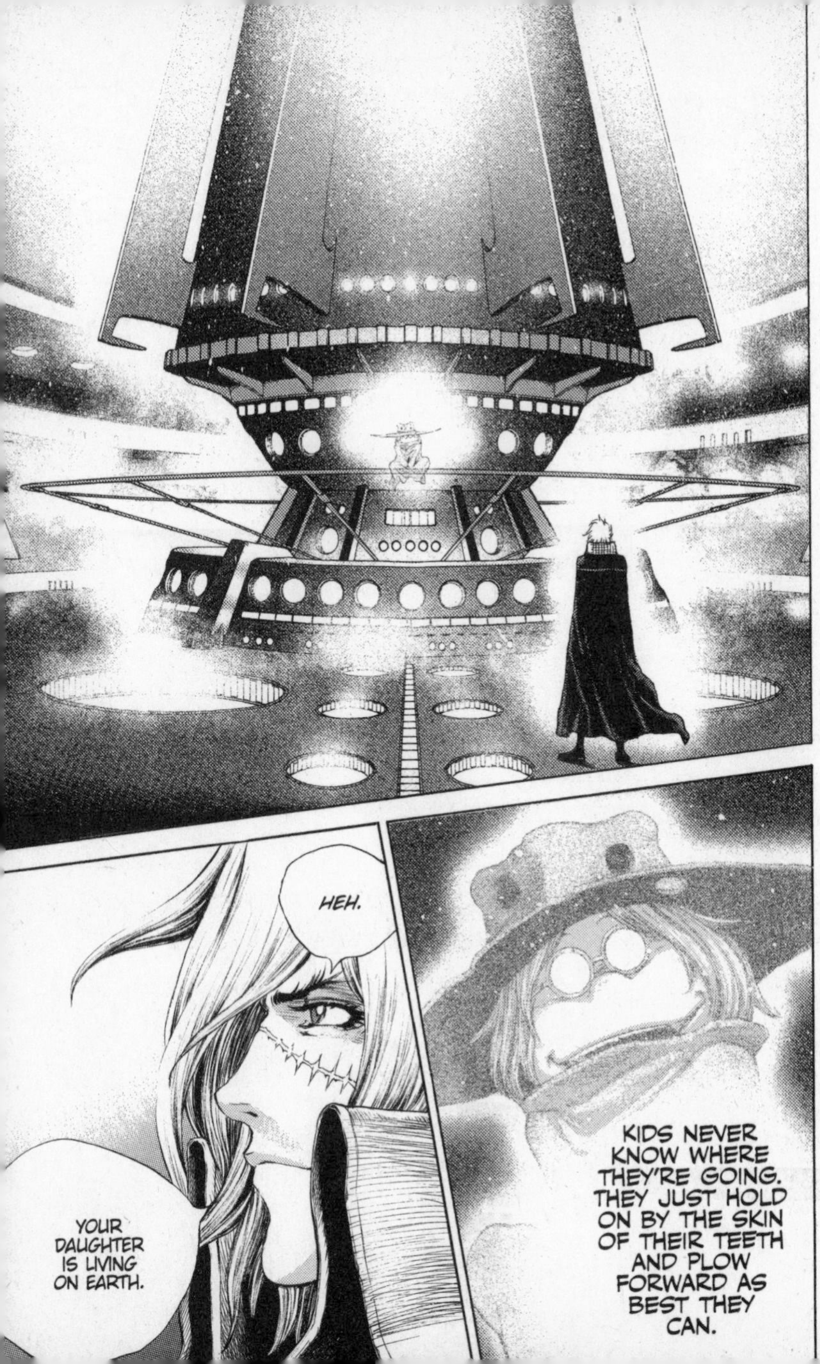
KIDS NEVER KNOW WHERE THEY'RE GOING. THEY JUST HOLD ON BY THE SKIN OF THEIR TEETH AND PLOW FORWARD AS BEST THEY CAN.
HEH.
YOUR DAUGHTER IS LIVING ON EARTH.

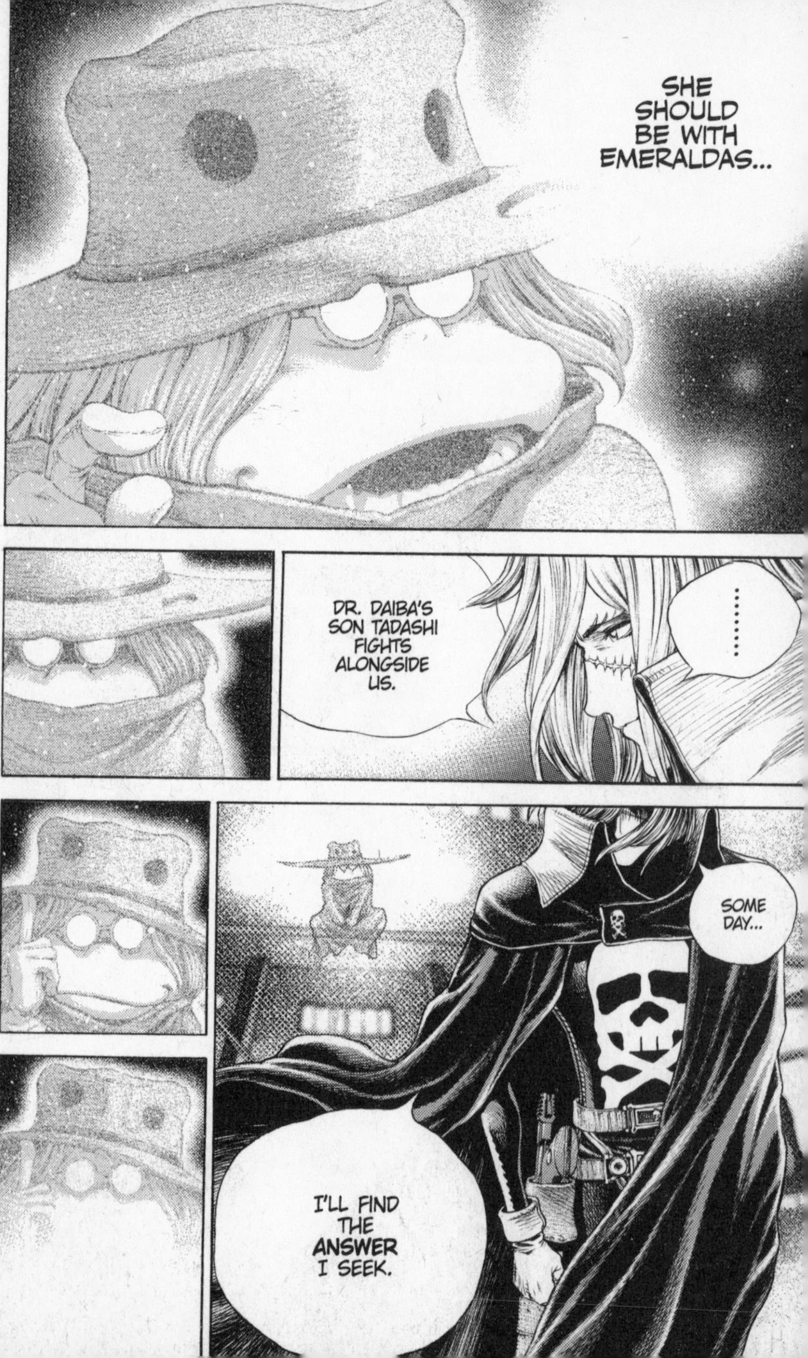
SHE SHOULD BE WITH EMERALDAS...
....
DR. DAIBA'S SON TADASHI FIGHTS ALONGSIDE US.
SOME DAY...
I'LL FIND THE ANSWER I SEEK.

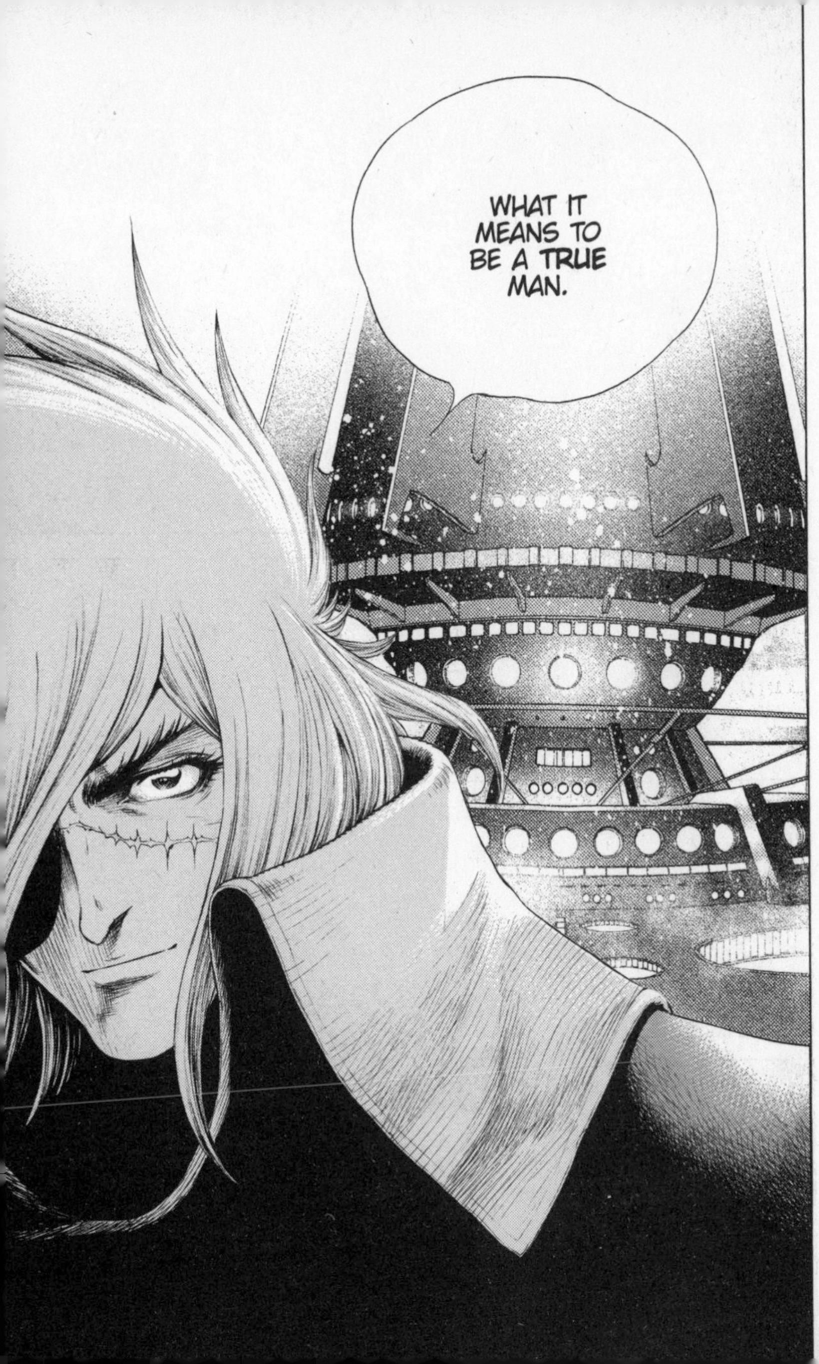
WHAT IT MEANS TO BE A TRUE MAN.

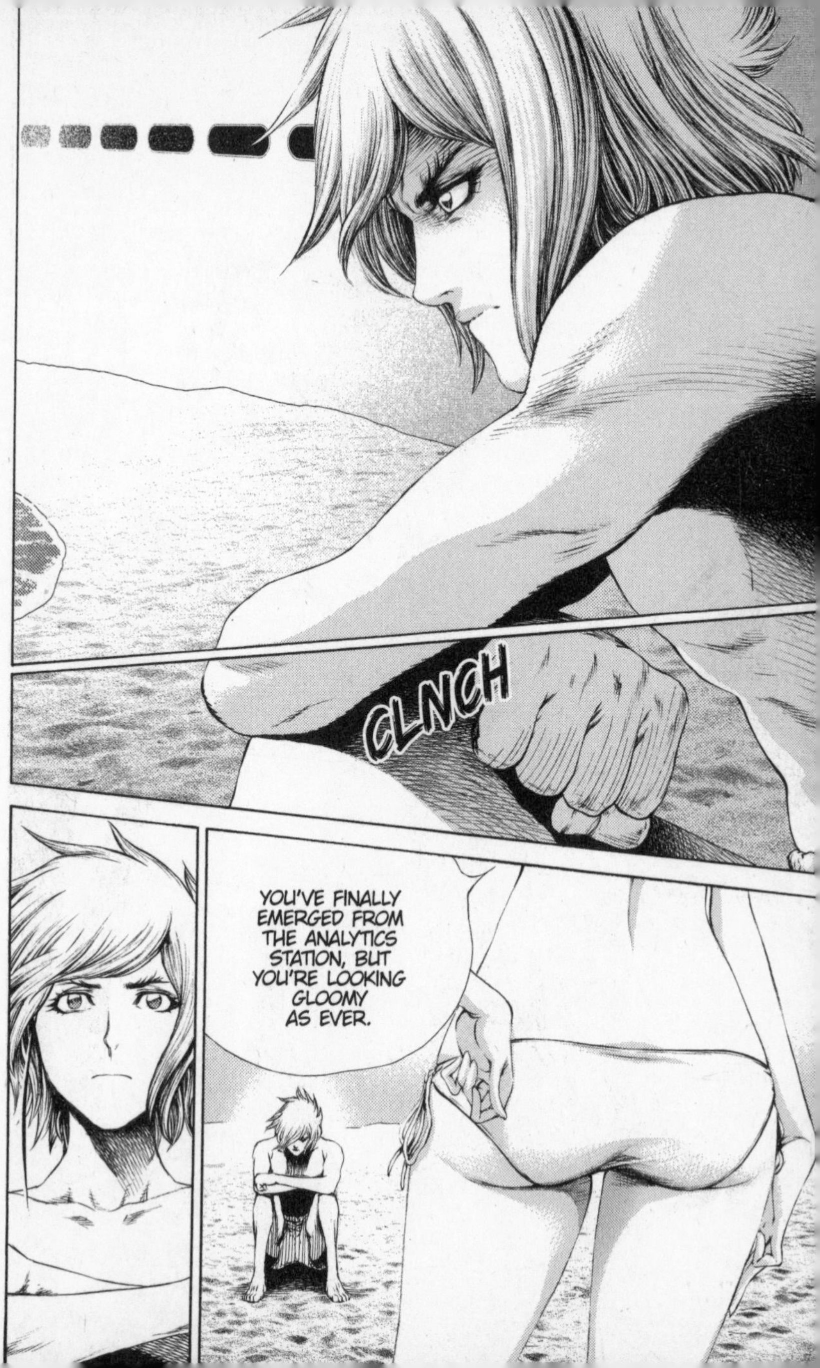
CLNCH
YOU'VE FINALLY EMERGED FROM THE ANALYTICS STATION, BUT YOU'RE LOOKING GLOOMY AS EVER.

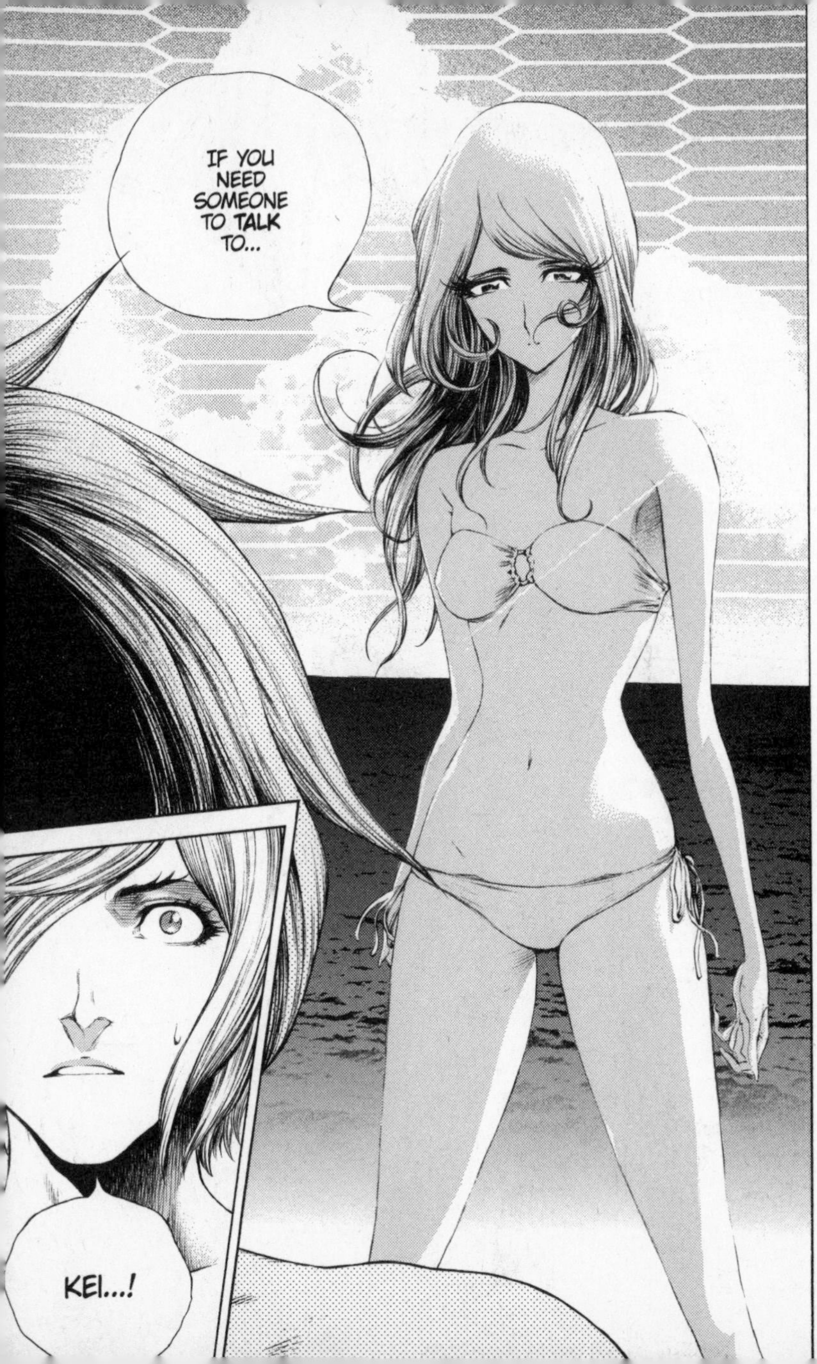
IF YOU NEED SOMEONE TO TALK TO...
KEI...!

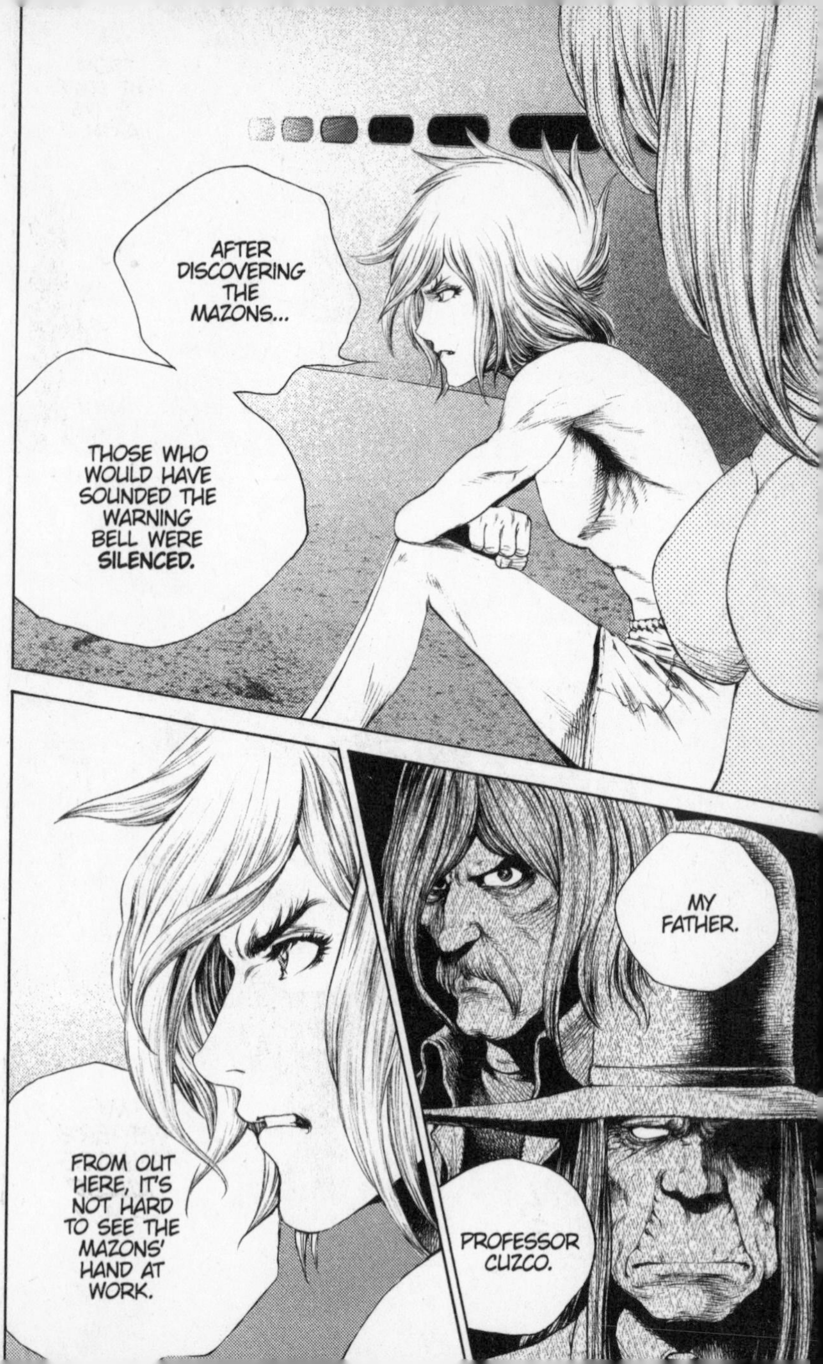
AFTER DISCOVERING THE MAZONS...
THOSE WHO WOULD HAVE SOUNDED THE WARNING BELL WERE SILENCED.
MY FATHER.
PROFESSOR CUZCO.
FROM OUT HERE, IT'S NOT HARD TO SEE THE MAZONS' HAND AT WORK.

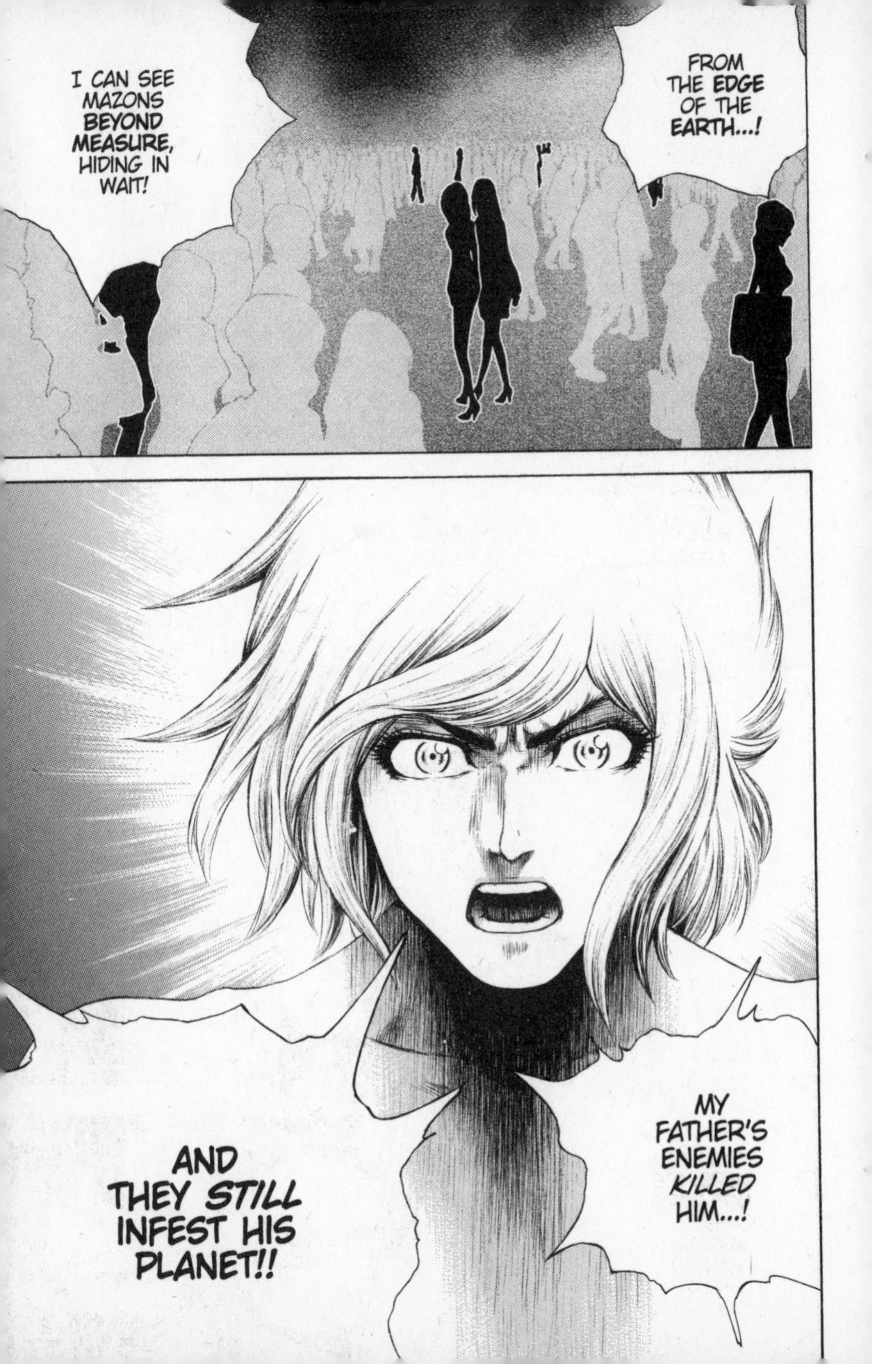
FROM THE EDGE OF THE EARTH...!
I CAN SEE MAZONS BEYOND MEASURE, HIDING IN WAIT!
MY FATHER'S ENEMIES *KILLED* HIM...!
AND THEY *STILL* INFEST HIS PLANET!!

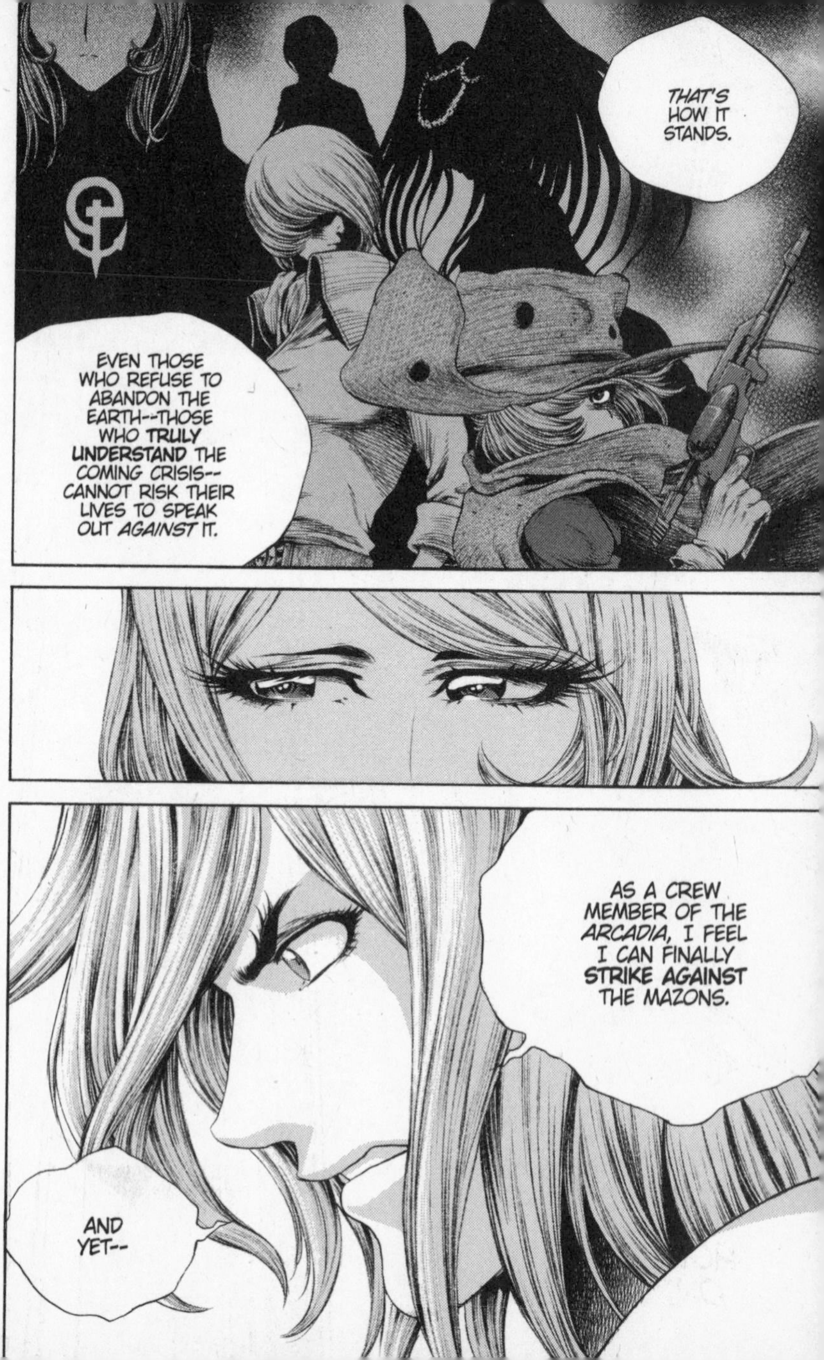
THAT'S HOW IT STANDS.
EVEN THOSE WHO REFUSE TO ABANDON THE EARTH--THOSE WHO **TRULY UNDERSTAND** THE COMING CRISIS--CANNOT RISK THEIR LIVES TO SPEAK OUT *AGAINST* IT.
AS A CREW MEMBER OF THE *ARCADIA*, I FEEL I CAN FINALLY **STRIKE AGAINST** THE MAZONS.
AND YET--

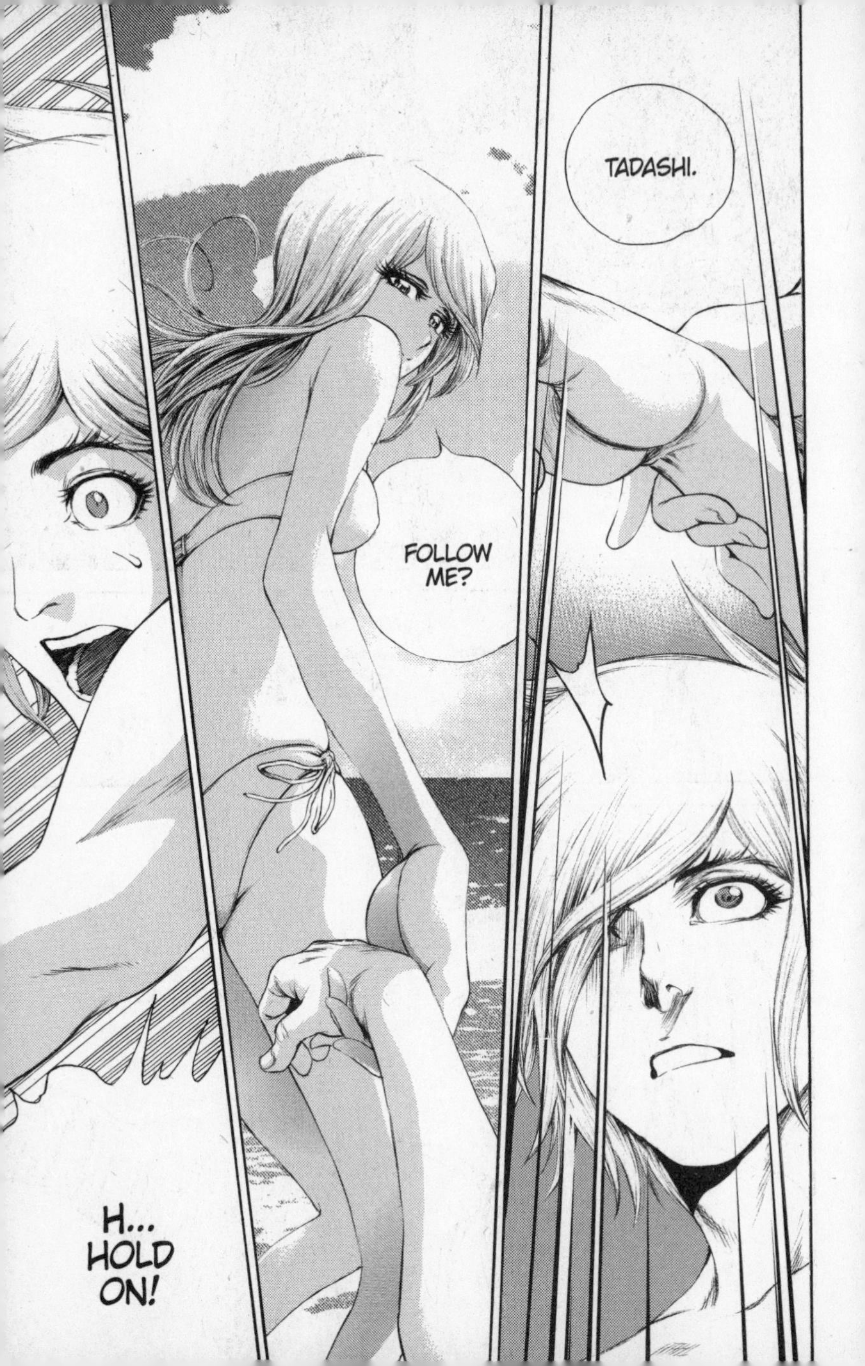
TADASHI.
FOLLOW ME?
H... HOLD ON!

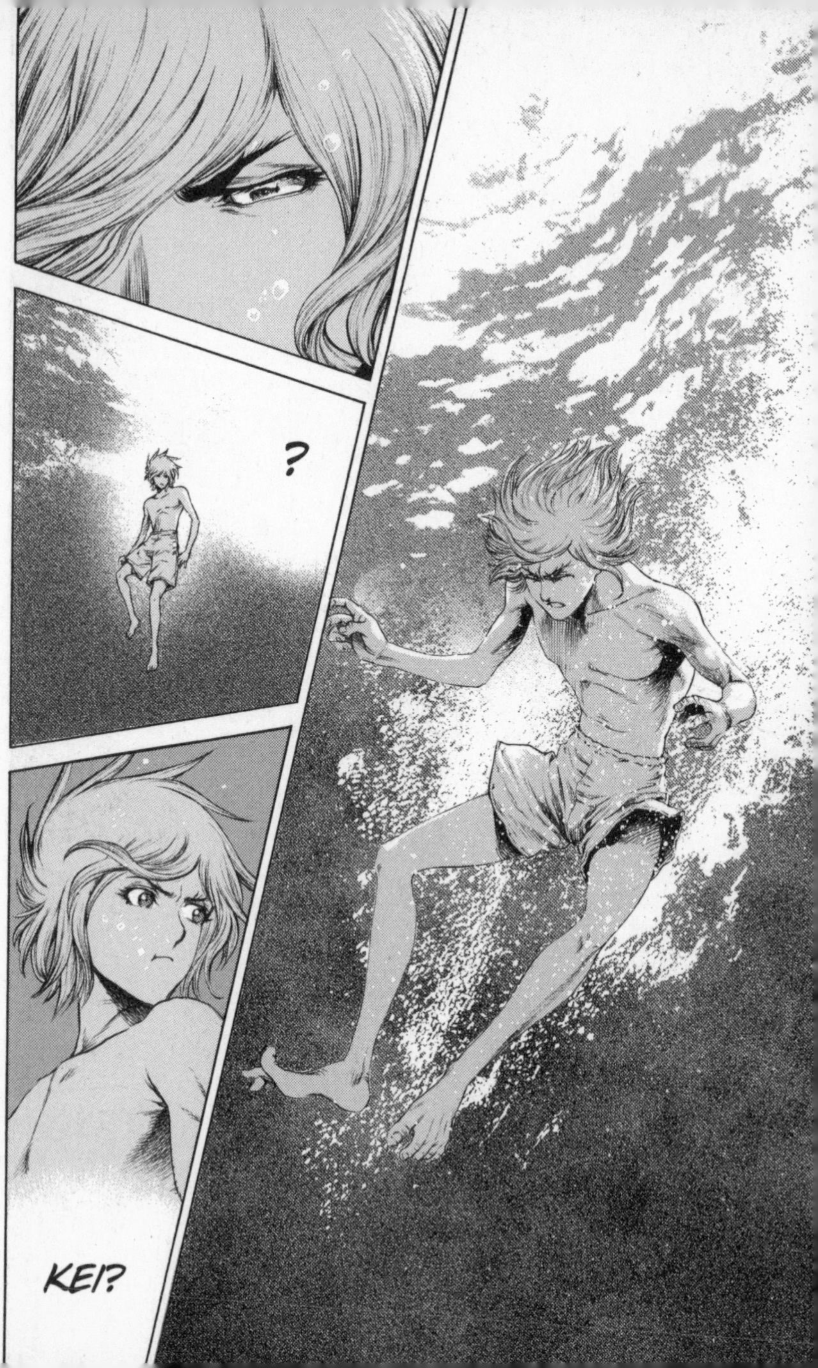
?
KEI?

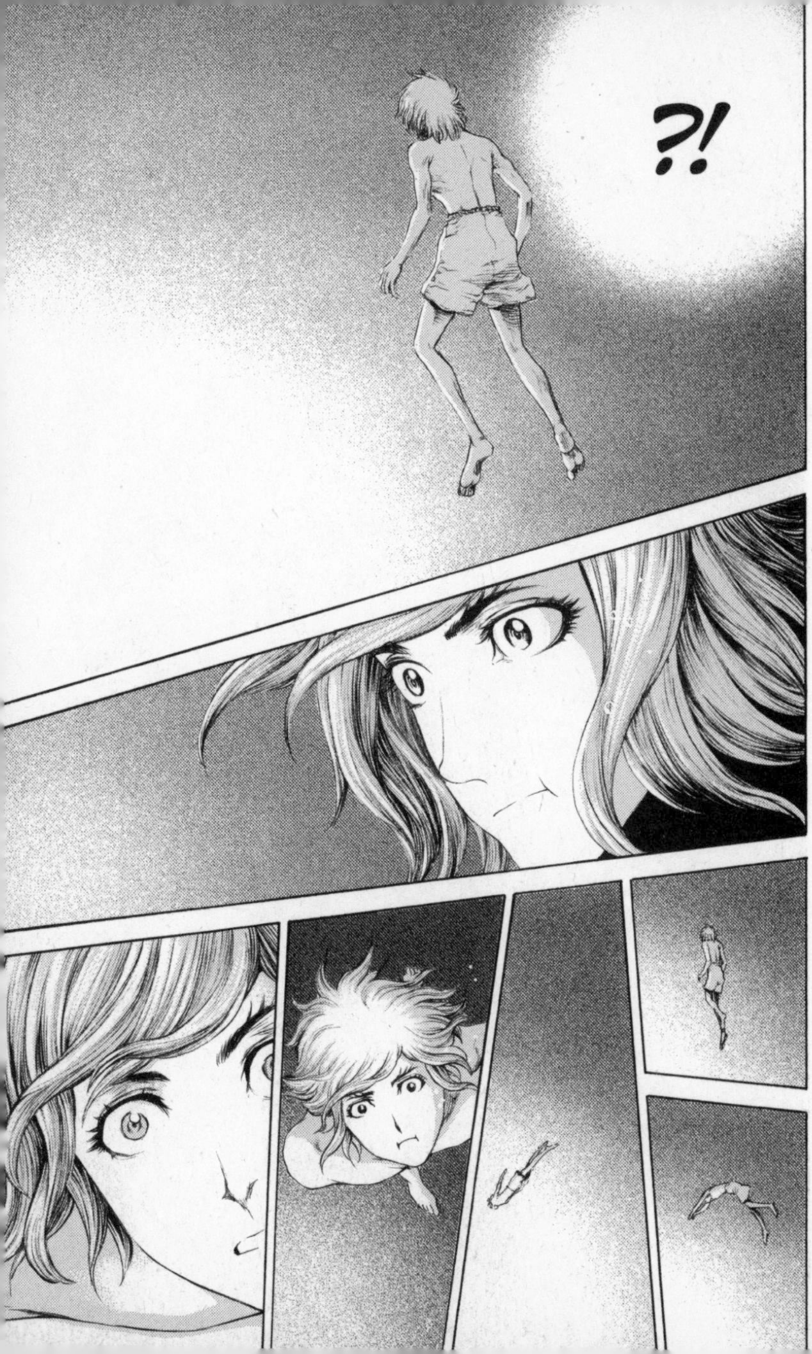
?!

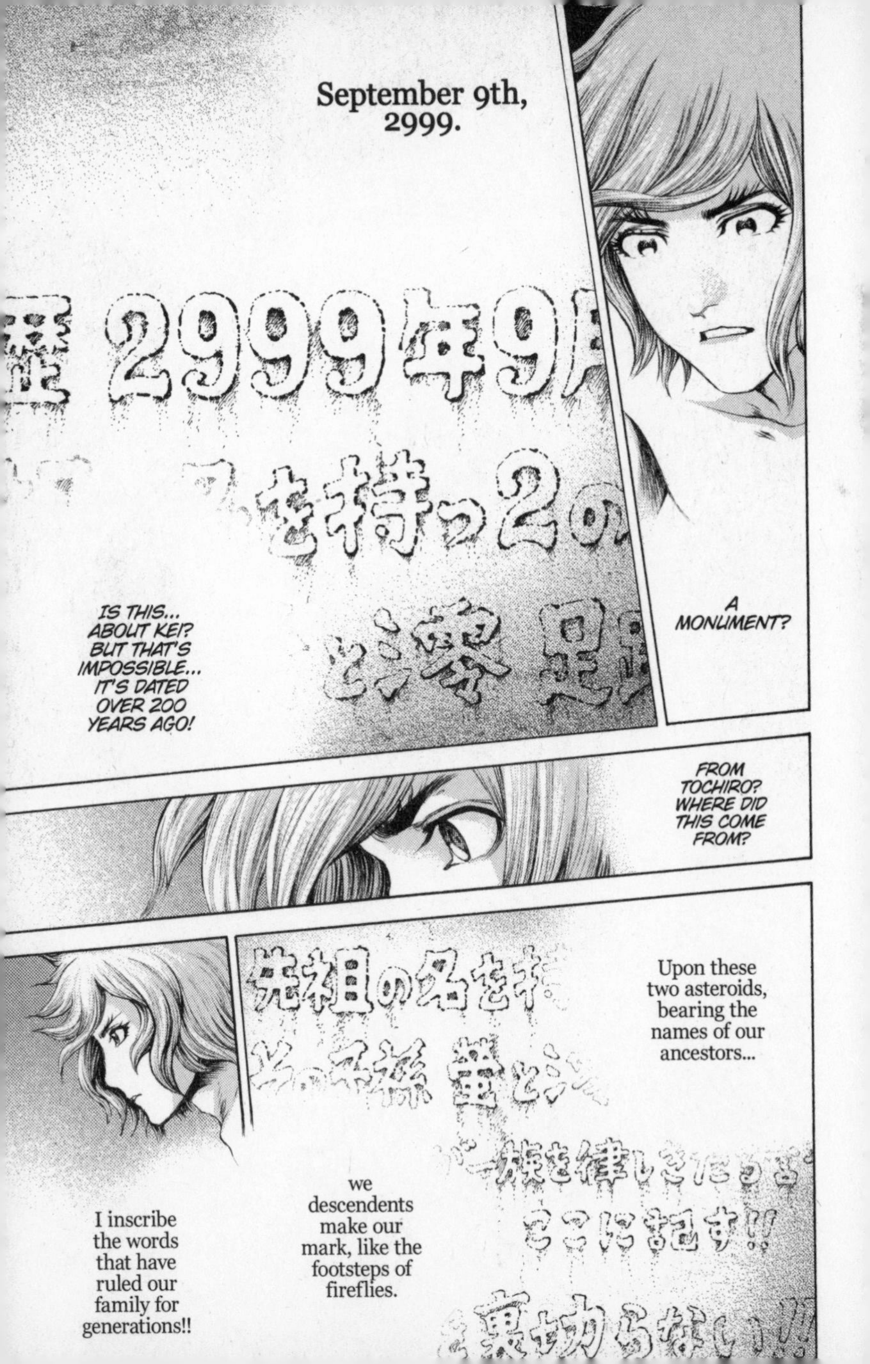
A MONUMENT?
September 9th, 2999.
IS THIS... ABOUT KEI? BUT THAT'S IMPOSSIBLE... IT'S DATED OVER 200 YEARS AGO!
FROM TOCHIRO? WHERE DID THIS COME FROM?
Upon these two asteroids, bearing the names of our ancestors...
we descendents make our mark, like the footsteps of fireflies.
I inscribe the words that have ruled our family for generations!!

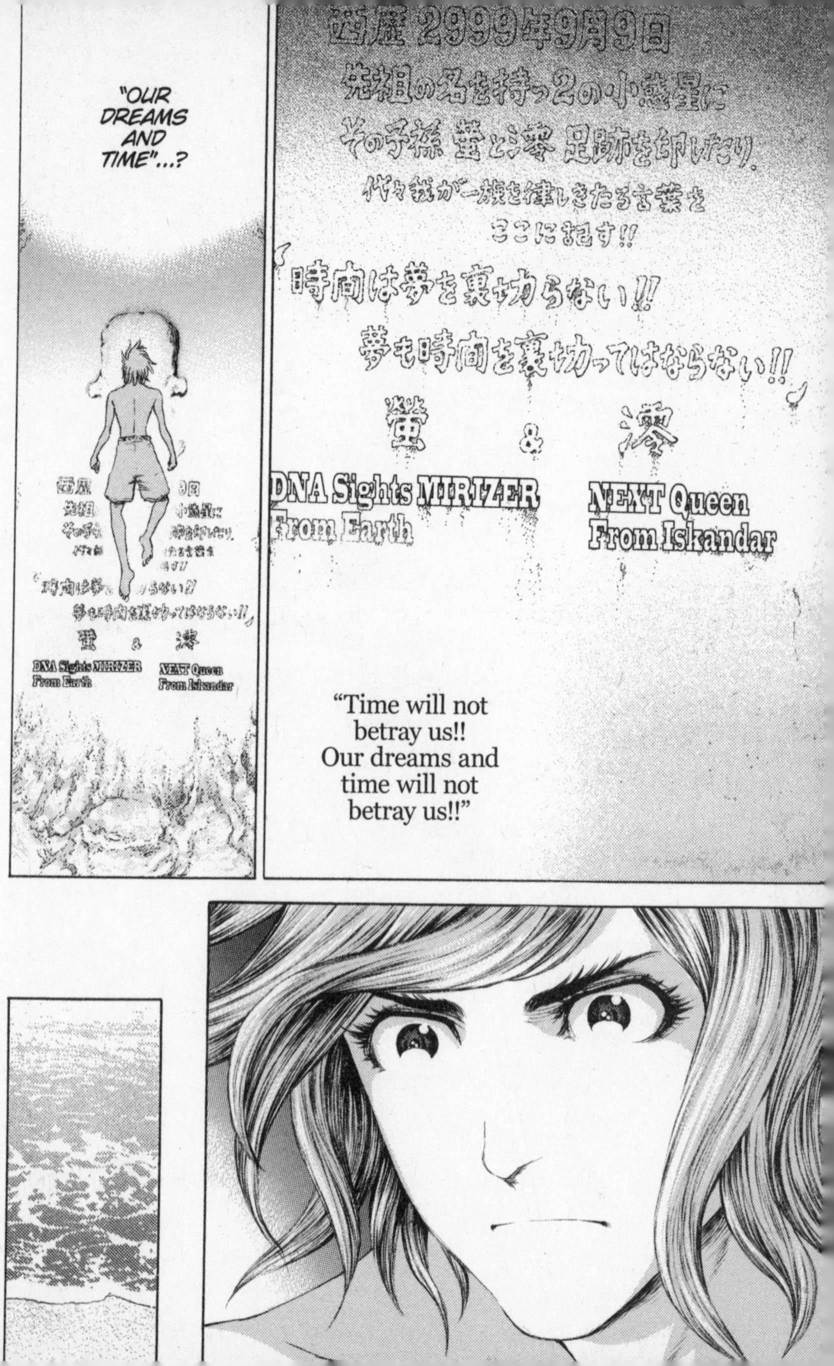

西暦2999年9月9日
先祖の名を持つ2の小惑星に
その子孫 蛍と澪 足跡を印したり。
代々我が一族を律しきたる言葉を
ここに記す!!
「時間は夢を裏切らない!!
夢も時間を裏切ってはならない!!」
蛍 & 澪
DNA Sights MIRIZER From Earth
NEXT Queen From Iskandar
"Time will not betray us!! Our dreams and time will not betray us!!"
"OUR DREAMS AND TIME"...?
DNA Sights MIRIZER From Earth
NEXT Queen From Iskandar

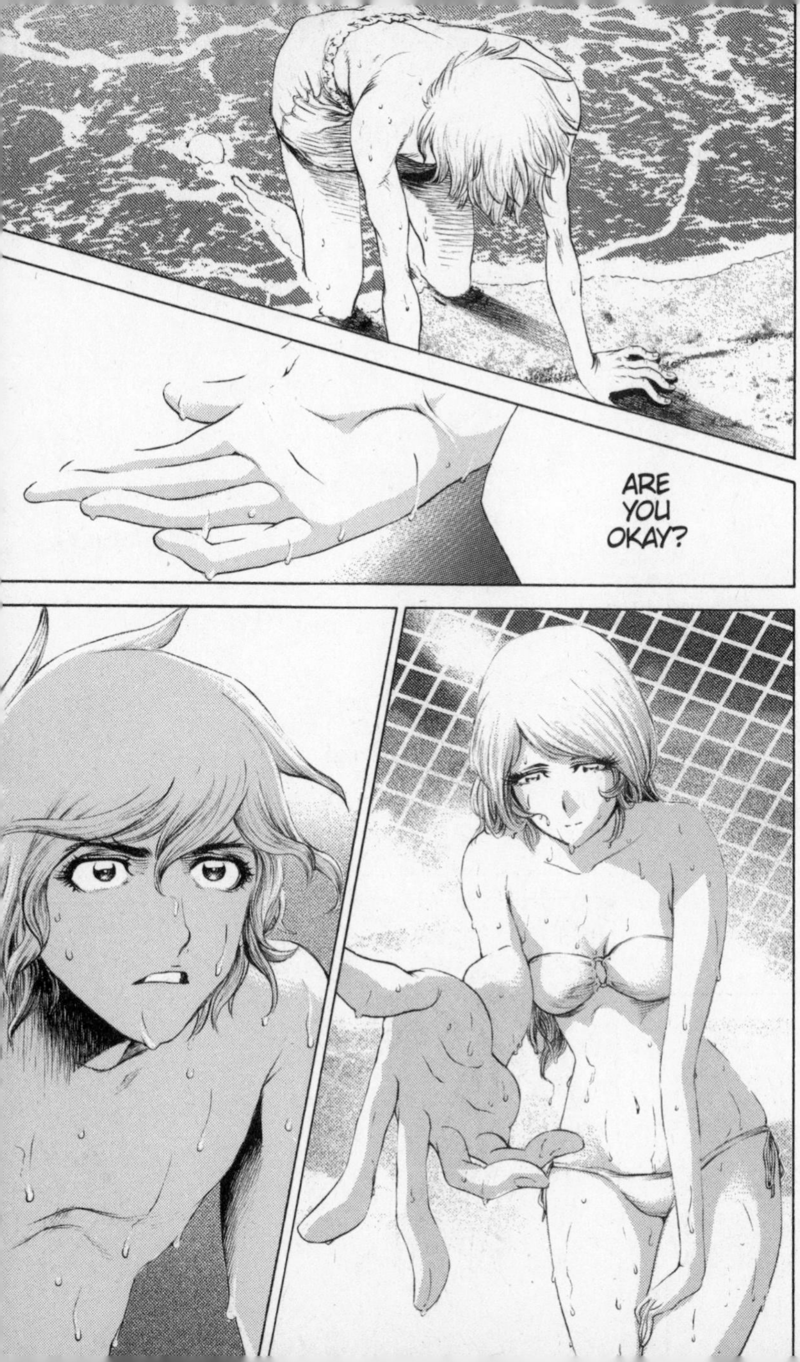
ARE YOU OKAY?

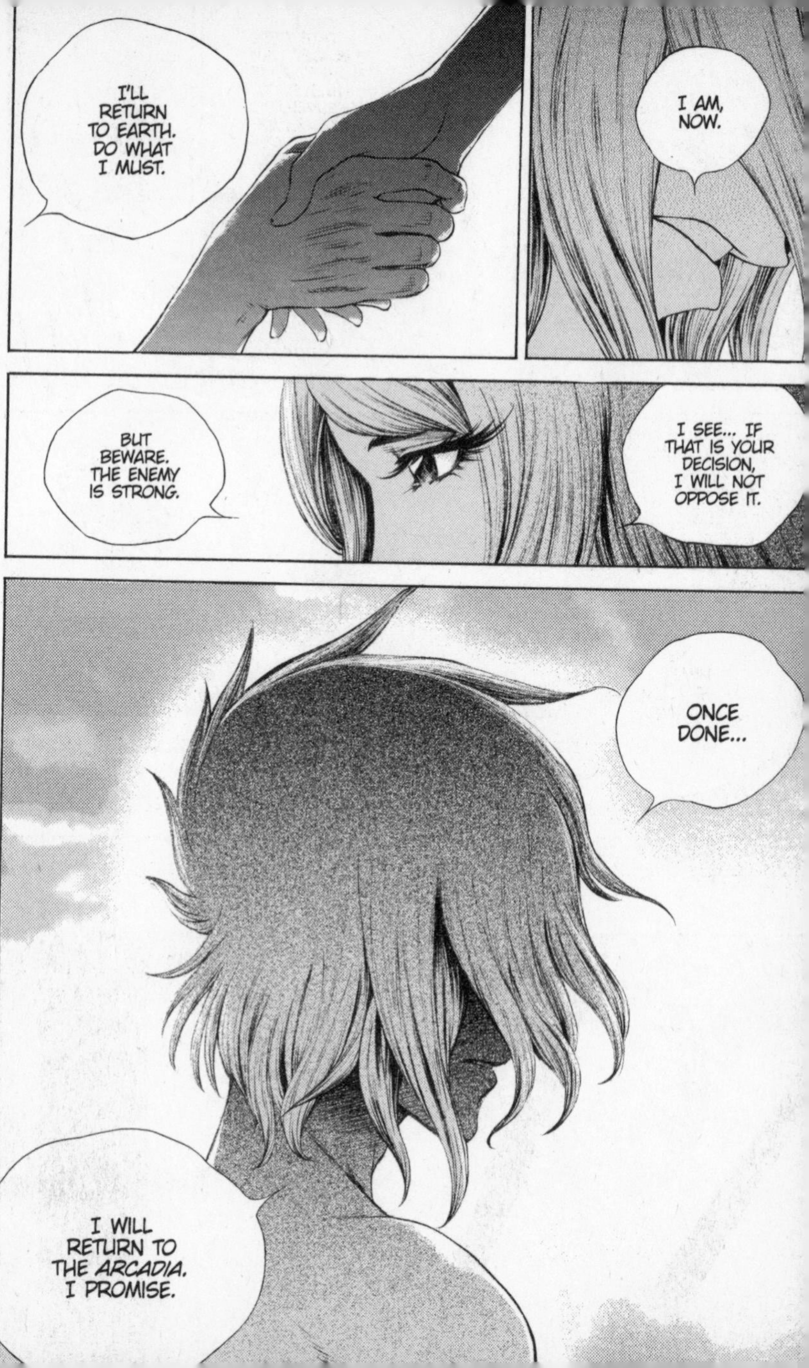
I AM, NOW.
I'LL RETURN TO EARTH. DO WHAT I MUST.
I SEE... IF THAT IS YOUR DECISION, I WILL NOT OPPOSE IT.
BUT BEWARE. THE ENEMY IS STRONG.
ONCE DONE...
I WILL RETURN TO THE *ARCADIA*. I PROMISE.

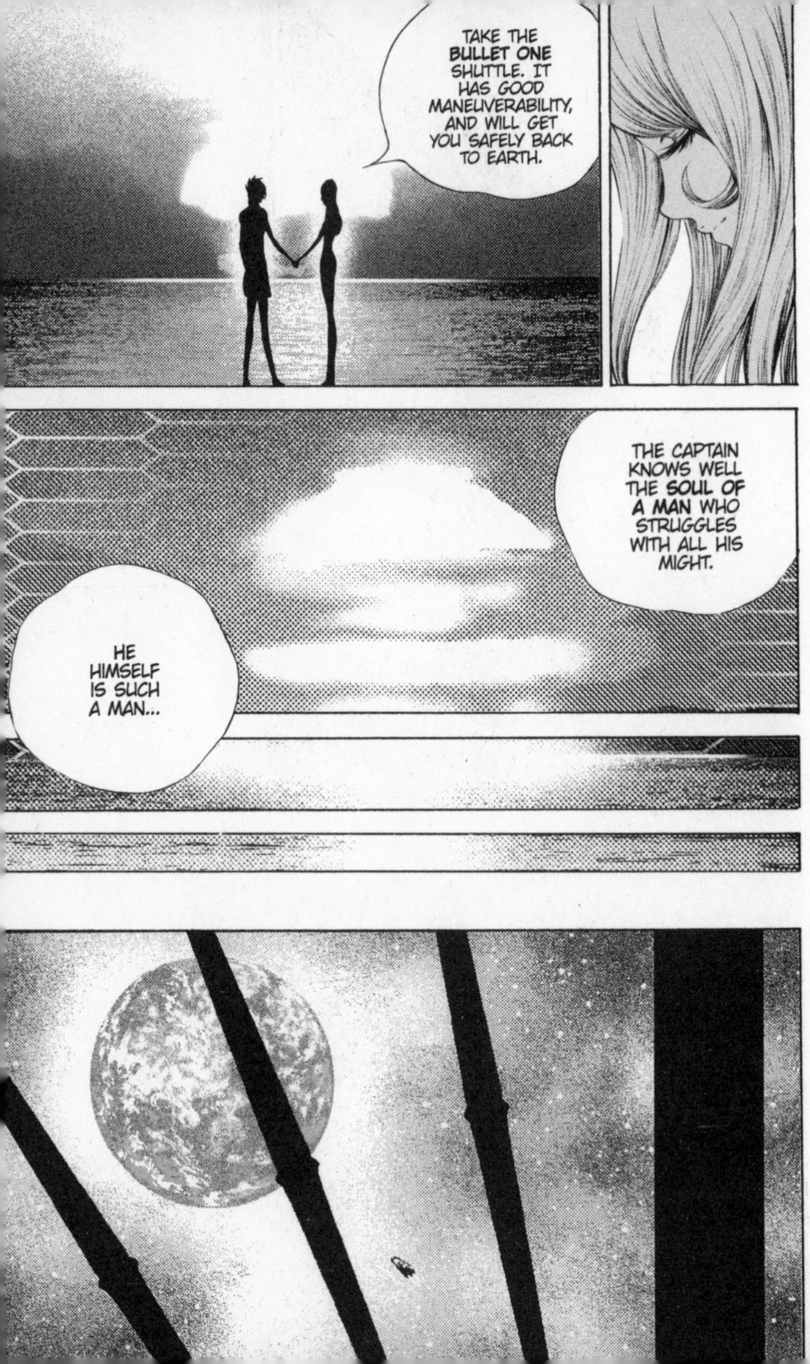
TAKE THE **BULLET ONE** SHUTTLE. IT HAS GOOD MANEUVERABILITY, AND WILL GET YOU SAFELY BACK TO EARTH.
THE CAPTAIN KNOWS WELL THE **SOUL OF A MAN** WHO STRUGGLES WITH ALL HIS MIGHT.
HE HIMSELF IS SUCH A MAN...

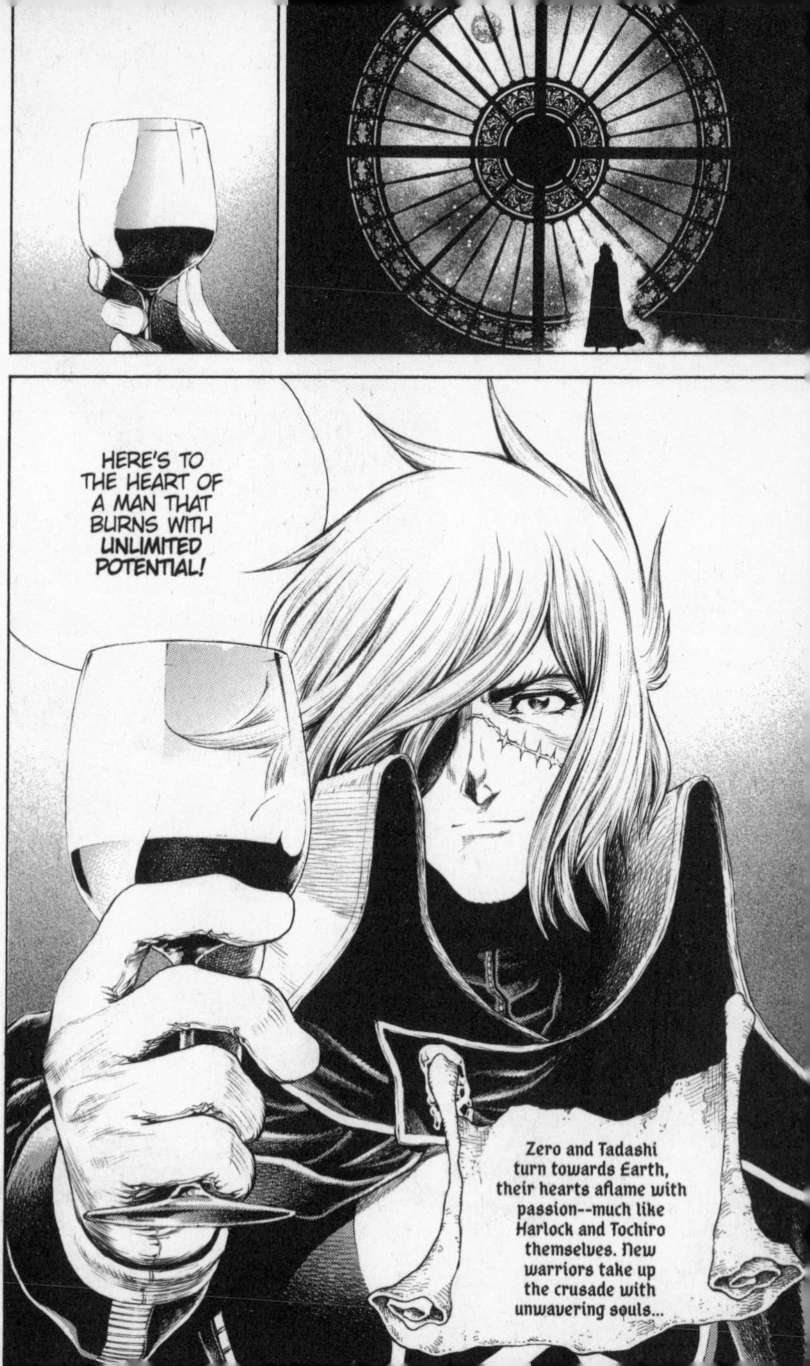
HERE'S TO THE HEART OF A MAN THAT BURNS WITH UNLIMITED POTENTIAL!
Zero and Tadashi turn towards Earth, their hearts aflame with passion--much like Harlock and Tochiro themselves. New warriors take up the crusade with unwavering souls...

CHAPTER 14 DECLARATION OF WAR

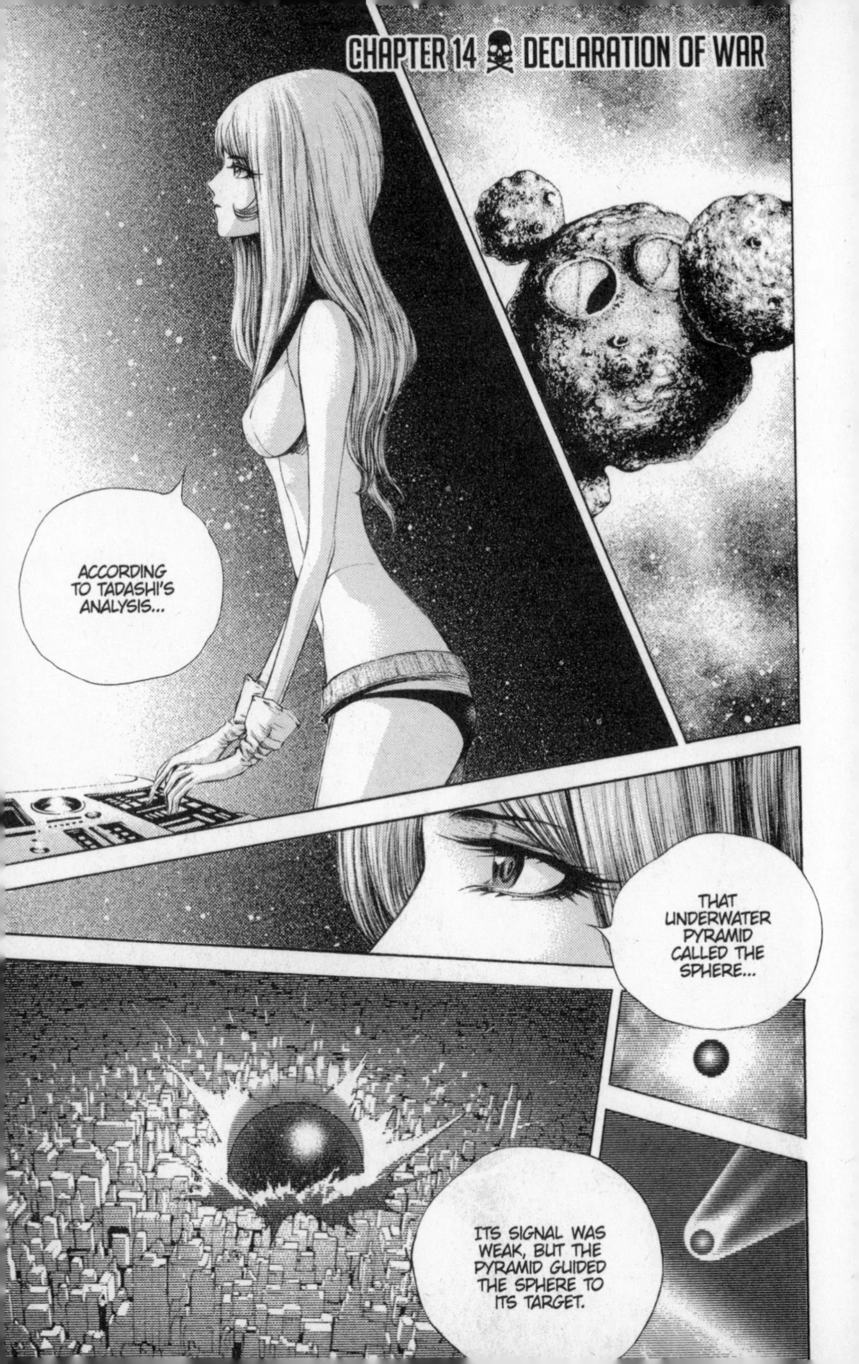
ACCORDING TO TADASHI'S ANALYSIS...
THAT UNDERWATER PYRAMID CALLED THE SPHERE...
ITS SIGNAL WAS WEAK, BUT THE PYRAMID GUIDED THE SPHERE TO ITS TARGET.

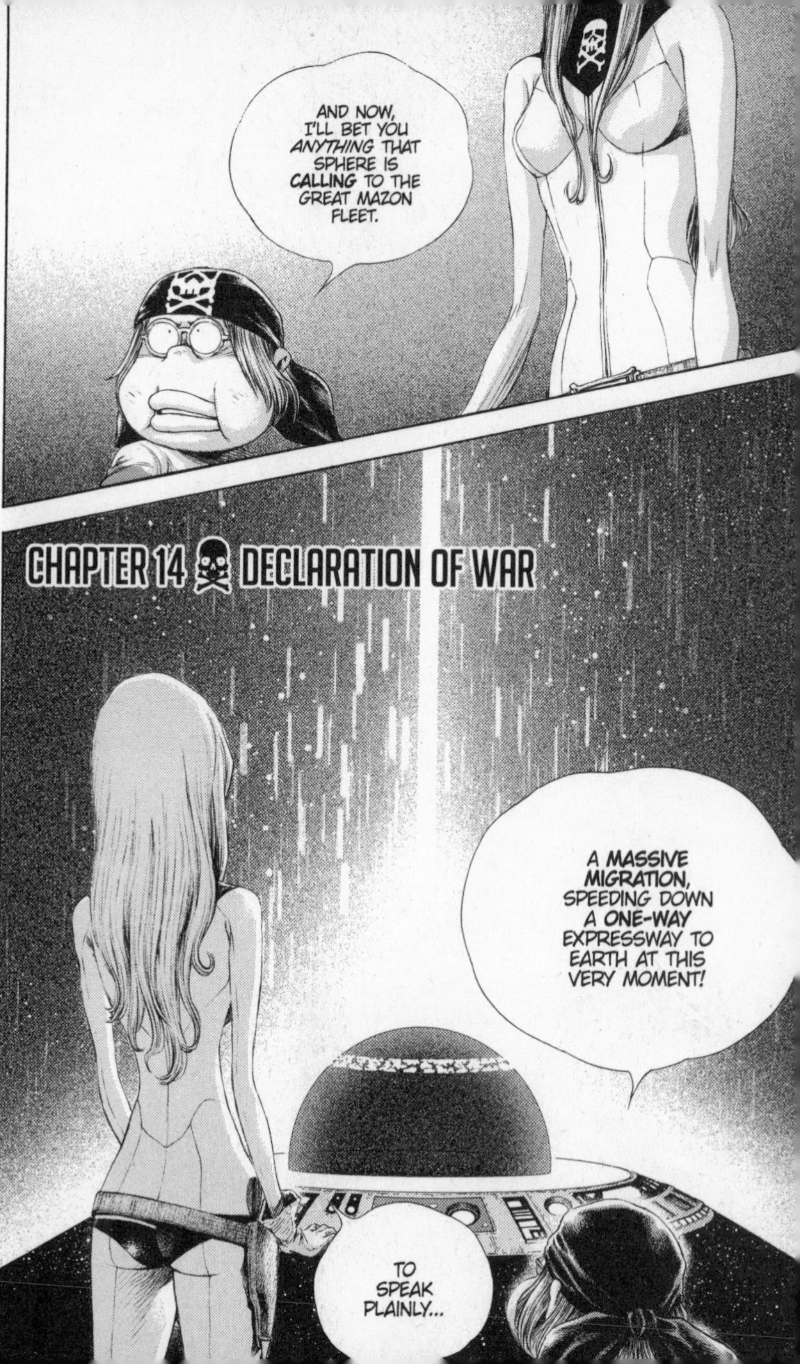
AND NOW, I'LL BET YOU *ANYTHING* THAT SPHERE IS **CALLING** TO THE GREAT MAZON FLEET.
CHAPTER 14 DECLARATION OF WAR
A MASSIVE MIGRATION, SPEEDING DOWN A ONE-WAY EXPRESSWAY TO EARTH AT THIS VERY MOMENT!
TO SPEAK PLAINLY...

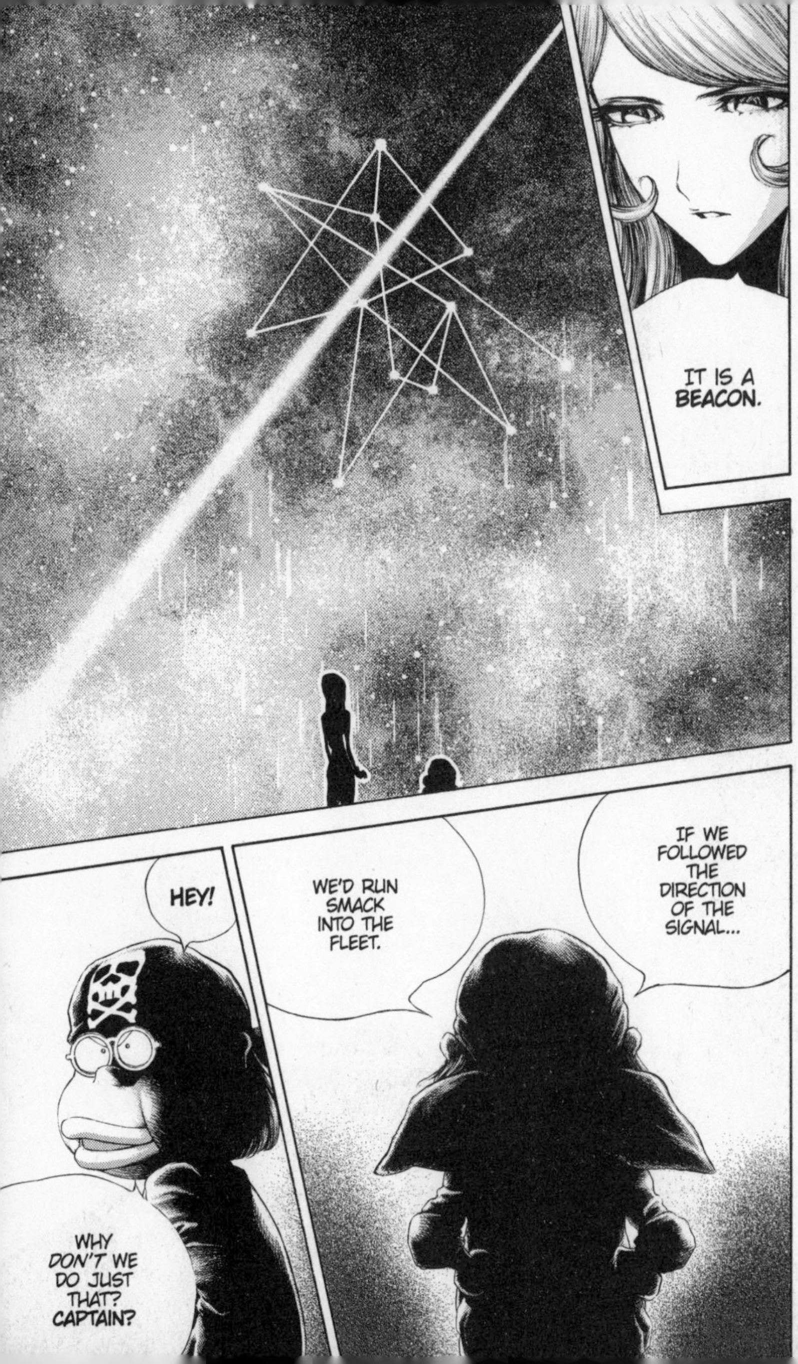
IT IS A BEACON.
IF WE FOLLOWED THE DIRECTION OF THE SIGNAL...
WE'D RUN SMACK INTO THE FLEET.
HEY!
WHY DON'T WE DO JUST THAT? CAPTAIN?

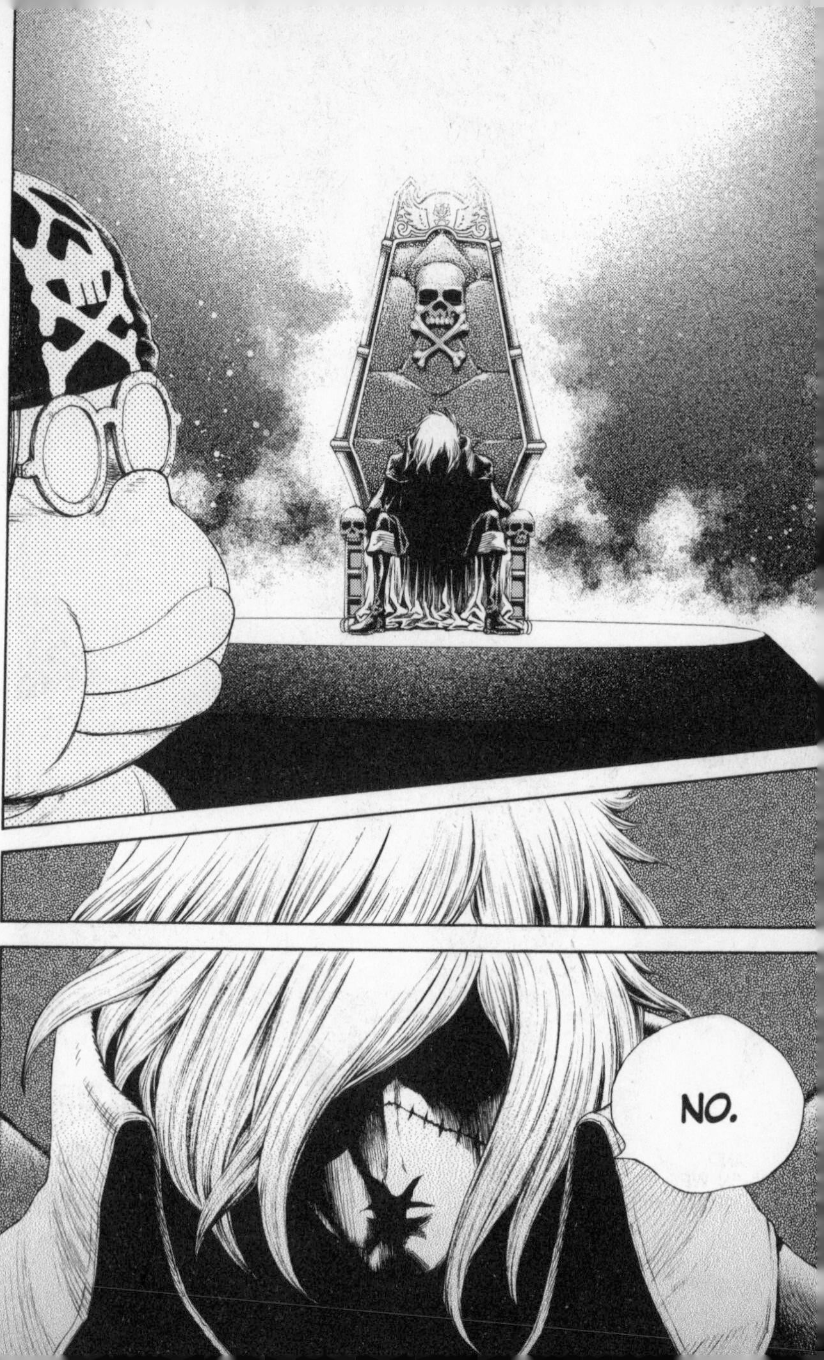
NO.

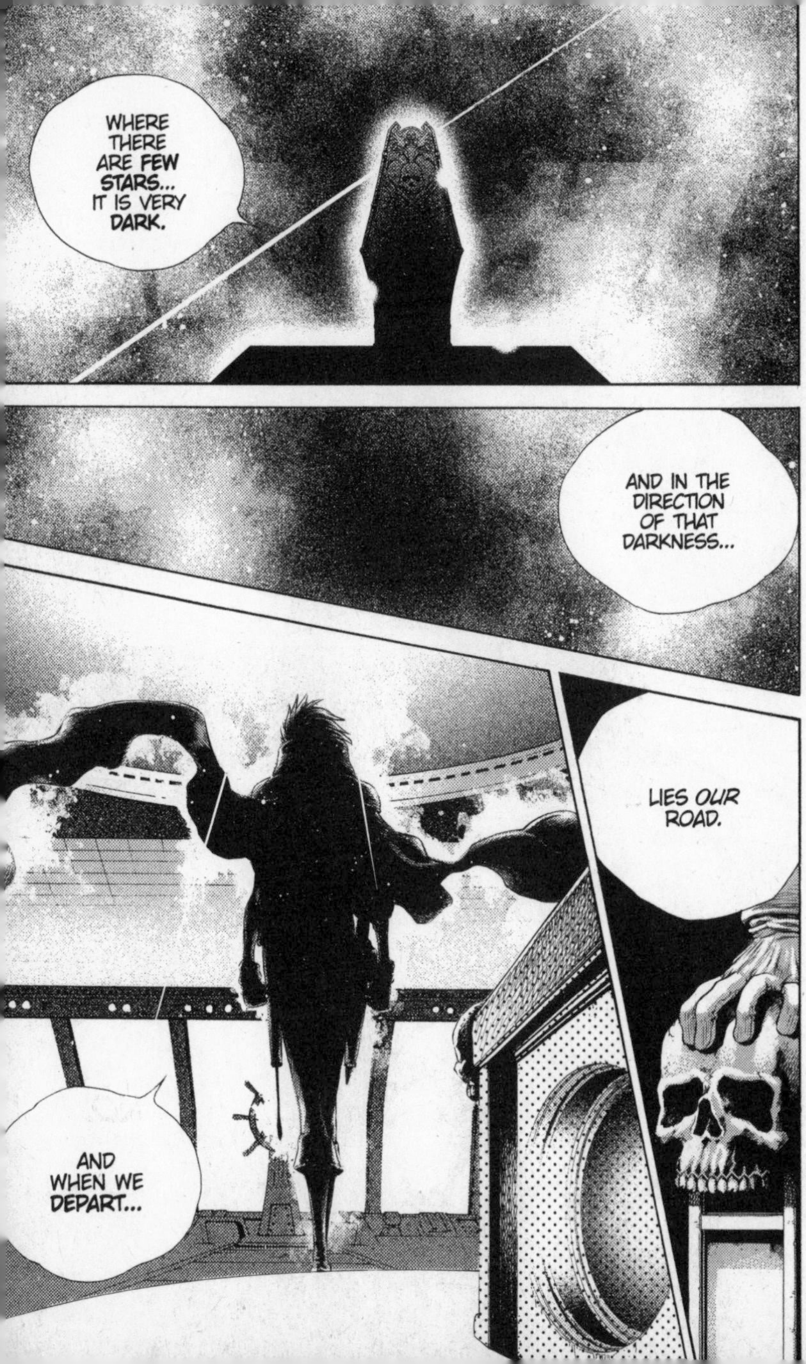
WHERE THERE ARE FEW STARS... IT IS VERY DARK.
AND IN THE DIRECTION OF THAT DARKNESS...
LIES OUR ROAD.
AND WHEN WE DEPART...

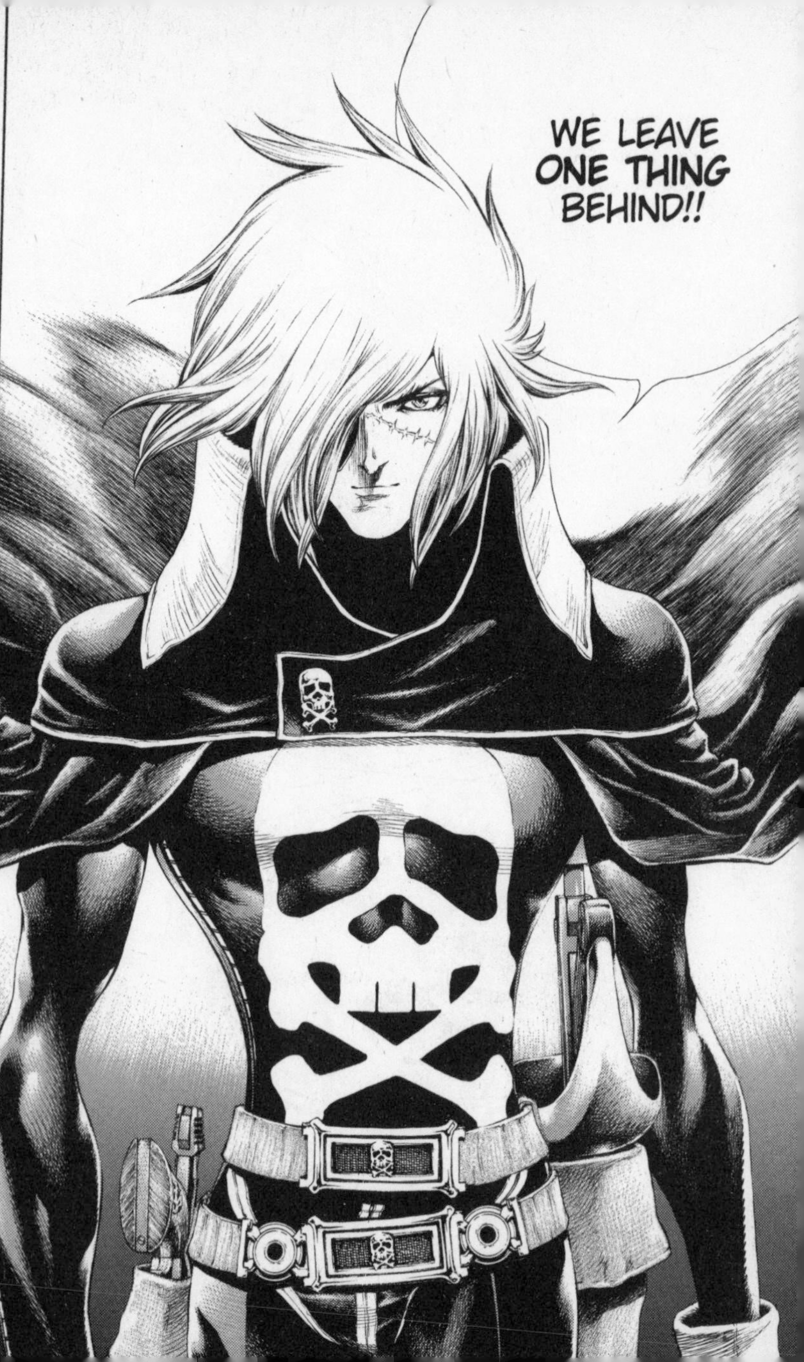
WE LEAVE ONE THING BEHIND!!

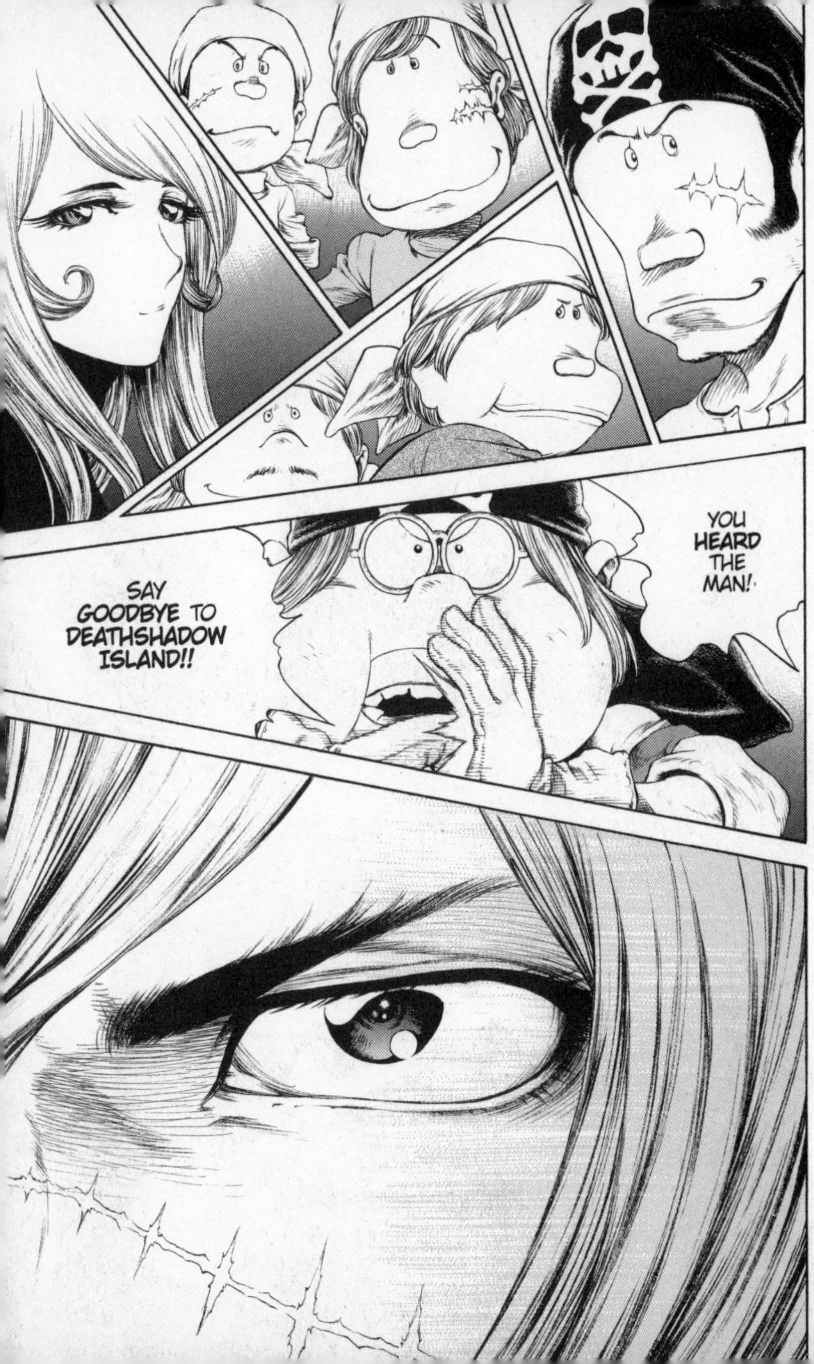
YOU HEARD THE MAN!
SAY GOODBYE TO DEATHSHADOW ISLAND!!

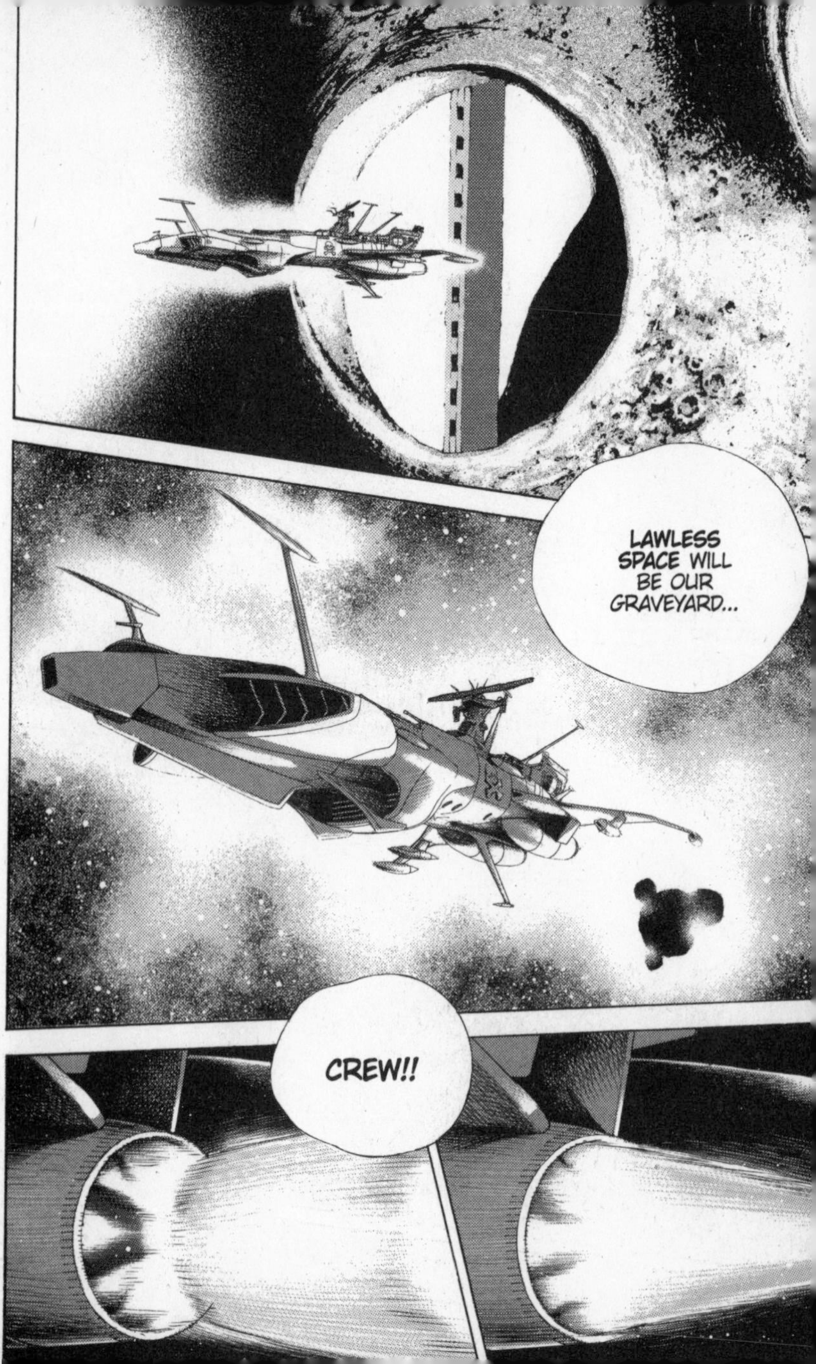
LAWLESS SPACE WILL BE OUR GRAVEYARD...
CREW!!

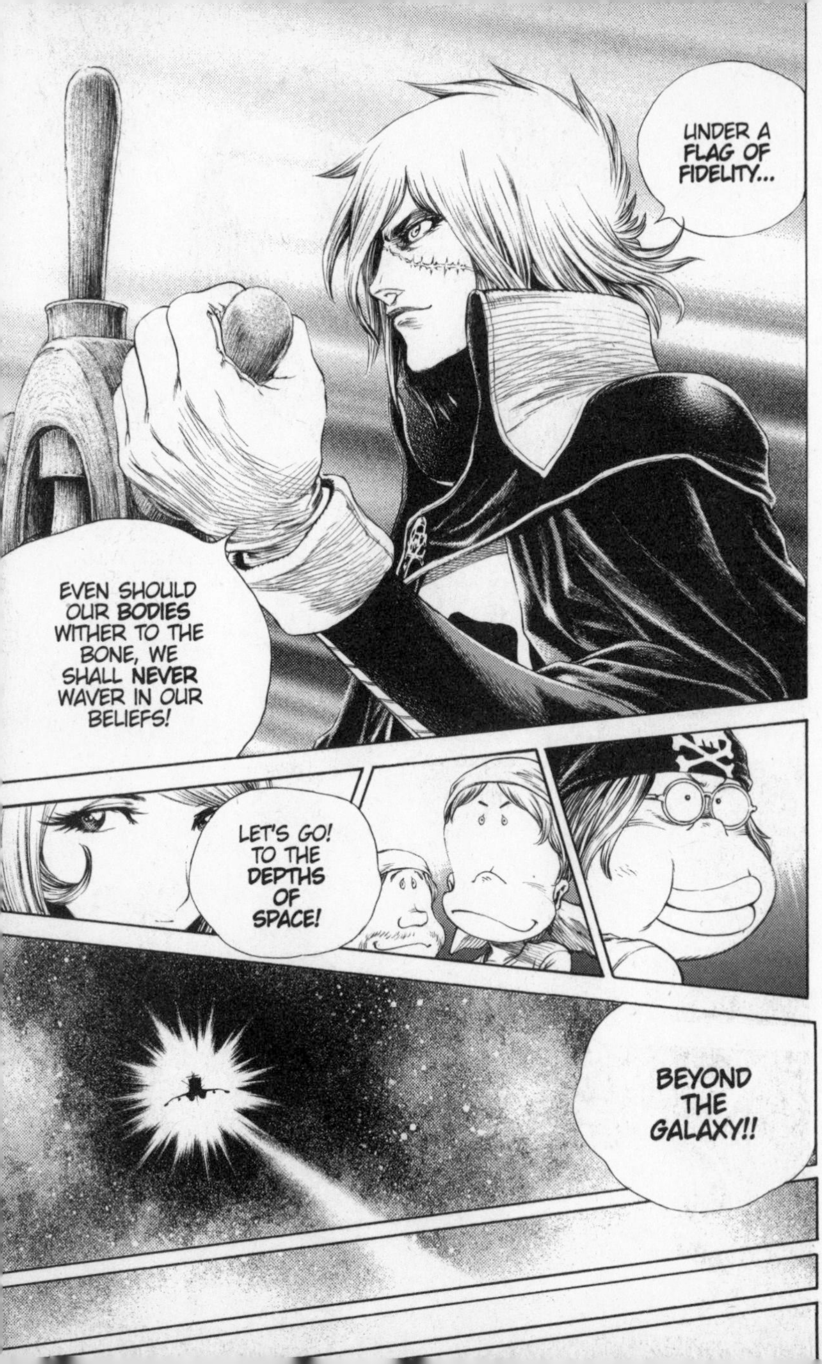
UNDER A FLAG OF FIDELITY...
EVEN SHOULD OUR BODIES WITHER TO THE BONE, WE SHALL NEVER WAVER IN OUR BELIEFS!
LET'S GO! TO THE DEPTHS OF SPACE!
BEYOND THE GALAXY!!

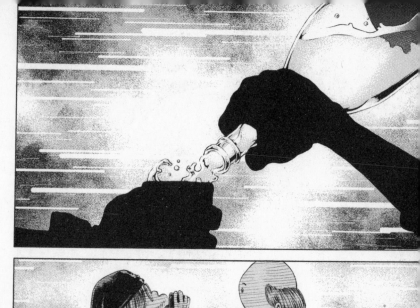

A LITTLE
LONELY
WITH
TADASHI
GONE,
EH?

I AIN'T
WORRIED...

WE'LL
BE BACK
SOON
ENOUGH.

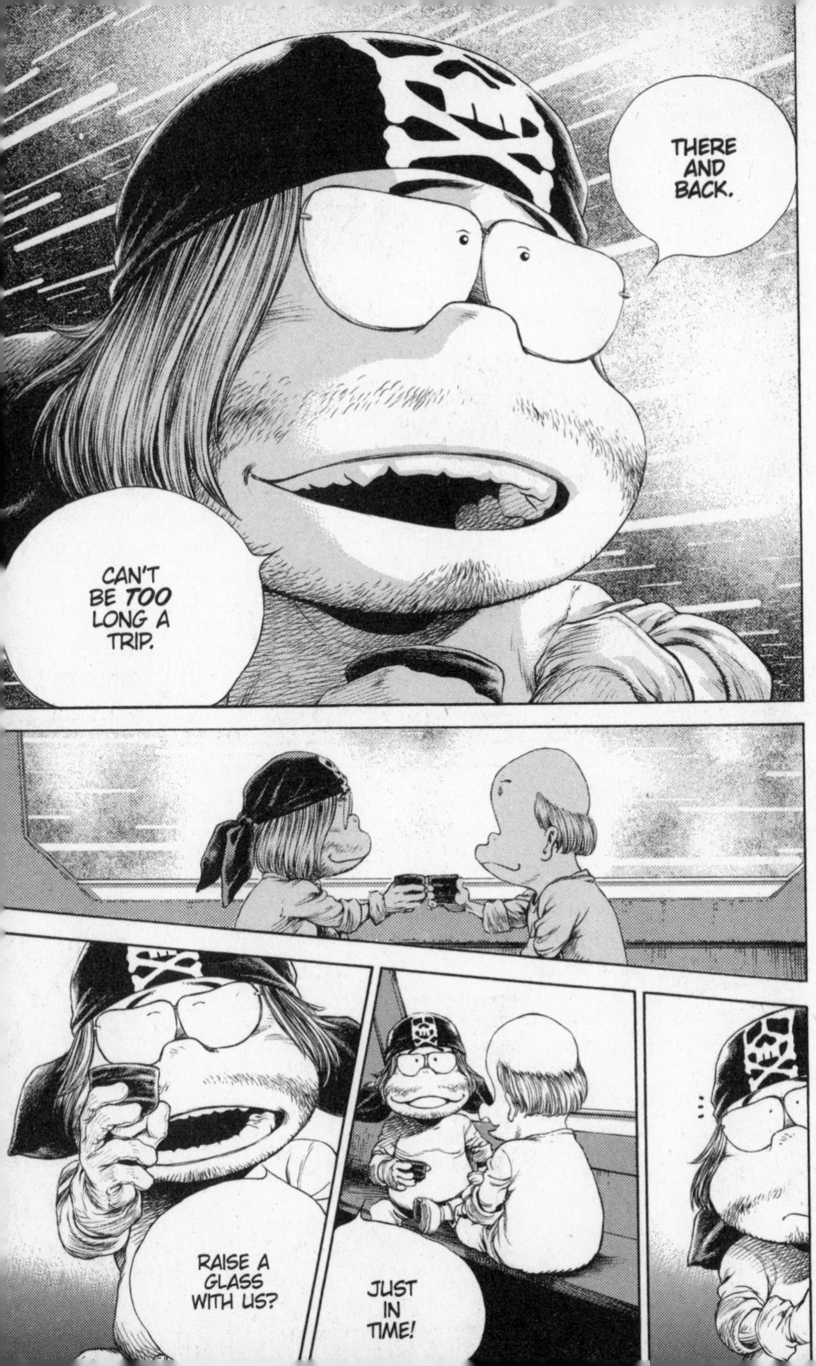
THERE AND BACK.
CAN'T BE *TOO* LONG A TRIP.
...
JUST IN TIME!
RAISE A GLASS WITH US?

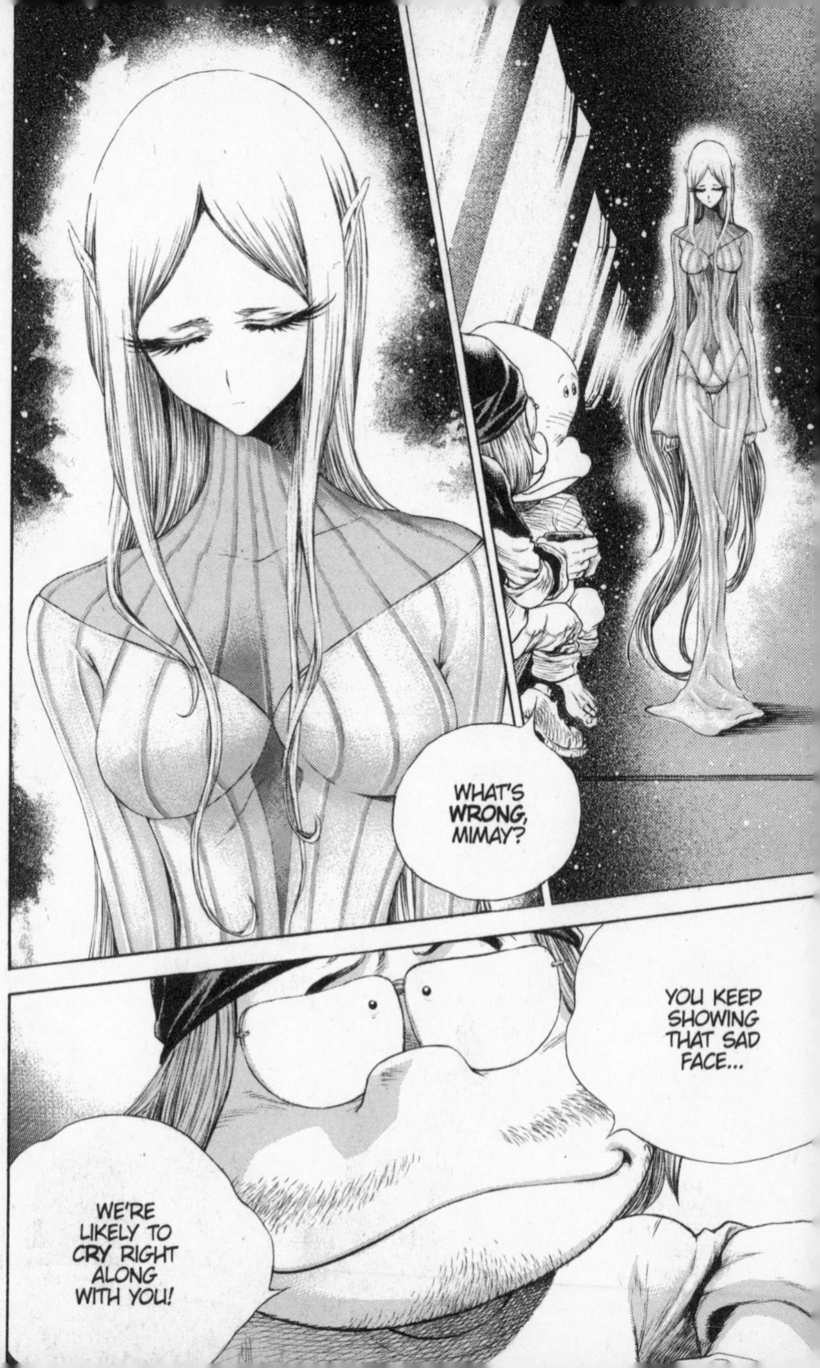
WHAT'S WRONG, MIMAY?
YOU KEEP SHOWING THAT SAD FACE...
WE'RE LIKELY TO CRY RIGHT ALONG WITH YOU!

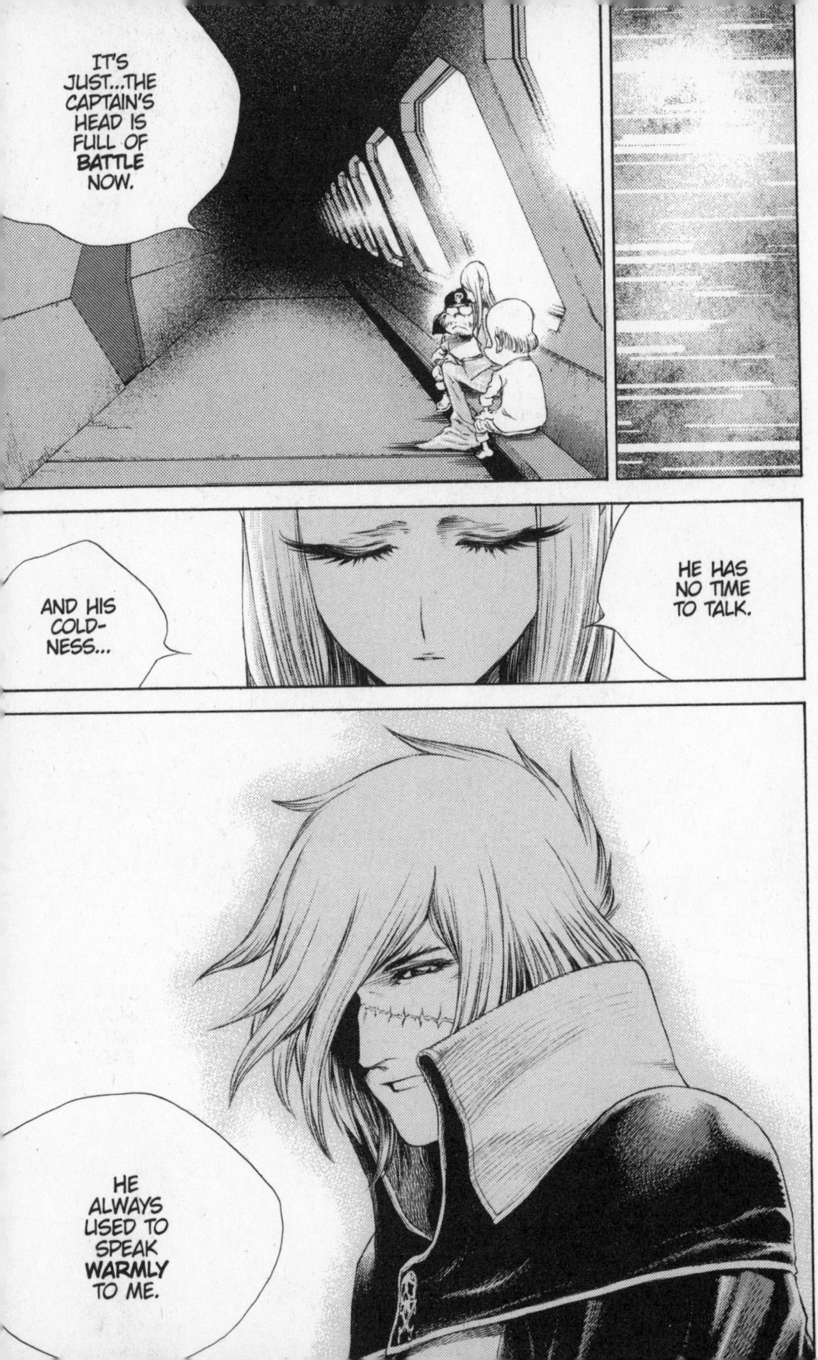
IT'S JUST...THE CAPTAIN'S HEAD IS FULL OF BATTLE NOW.
HE HAS NO TIME TO TALK.
AND HIS COLD-NESS...
HE ALWAYS USED TO SPEAK WARMLY TO ME.

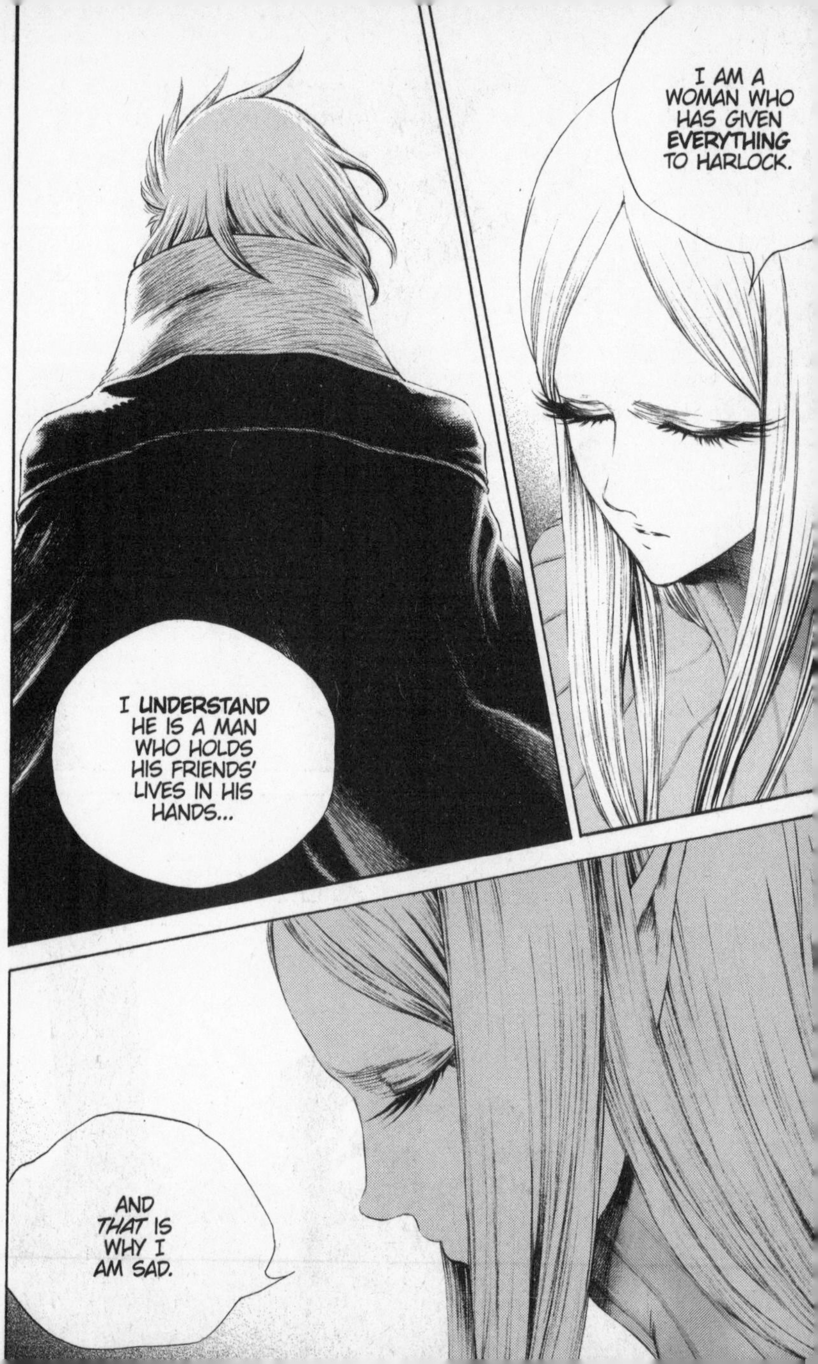
I AM A WOMAN WHO HAS GIVEN EVERYTHING TO HARLOCK.
I UNDERSTAND HE IS A MAN WHO HOLDS HIS FRIENDS' LIVES IN HIS HANDS...
AND *THAT* IS WHY I AM SAD.

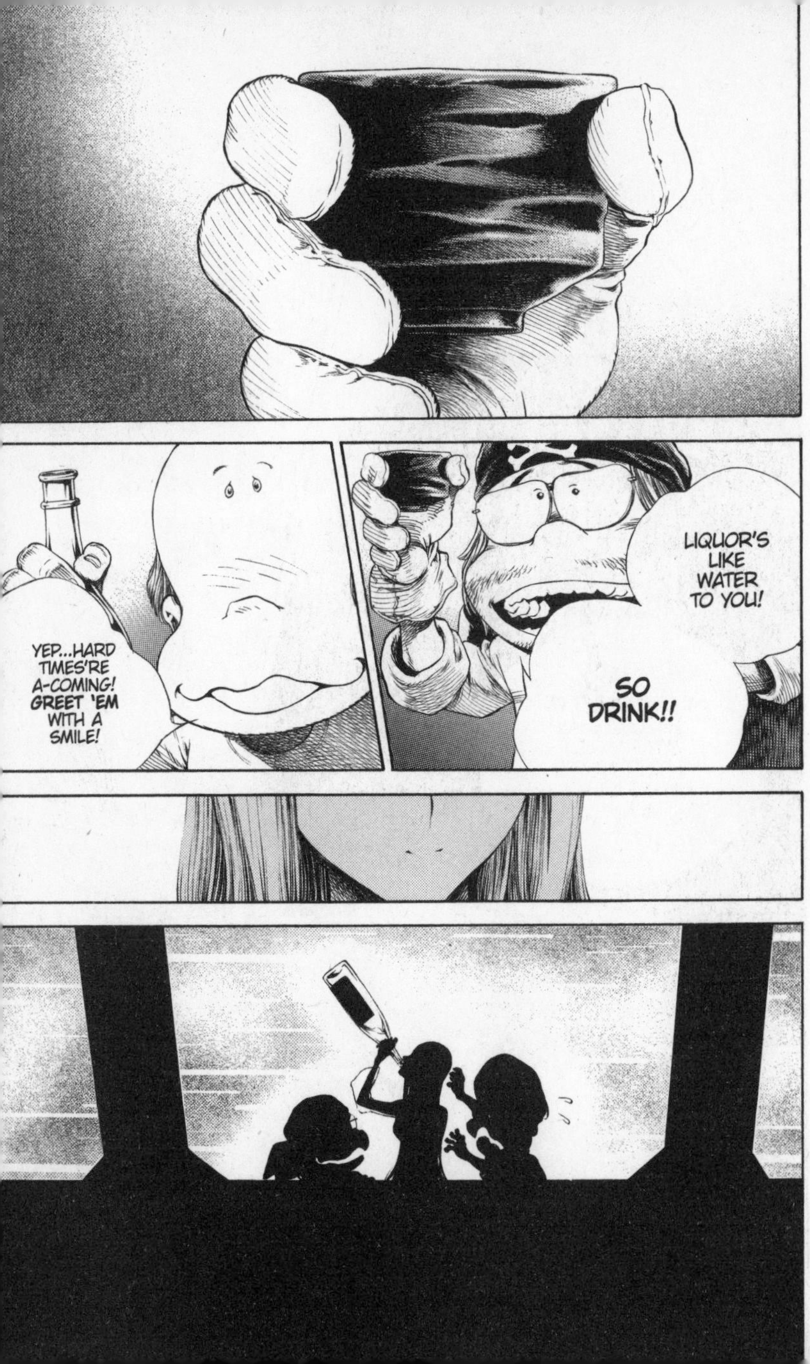
LIQUOR'S LIKE WATER TO YOU!
SO DRINK!!
YEP...HARD TIMES'RE A-COMING! GREET 'EM WITH A SMILE!

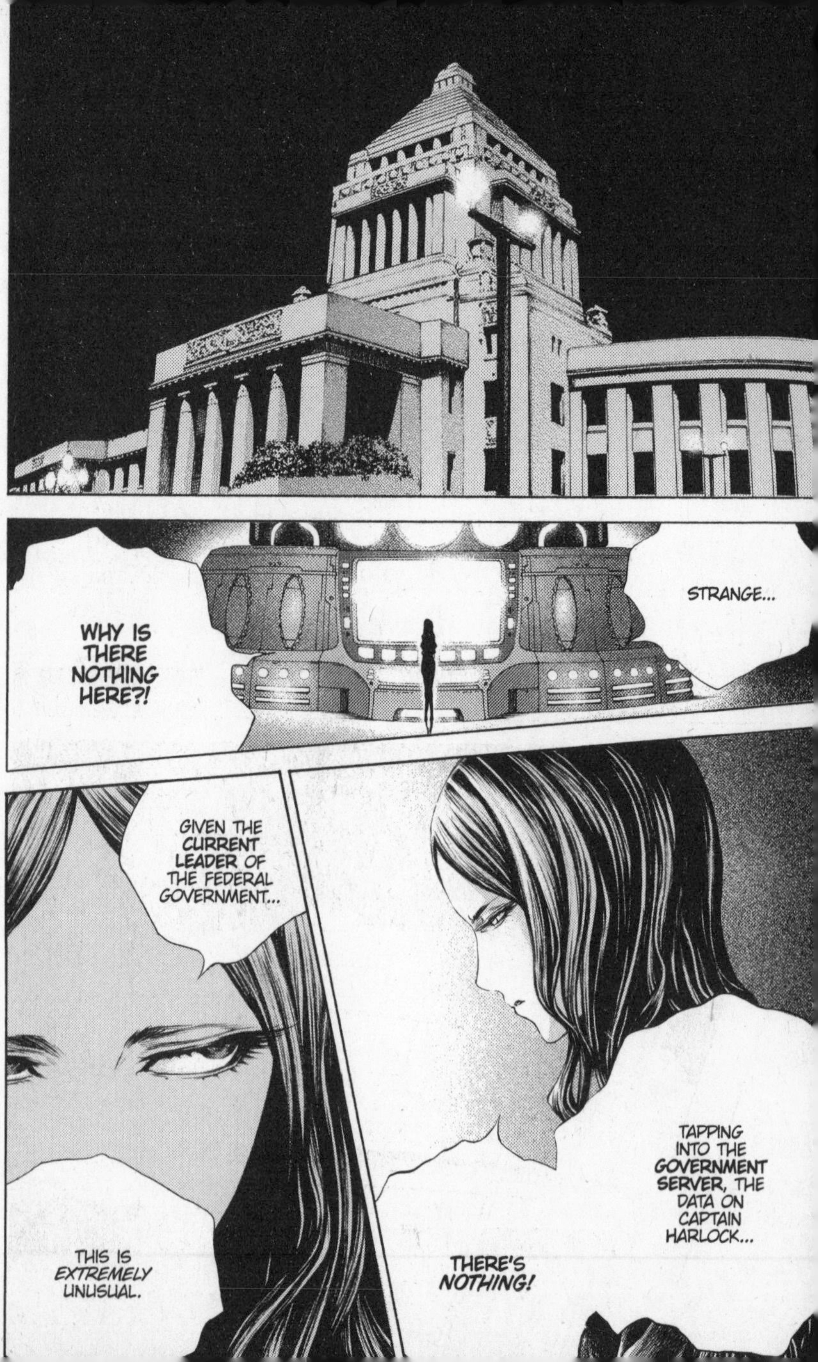
STRANGE...
WHY IS THERE NOTHING HERE?!
TAPPING INTO THE GOVERNMENT SERVER, THE DATA ON CAPTAIN HARLOCK...
THERE'S NOTHING!
GIVEN THE CURRENT LEADER OF THE FEDERAL GOVERNMENT...
THIS IS EXTREMELY UNUSUAL.

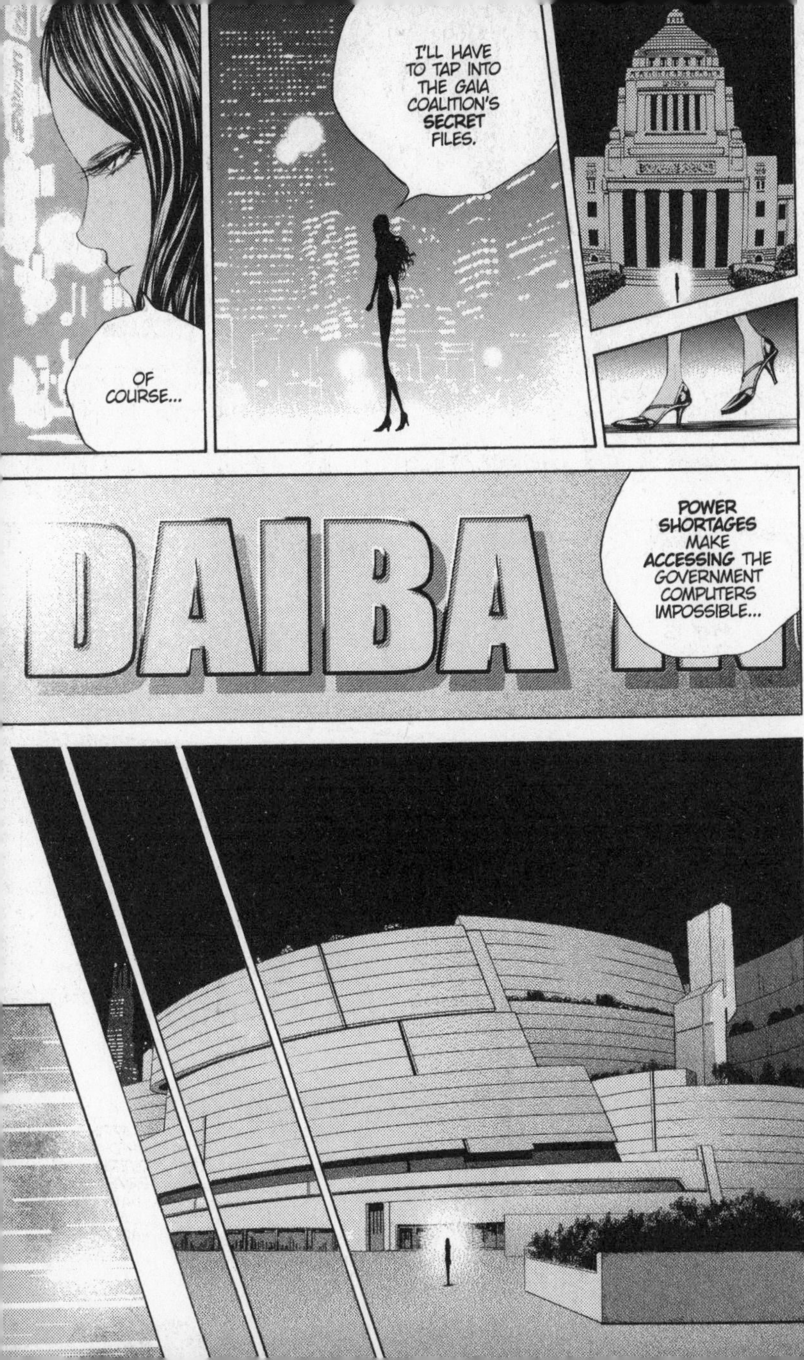
I'LL HAVE TO TAP INTO THE GAIA COALITION'S SECRET FILES.
OF COURSE...
POWER SHORTAGES MAKE ACCESSING THE GOVERNMENT COMPUTERS IMPOSSIBLE...
DAIBA

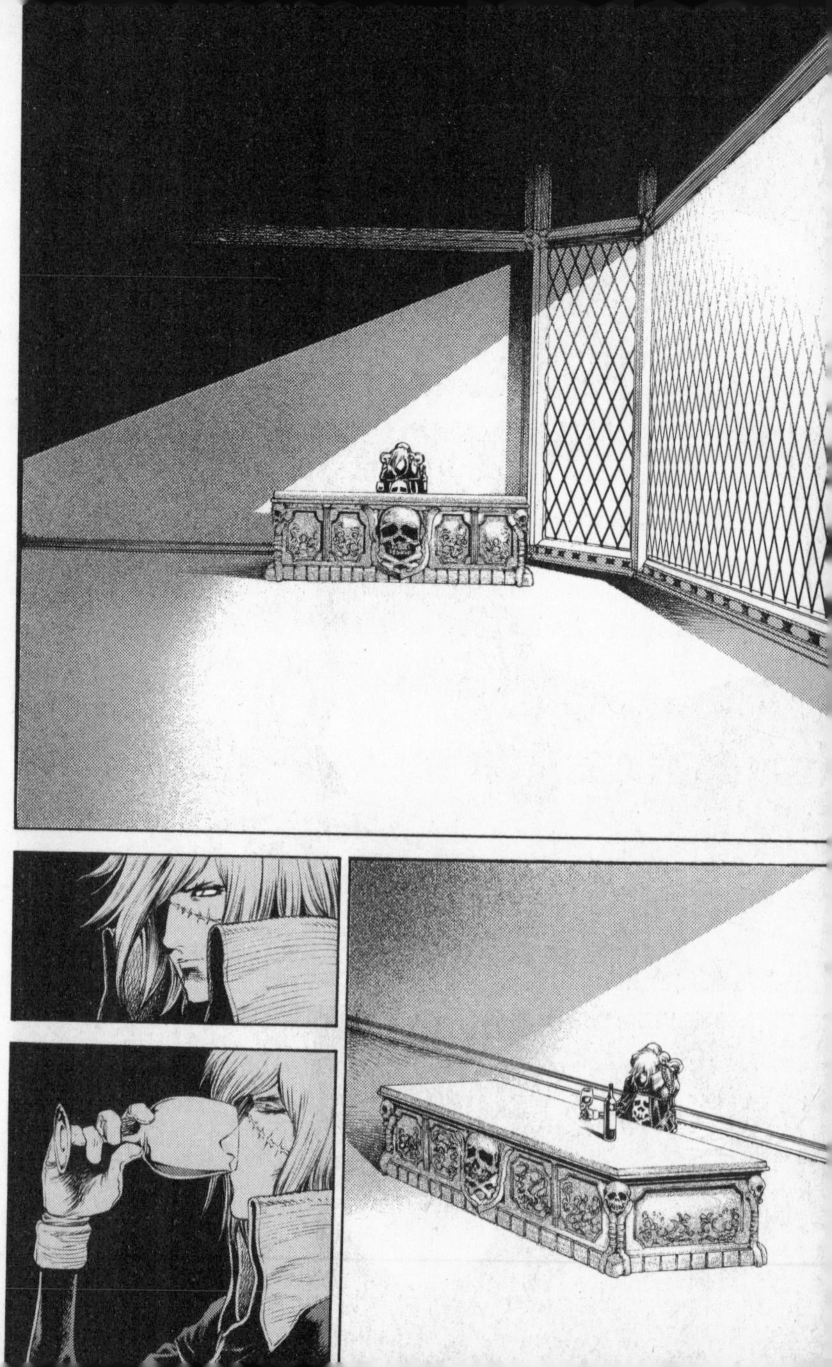

WELL
NOW.

I DIDN'T
COME
HERE TO
FIGHT.

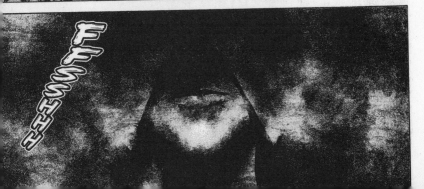

FFSSSHHH

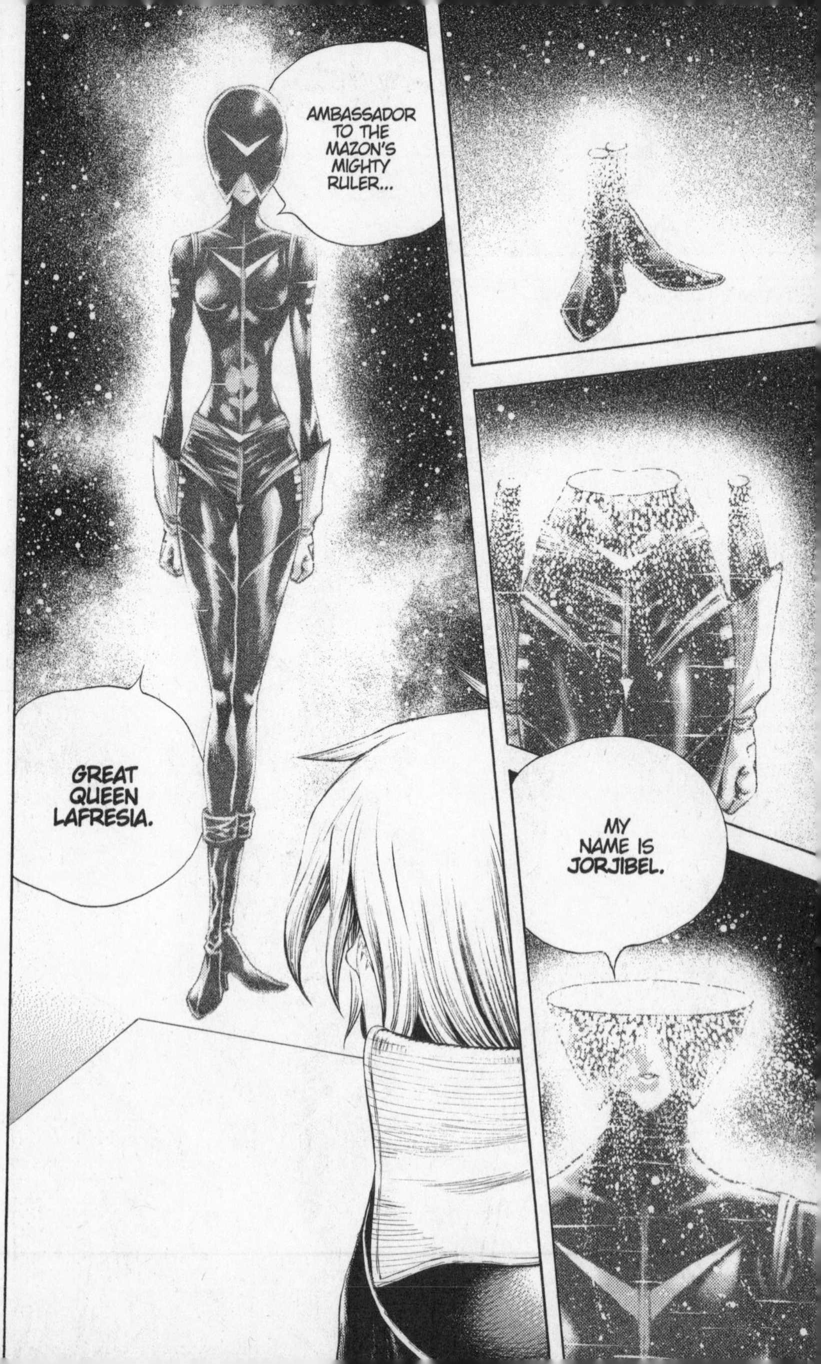
MY NAME IS JORJIBEL.
AMBASSADOR TO THE MAZON'S MIGHTY RULER...
GREAT QUEEN LAFRESIA.

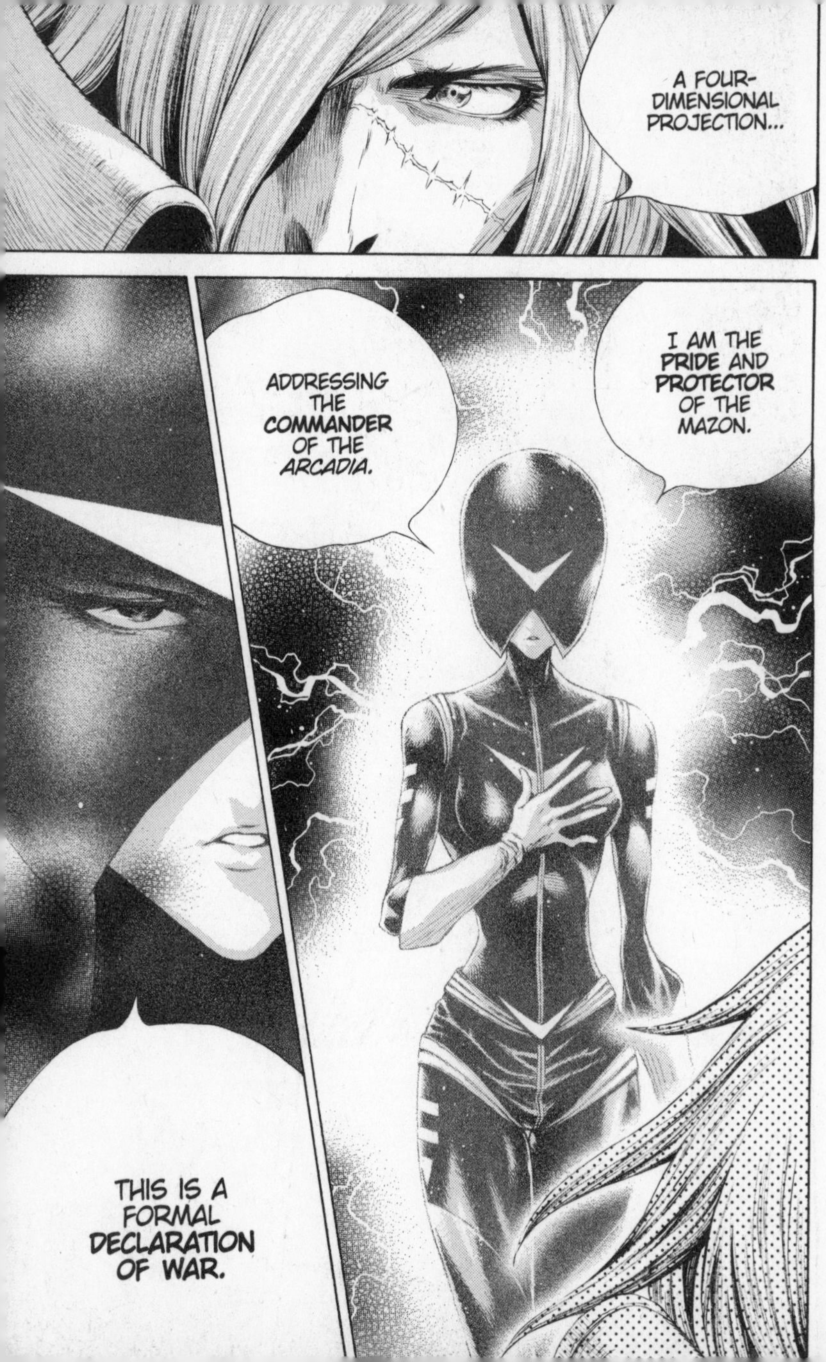
A FOUR-DIMENSIONAL PROJECTION...
I AM THE PRIDE AND PROTECTOR OF THE MAZON.
ADDRESSING THE COMMANDER OF THE ARCADIA.
THIS IS A FORMAL DECLARATION OF WAR.

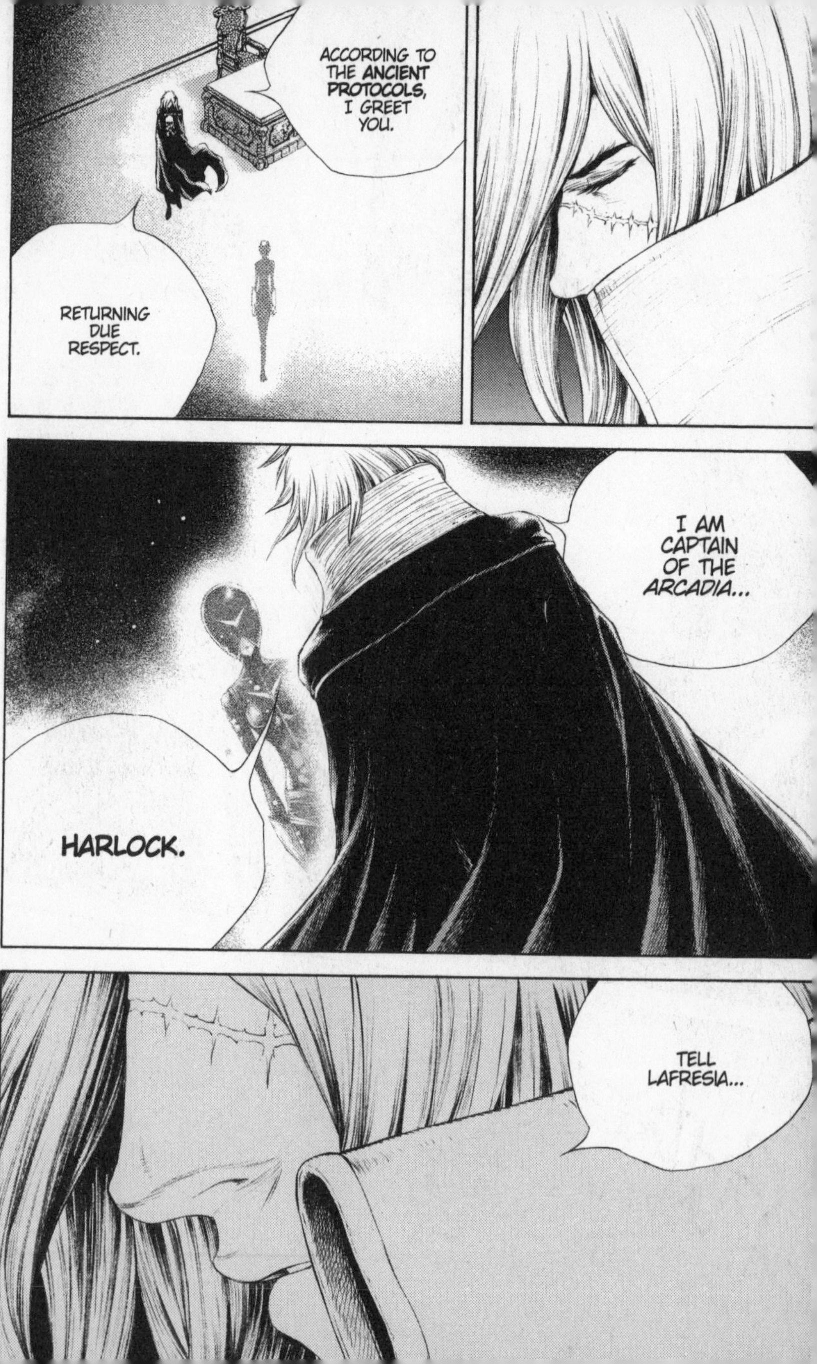
ACCORDING TO THE ANCIENT PROTOCOLS, I GREET YOU.
RETURNING DUE RESPECT.
I AM CAPTAIN OF THE ARCADIA...
HARLOCK.
TELL LAFRESIA...

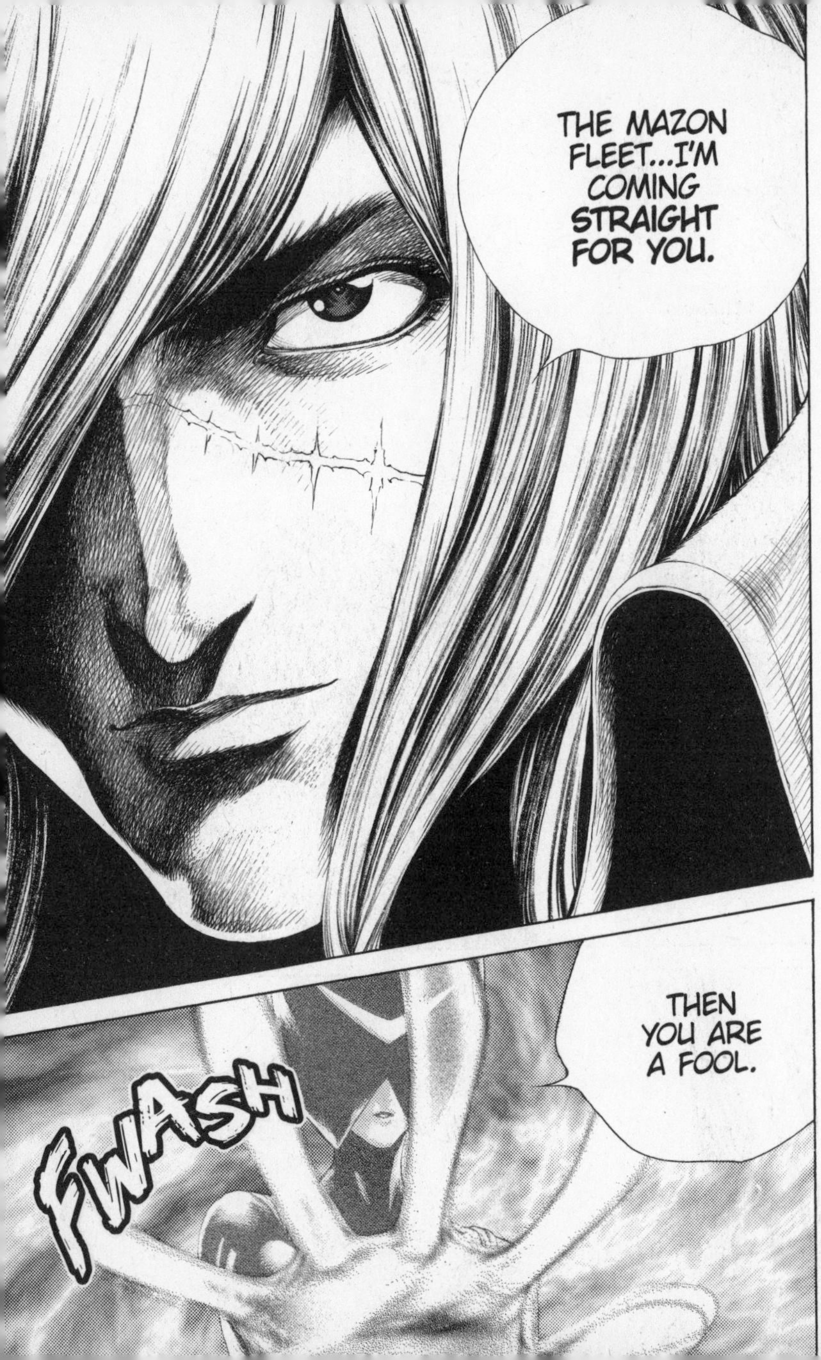
THE MAZON FLEET...I'M COMING STRAIGHT FOR YOU.
THEN YOU ARE A FOOL.
FWASH

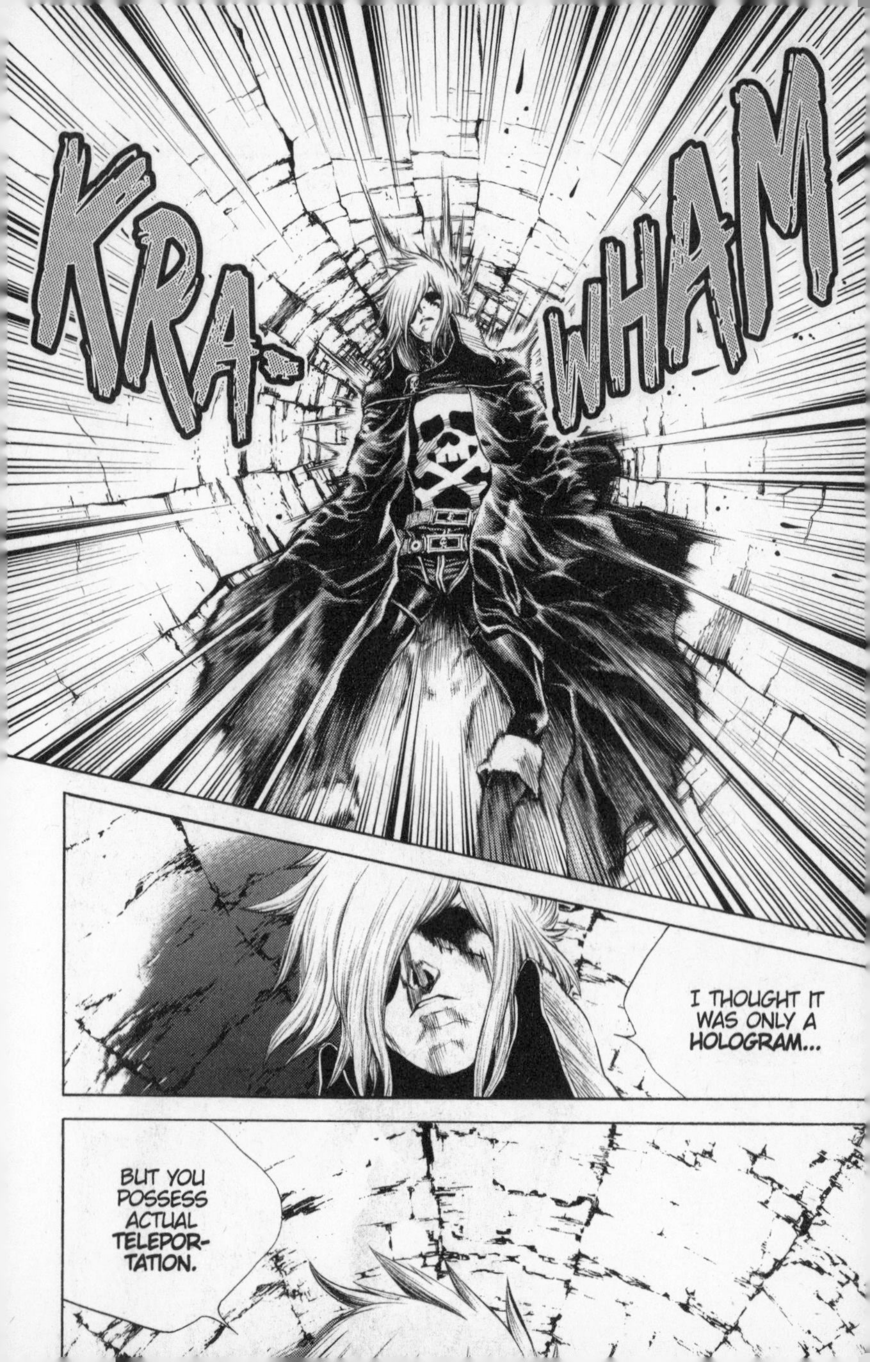
KRA-WHAM
I THOUGHT IT WAS ONLY A HOLOGRAM...
BUT YOU POSSESS ACTUAL TELEPORTATION.

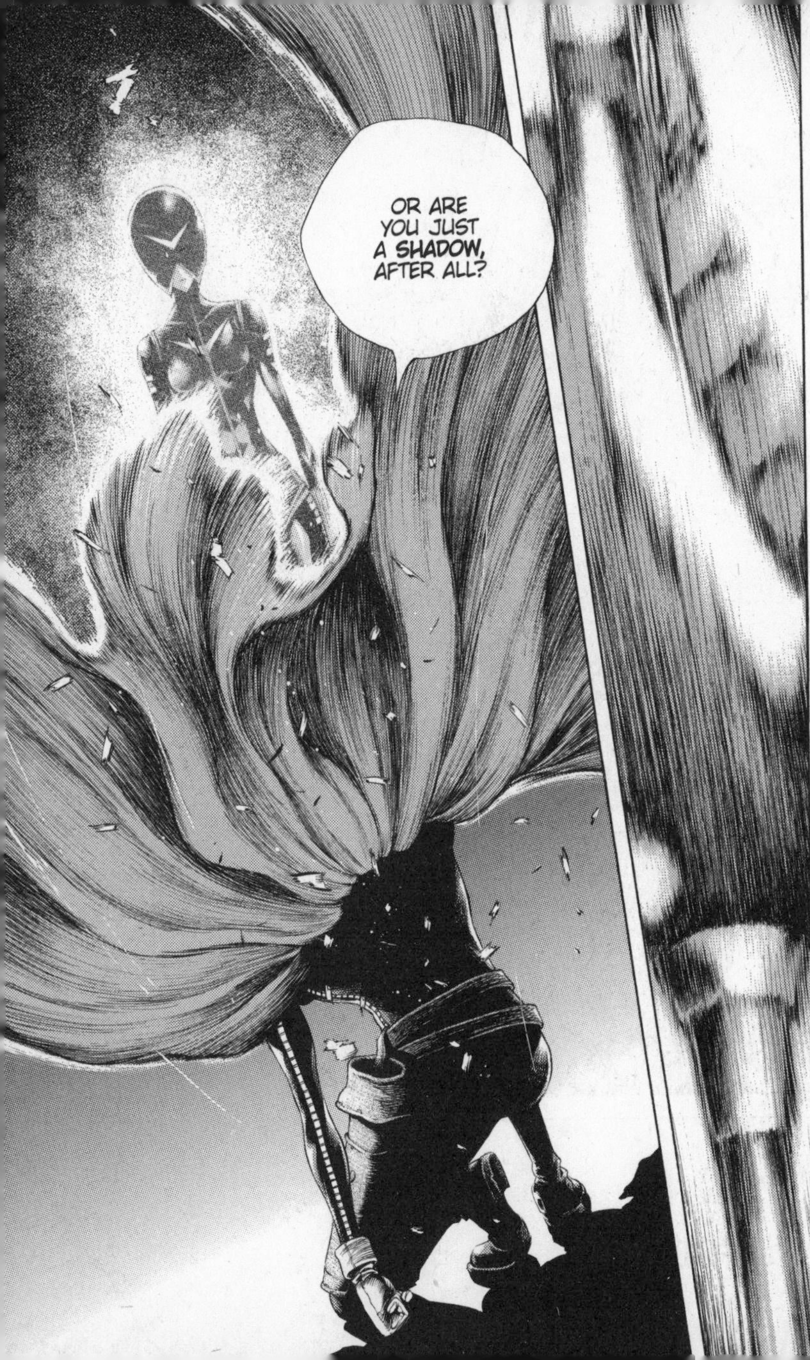
OR ARE YOU JUST A SHADOW, AFTER ALL?

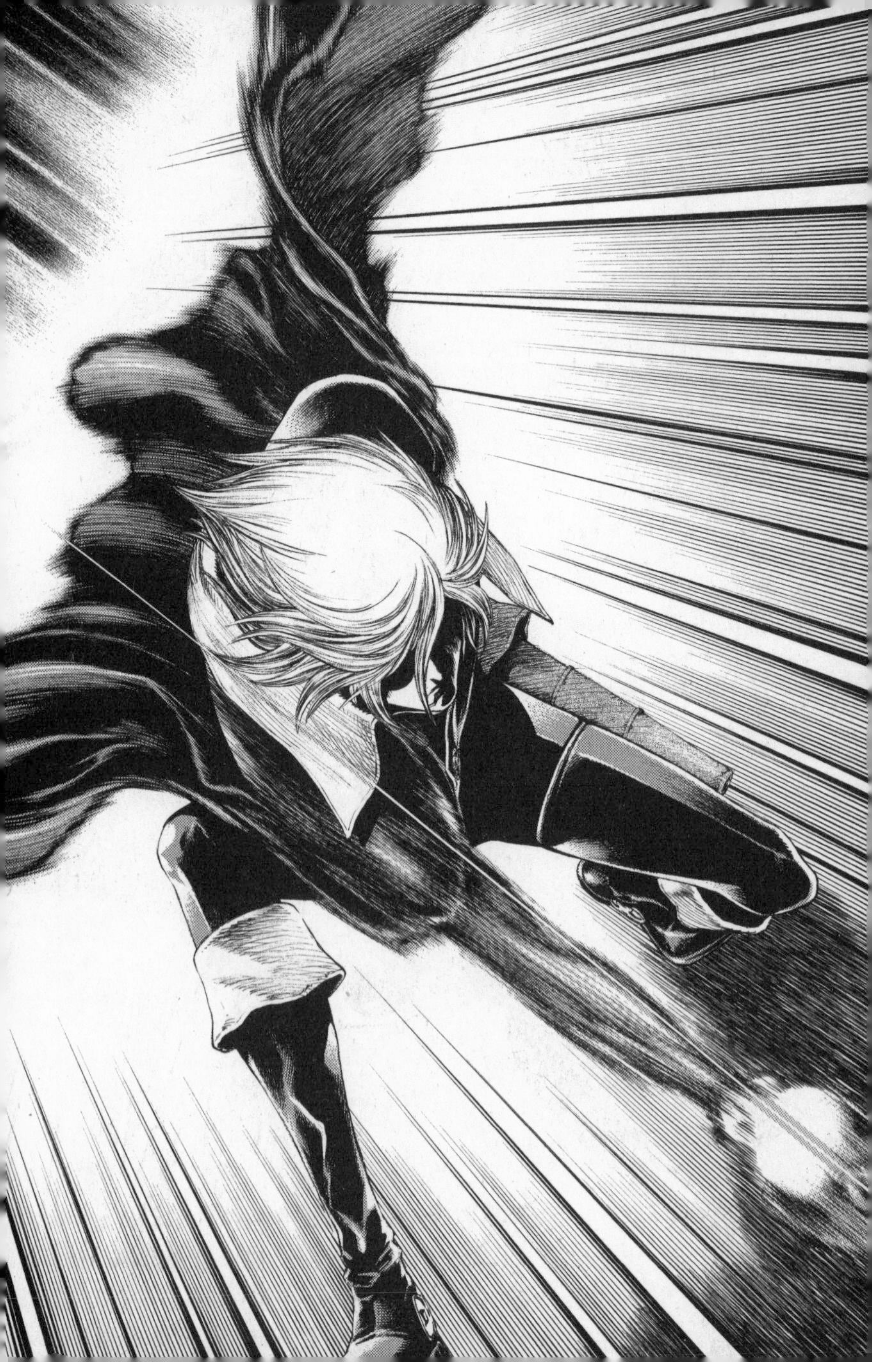

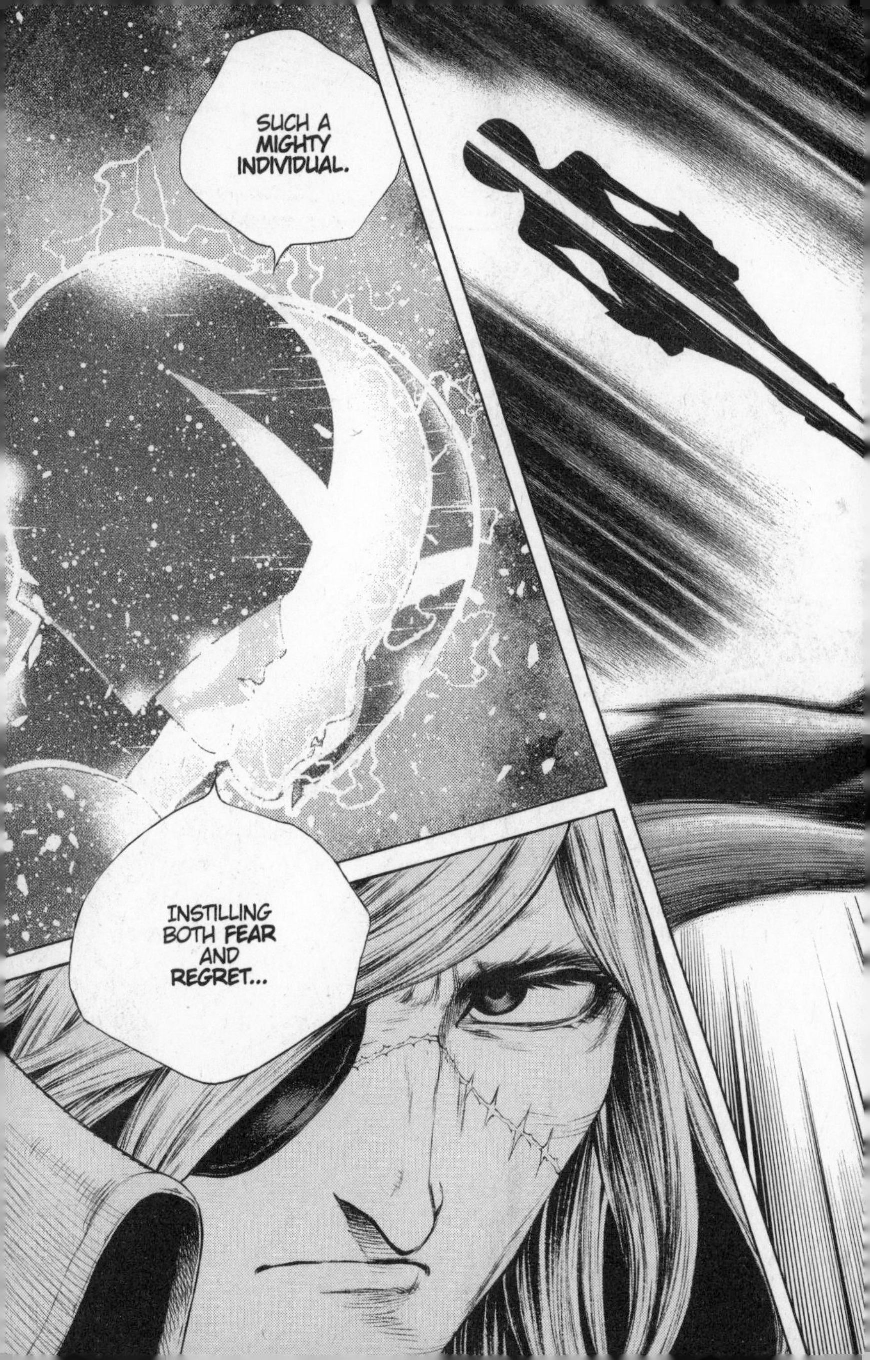
SUCH A MIGHTY INDIVIDUAL.
INSTILLING BOTH FEAR AND REGRET...

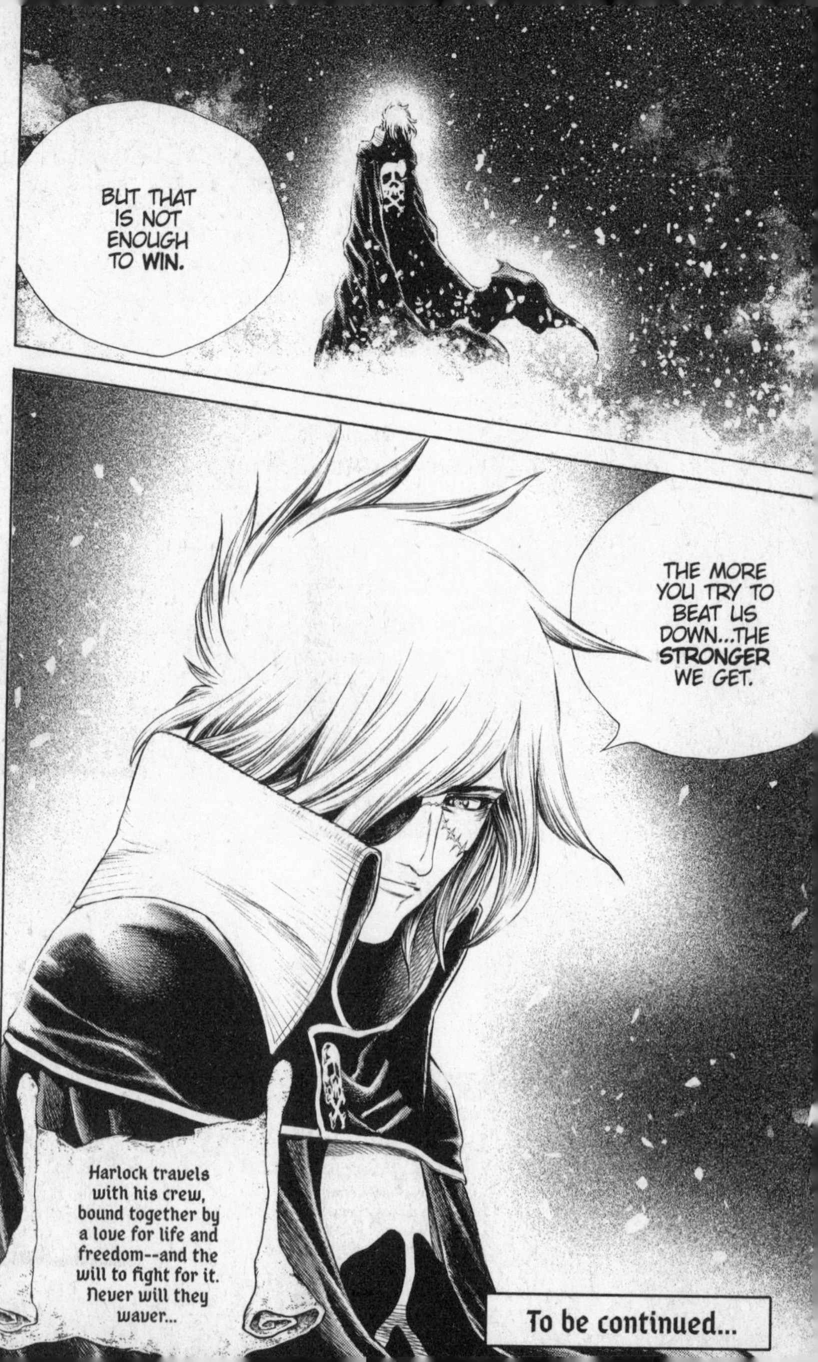
BUT THAT IS NOT ENOUGH TO WIN.
THE MORE YOU TRY TO BEAT US DOWN...THE STRONGER WE GET.
Harlock travels with his crew, bound together by a love for life and freedom--and the will to fight for it. Never will they waver...
To be continued...